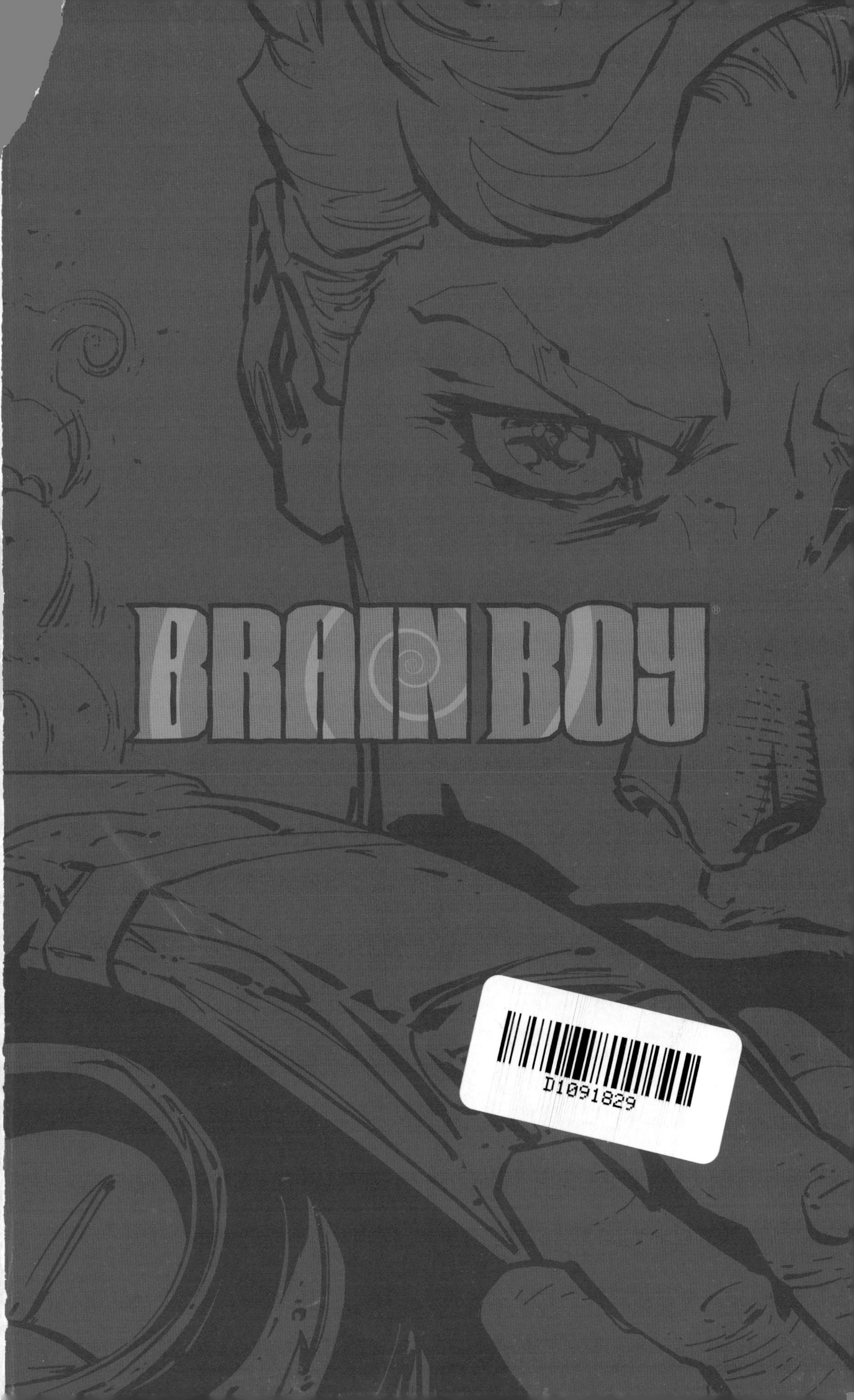
BRAIN BOY®

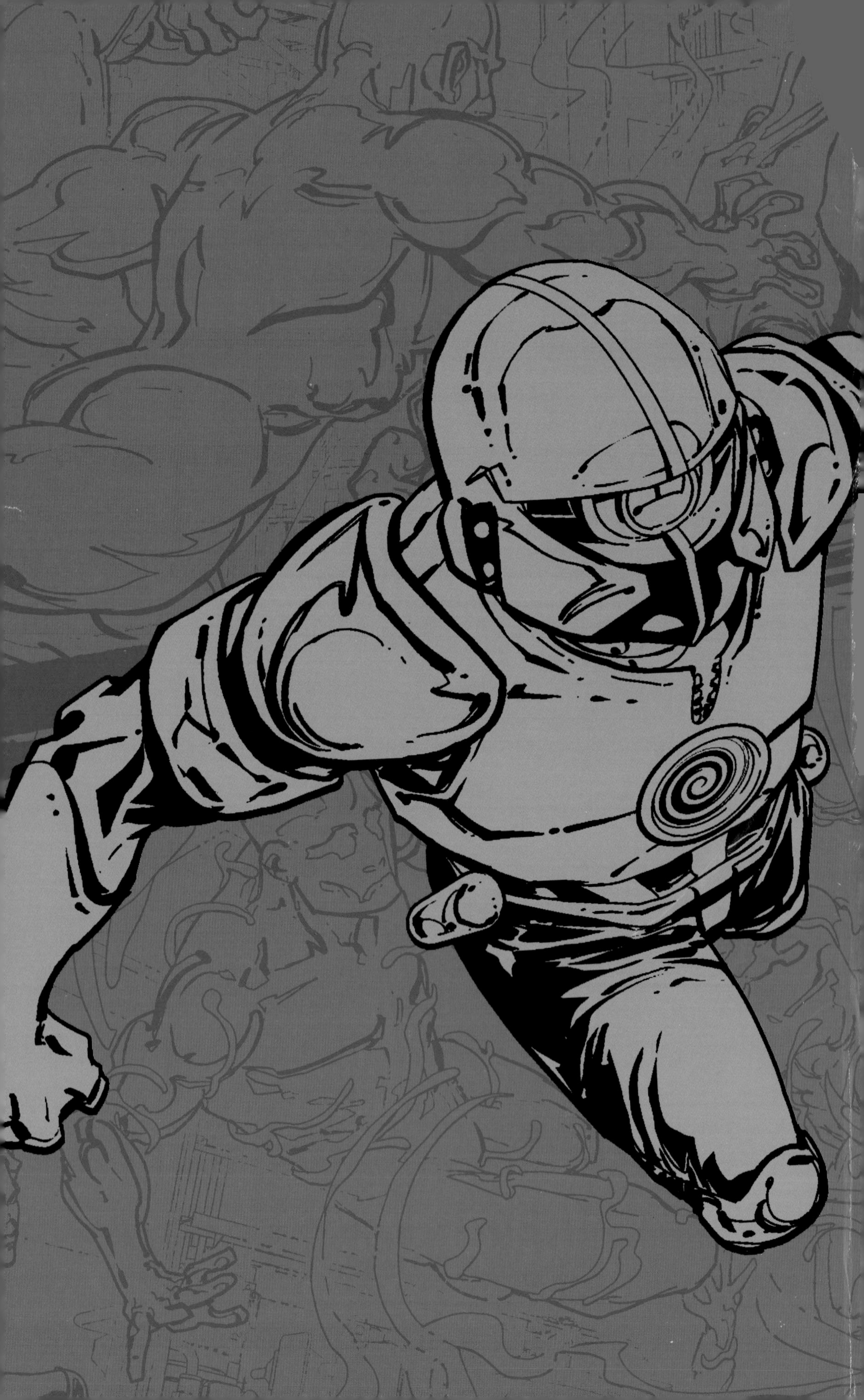

BRAIN BOY

VOLUME 2: THE MEN FROM G.E.S.T.A.L.T.

STORY BY

FRED VAN LENTE

ART BY

FREDDIE WILLIAMS II

COLORS BY

JEREMY COLWELL

LETTERS BY

NATE PIEKOS OF BLAMBOT®

COVER AND CHAPTER BREAK ART BY

FREDDIE WILLIAMS II AND DAN SCOTT

DARK HORSE BOOKS

PUBLISHER......................**MIKE RICHARDSON**

EDITOR...........................**JIM GIBBONS**

ASSISTANT EDITOR.........**SPENCER CUSHING**

DIGITAL PRODUCTION.........**ALLYSON HALLER**

COLLECTION DESIGNER..................**NICK JAMES**

Special thanks to Mike Richardson, Randy Stradley, and Scott Allie.

Mike Richardson, President and Publisher | Neil Hankerson, Executive Vice President | Tom Weddle, Chief Financial Officer | Randy Stradley, Vice President of Publishing | Michael Martens, Vice President of Book Trade Sales | Anita Nelson, Vice President of Business Affairs | Scott Allie, Editor in Chief | Matt Parkinson, Vice President of Marketing | David Scroggy, Vice President of Product Development | Dale LaFountain, Vice President of Information Technology | Darlene Vogel, Senior Director of Print, Design, and Production | Ken Lizzi, General Counsel | Davey Estrada, Editorial Director | Chris Warner, Senior Books Editor | Diana Schutz, Executive Editor | Cary Grazzini, Director of Print and Development | Lia Ribacchi, Art Director | Cara Niece, Director of Scheduling | Mark Bernardi, Director of Digital Publishing

Published by Dark Horse Books
A division of Dark Horse Comics, Inc.
10956 SE Main Street
Milwaukie, OR 97222

First edition: December 2014
ISBN 978-1-61655-506-1

1 3 5 7 9 10 8 6 4 2
Printed in China

International Licensing: (503) 905-2377
Comic Shop Locator Service: (888) 266-4226

BRAIN BOY VOLUME 2: THE MEN FROM G.E.S.T.A.L.T.

Brain Boy® © 2014 Dark Horse Comics, Inc. Dark Horse Books® and the Dark Horse logo are registered trademarks of Dark Horse Comics, Inc. All rights reserved. No portion of this publication may be reproduced or transmitted, in any form or by any means, without the express written permission of Dark Horse Comics, Inc. Names, characters, places, and incidents featured in this publication either are the product of the author's imagination or are used fictitiously. Any resemblance to actual persons (living or dead), events, institutions, or locales, without satiric intent, is coincidental.

This volume collects Brain Boy: The Men from G.E.S.T.A.L.T. #1–#4, from the ongoing comic series from Dark Horse Comics.

Library of Congress Cataloging-in-Publication Data

Van Lente, Fred, author.
Brain Boy. Volume 2, The men from G.E.S.T.A.L.T. / story by Fred Van Lente ; art by Freddie Williams II ; colors by Jeremy Colwell ; letters by Nate Piekos of BLAMBOT ; cover by Freddie Williams II and Dan Scott ; chapter break art by Freddie Williams II and Dan Scott. -- First edition.
pages cm
Summary: Brain Boy's new mission pits him against a doomsday cult leader with a political agenda that poses a direct threat to the president so the psychic spy from the U.S. Secret Service will have no choice but to go head to head--brain to brain--with the mysterious Men from G.E.S.T.A.L.T.
ISBN 978-1-61655-506-1 (paperback)
1. Graphic novels. [1. Graphic novels. 2. Spies--Fiction. 3. Psychic ability--Fiction. 4. Superheroes--Fiction.] I. Williams, Freddie E., 1977- illustrator. II. Scott, Dan, 1973- illustrator. III. Title. IV. Title: Men from G.E.S.T.A.L.T.

PZ7.7.V26Br 2014
741.5'973--dc23
2014025754

CHAPTER 1

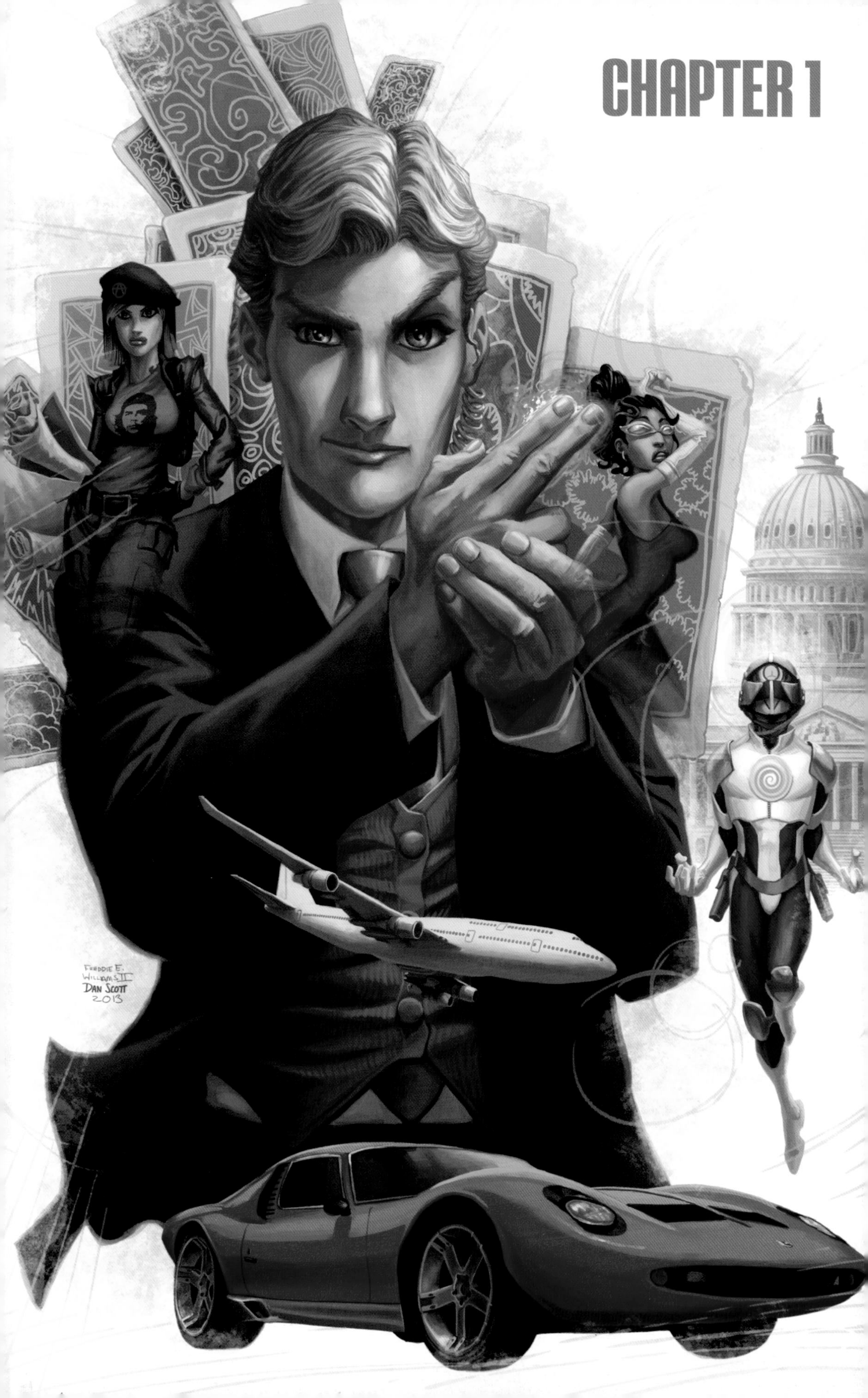
FREDDIE E. WILLIAMS II
DAN SCOTT
2013

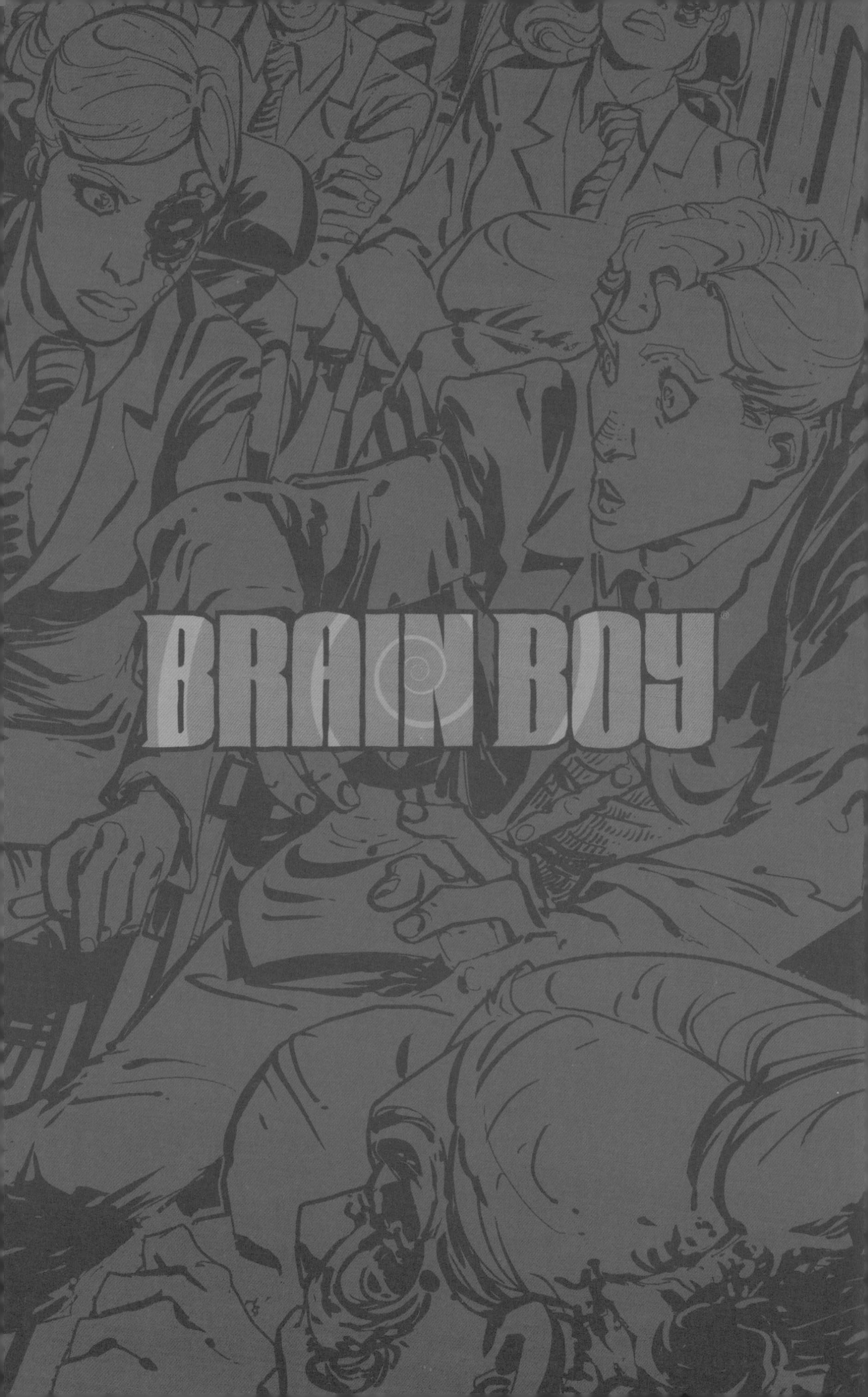
BRAIN BOY

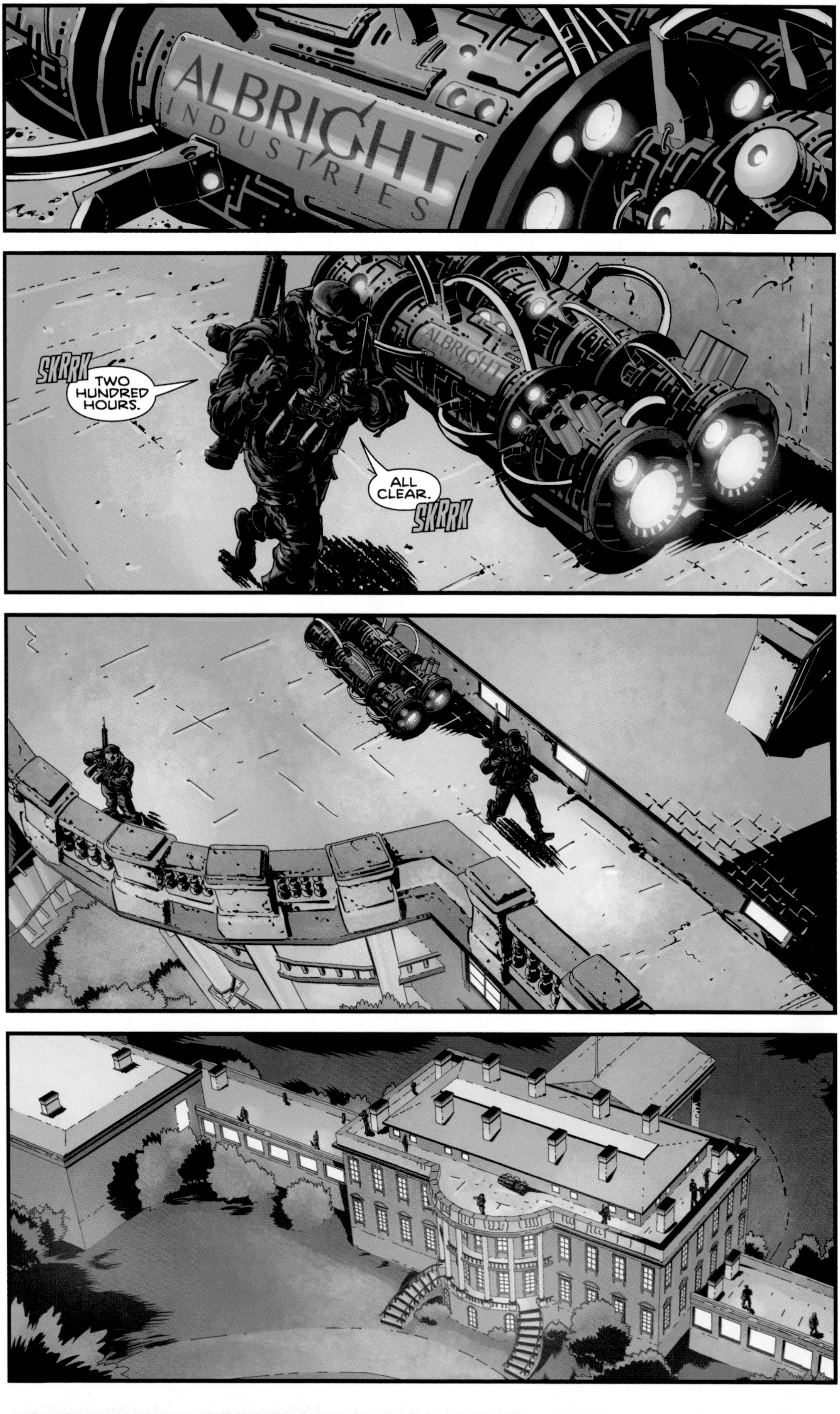
ALBRIGHT INDUSTRIES
SKRRK
TWO HUNDRED HOURS.
ALL CLEAR.
SKRRK

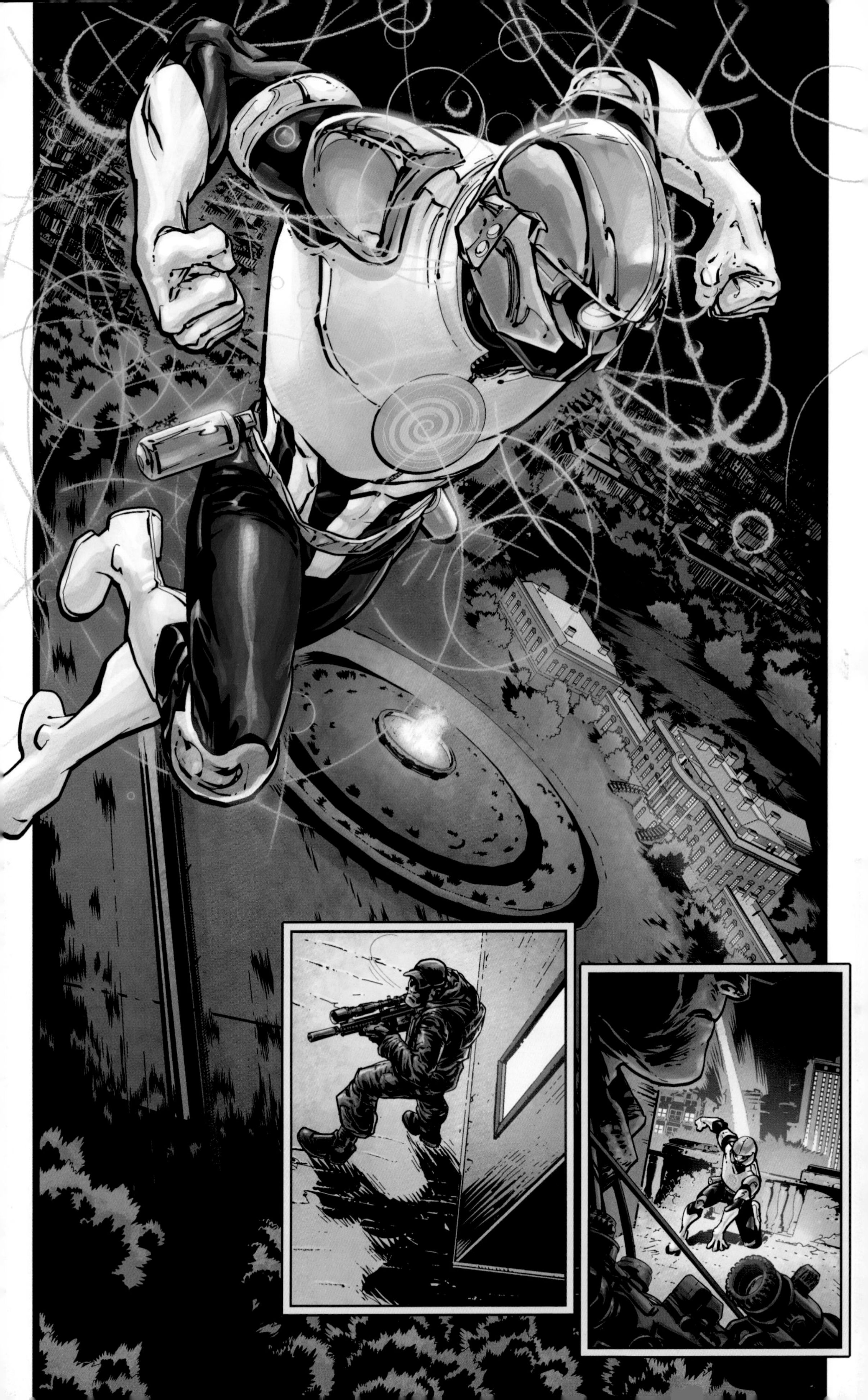

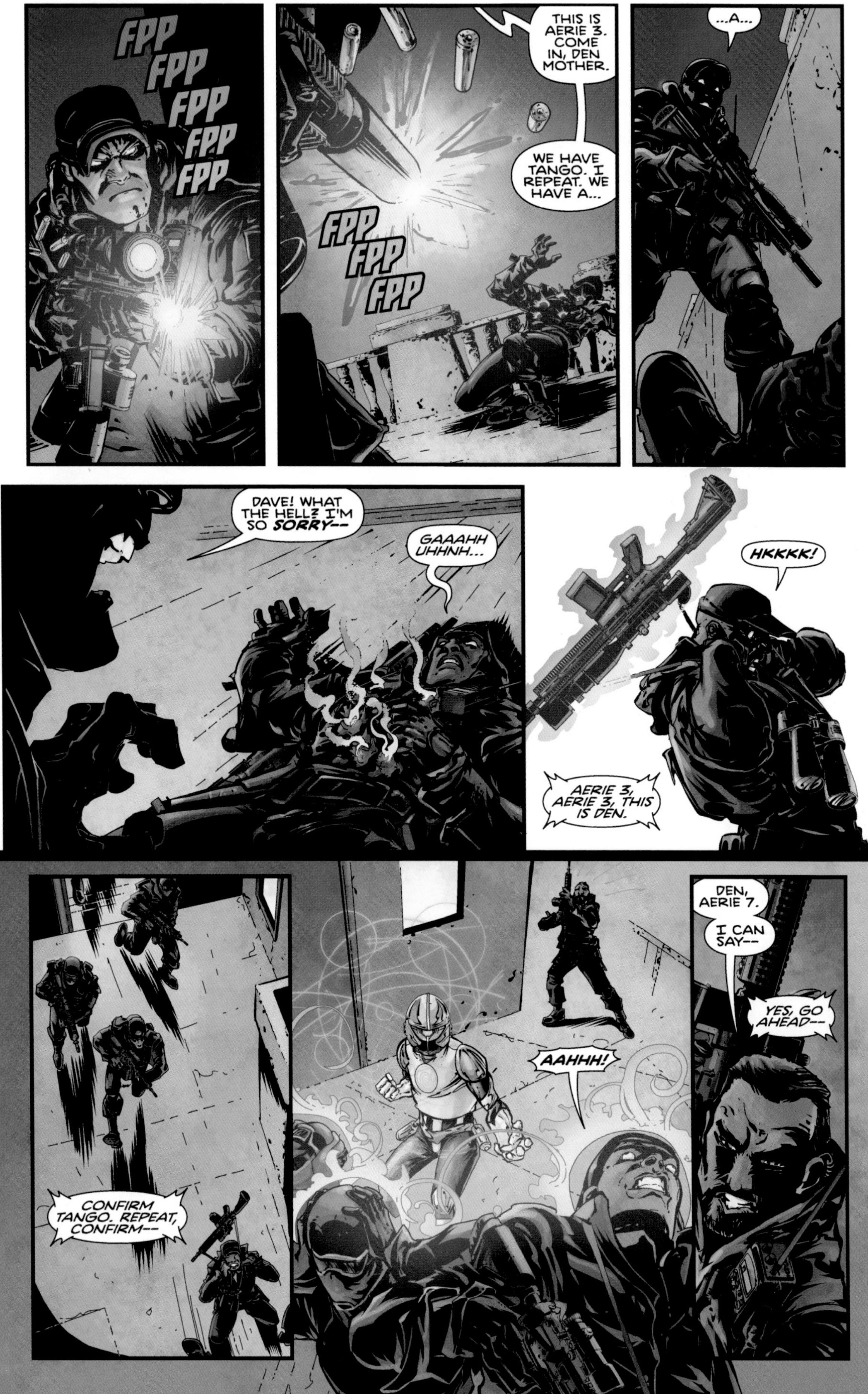
FPP FPP FPP FPP FPP
THIS IS AERIE 3. COME IN, DEN MOTHER.
WE HAVE TANGO. I REPEAT. WE HAVE A...
FPP FPP FPP
...A...
DAVE! WHAT THE HELL? I'M SO SORRY--
GAAAHH UHHNH...
HKKKK!
AERIE 3, AERIE 3, THIS IS DEN.
CONFIRM TANGO. REPEAT, CONFIRM--
AAHHH!
DEN, AERIE 7.
I CAN SAY--
YES, GO AHEAD--

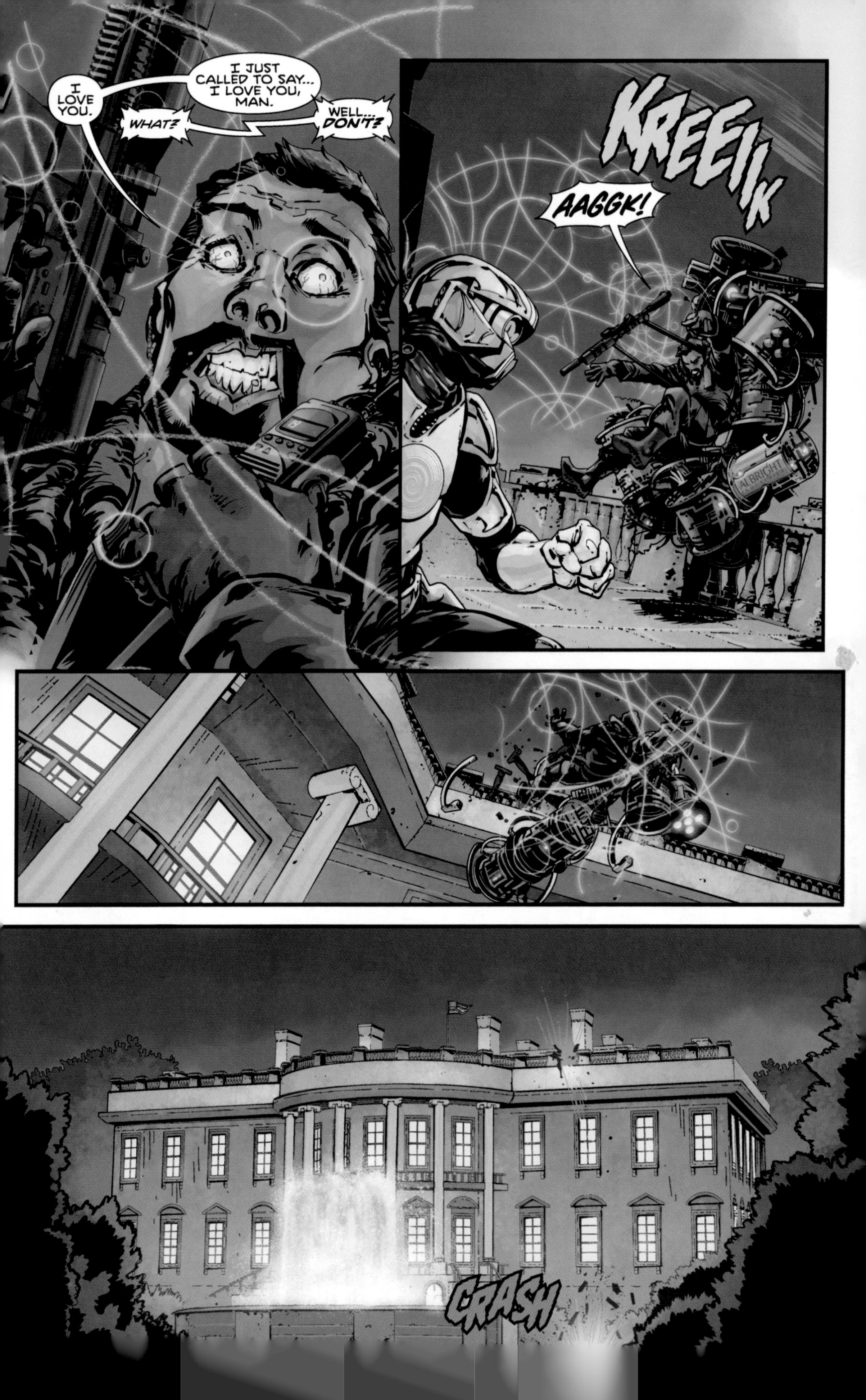
I JUST CALLED TO SAY... I LOVE YOU, MAN.
I LOVE YOU.
WHAT?
WELL... DON'T?
KREEIIK
AAGGK!
ALBRIGHT
CRASH

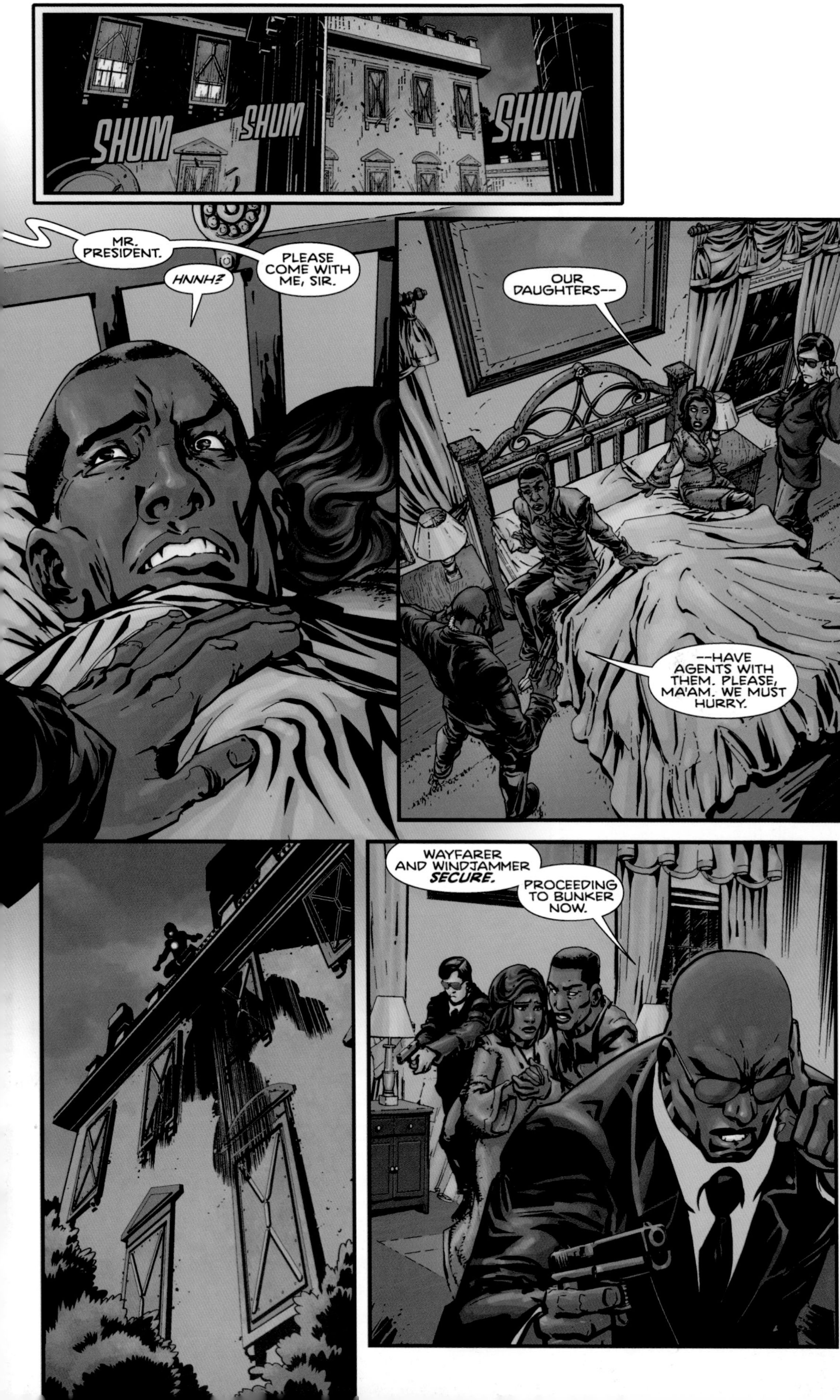
SHUM
SHUM
SHUM
MR. PRESIDENT.
HNNH?
PLEASE COME WITH ME, SIR.
OUR DAUGHTERS--
--HAVE AGENTS WITH THEM. PLEASE, MA'AM. WE MUST HURRY.
WAYFARER AND WINDJAMMER SECURE.
PROCEEDING TO BUNKER NOW.

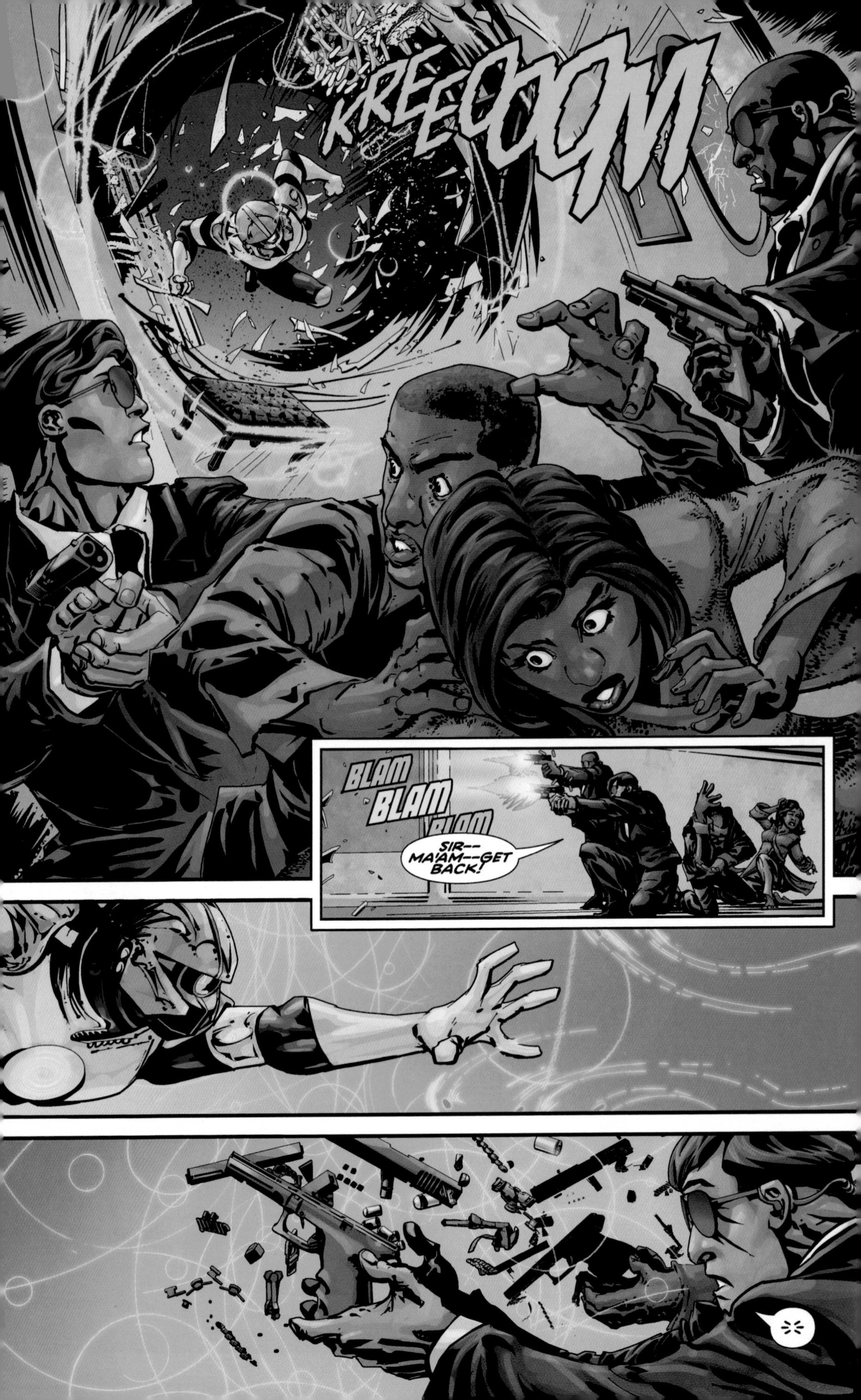
KREEOOOM
BLAM
BLAM
BLAM
SIR-- MA'AM--GET BACK!

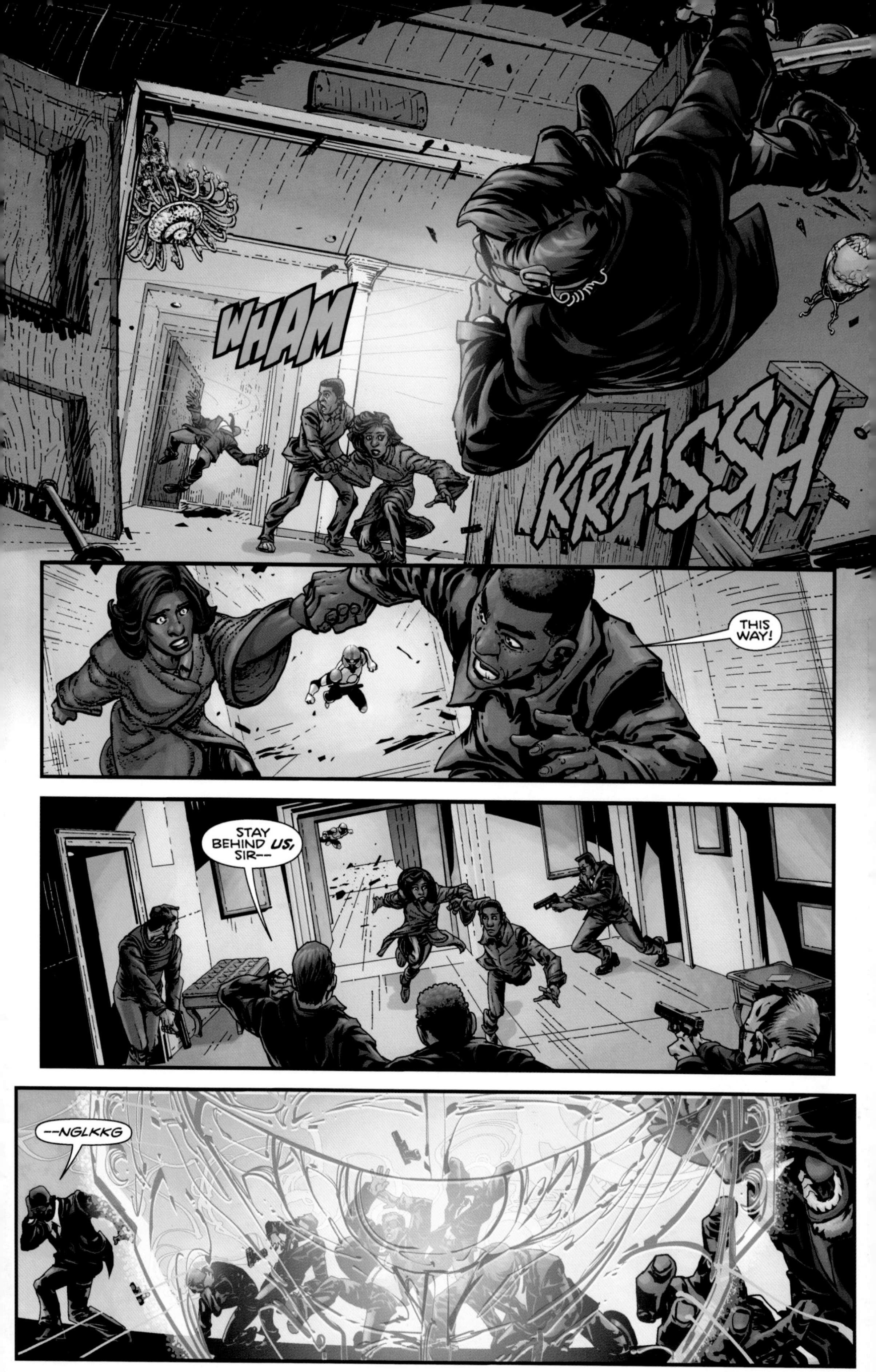
WHAM
KRASSH
THIS WAY!
STAY BEHIND US, SIR--
--NGLKKG

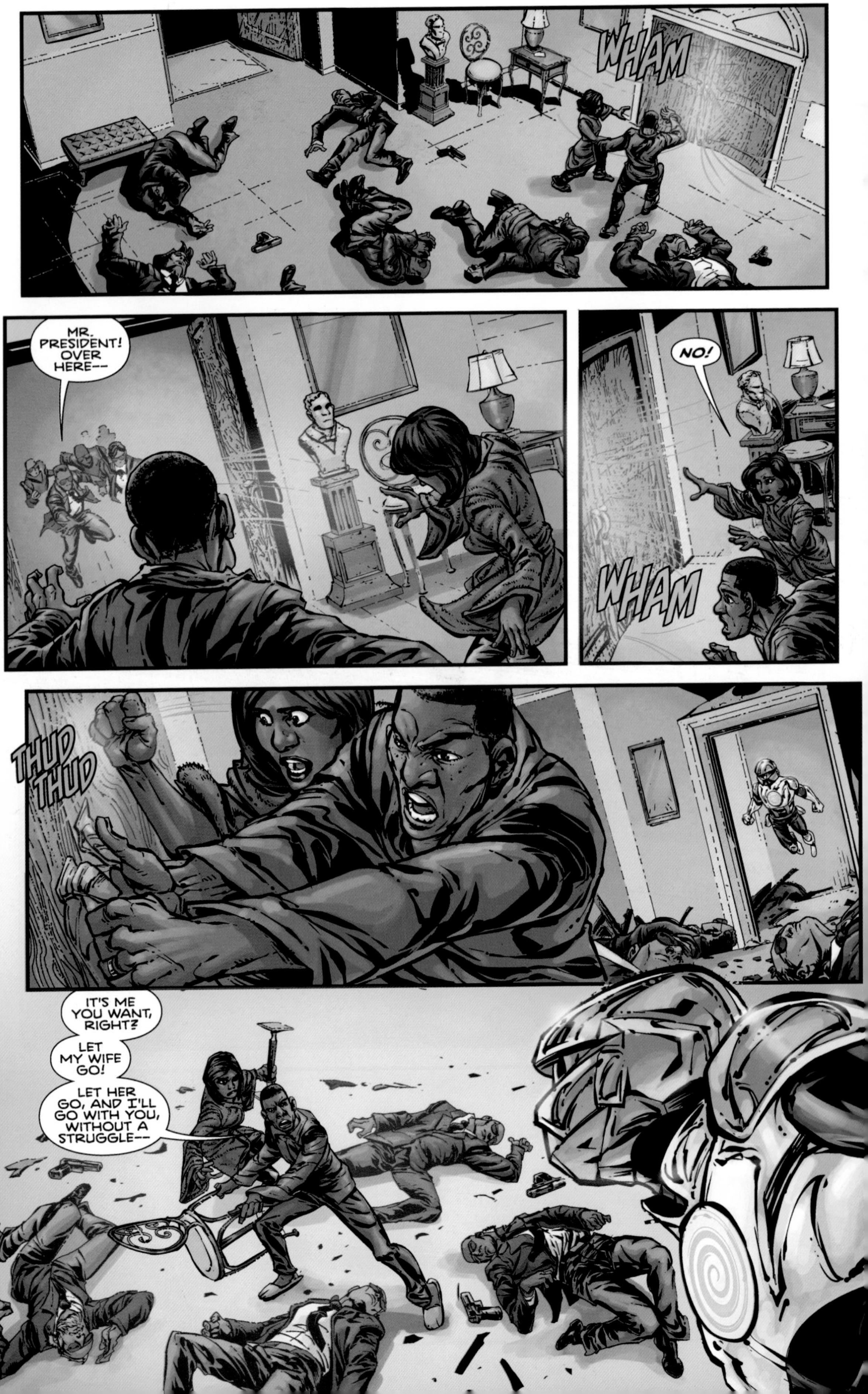
WHAM
MR. PRESIDENT! OVER HERE--
NO!
WHAM
THUD THUD
IT'S ME YOU WANT, RIGHT?
LET MY WIFE GO!
LET HER GO, AND I'LL GO WITH YOU, WITHOUT A STRUGGLE--

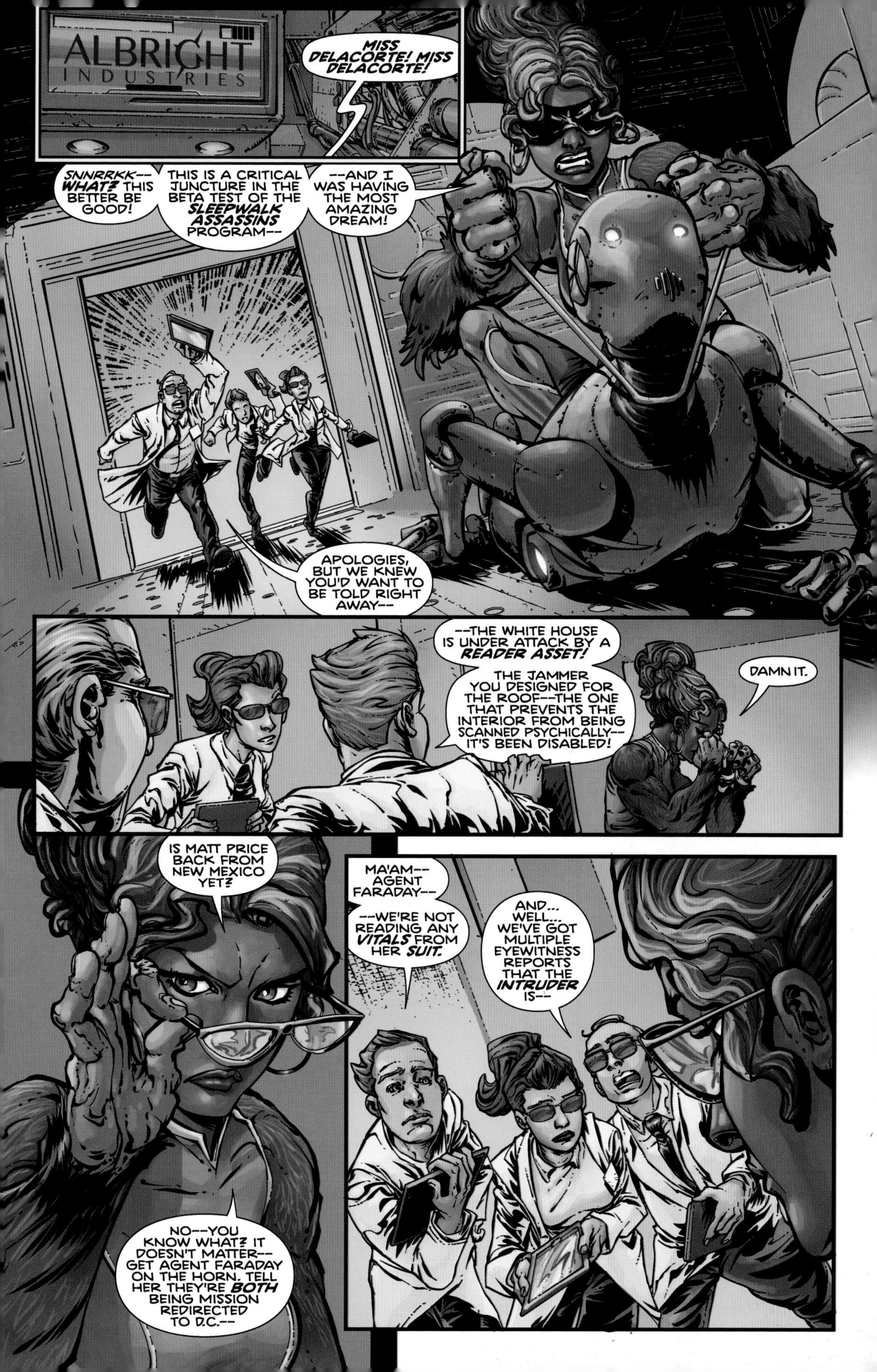
ALBRIGHT INDUSTRIES
MISS DELACORTE! MISS DELACORTE!
SNNRRKK-- WHAT? THIS BETTER BE GOOD!
THIS IS A CRITICAL JUNCTURE IN THE BETA TEST OF THE SLEEPWALK ASSASSINS PROGRAM--
--AND I WAS HAVING THE MOST AMAZING DREAM!
APOLOGIES, BUT WE KNEW YOU'D WANT TO BE TOLD RIGHT AWAY--
--THE WHITE HOUSE IS UNDER ATTACK BY A READER ASSET!
THE JAMMER YOU DESIGNED FOR THE ROOF--THE ONE THAT PREVENTS THE INTERIOR FROM BEING SCANNED PSYCHICALLY--IT'S BEEN DISABLED!
DAMN IT.
IS MATT PRICE BACK FROM NEW MEXICO YET?
NO--YOU KNOW WHAT? IT DOESN'T MATTER--GET AGENT FARADAY ON THE HORN. TELL HER THEY'RE BOTH BEING MISSION REDIRECTED TO D.C.--
MA'AM--AGENT FARADAY--
--WE'RE NOT READING ANY VITALS FROM HER SUIT.
AND... WELL... WE'VE GOT MULTIPLE EYEWITNESS REPORTS THAT THE INTRUDER IS--

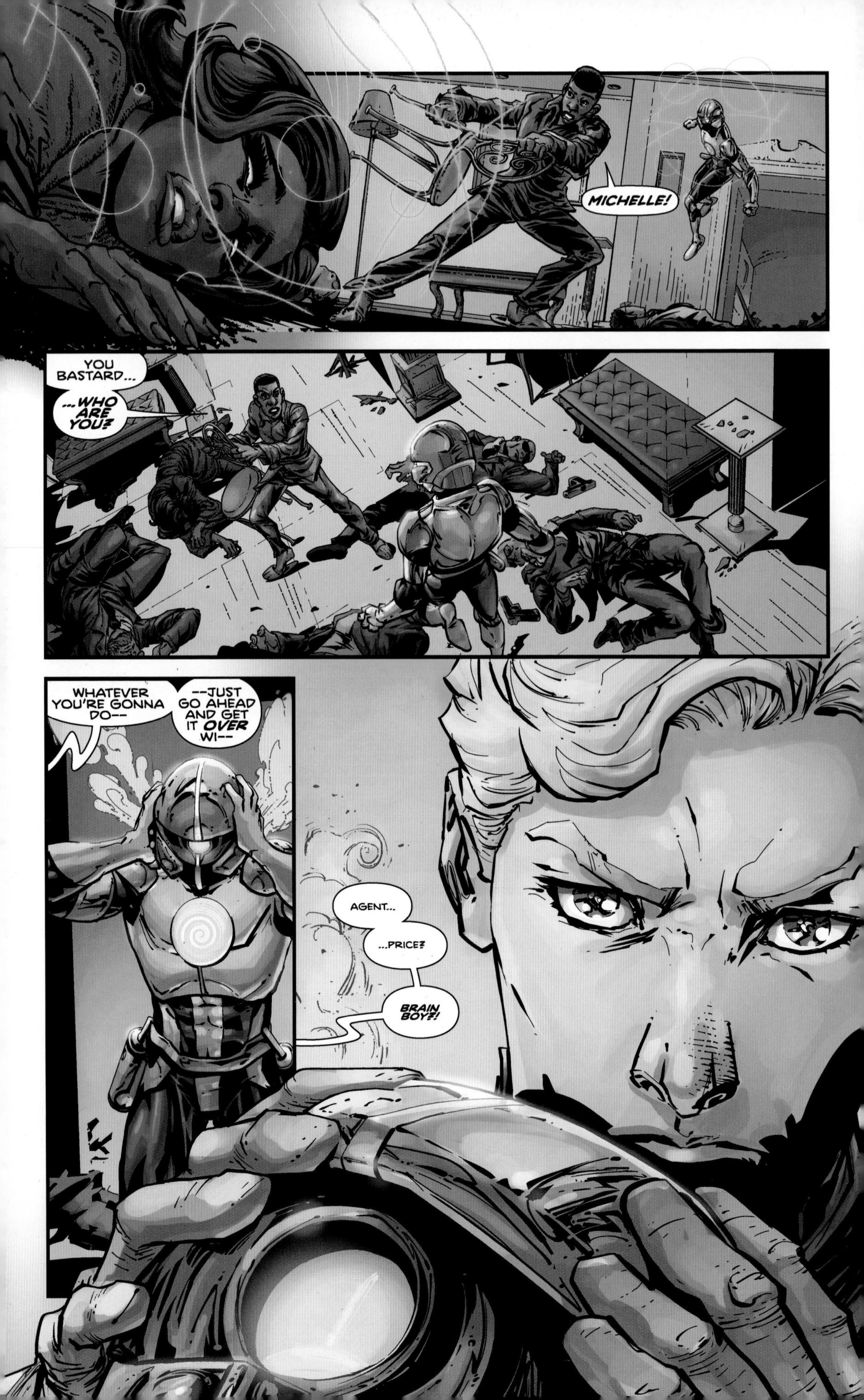
MICHELLE!
YOU BASTARD...
...WHO ARE YOU?
WHATEVER YOU'RE GONNA DO--
--JUST GO AHEAD AND GET IT OVER WI--
AGENT...
...PRICE?
BRAIN BOY?!

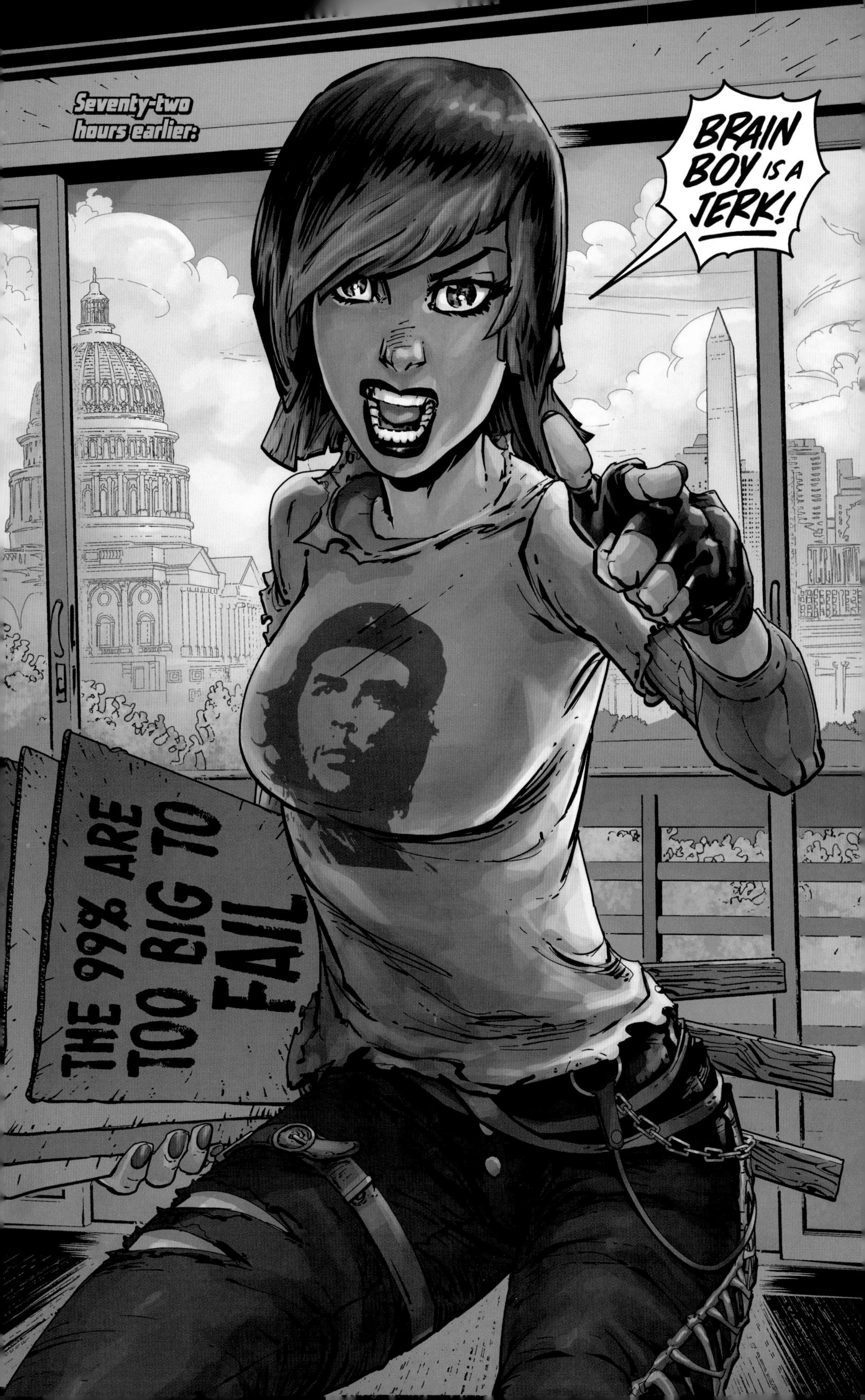
Seventy-two hours earlier:
BRAIN BOY IS A JERK!
THE 99% ARE TOO BIG TO FAIL

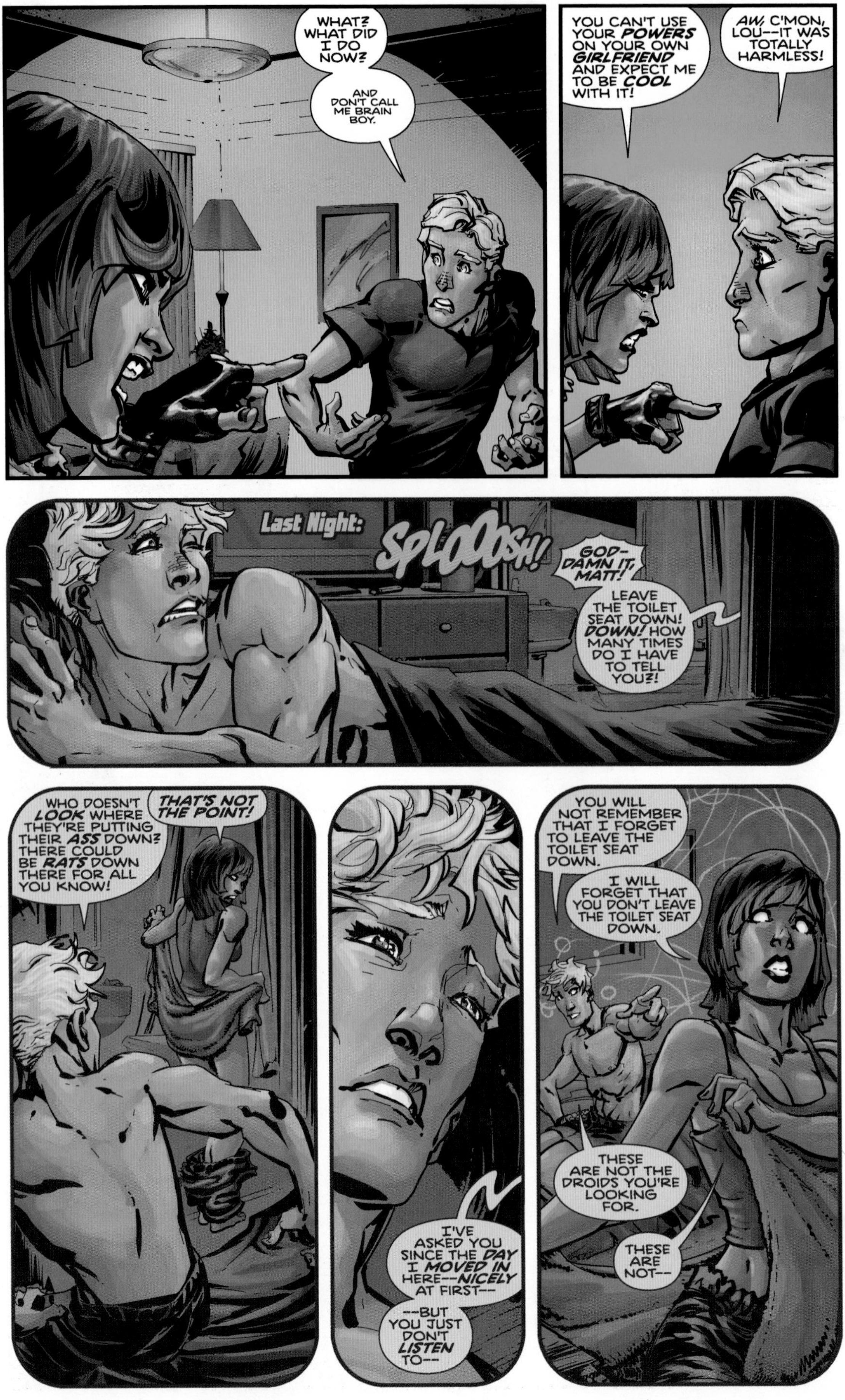
WHAT? WHAT DID I DO NOW?
AND DON'T CALL ME BRAIN BOY.
YOU CAN'T USE YOUR POWERS ON YOUR OWN GIRLFRIEND AND EXPECT ME TO BE COOL WITH IT!
AW, C'MON, LOU--IT WAS TOTALLY HARMLESS!
Last Night:
SPLOOOSH!
GOD-DAMN IT, MATT!
LEAVE THE TOILET SEAT DOWN! DOWN! HOW MANY TIMES DO I HAVE TO TELL YOU?!
WHO DOESN'T LOOK WHERE THEY'RE PUTTING THEIR ASS DOWN? THERE COULD BE RATS DOWN THERE FOR ALL YOU KNOW!
THAT'S NOT THE POINT!
I'VE ASKED YOU SINCE THE DAY I MOVED IN HERE--NICELY AT FIRST--
--BUT YOU JUST DON'T LISTEN TO--
YOU WILL NOT REMEMBER THAT I FORGET TO LEAVE THE TOILET SEAT DOWN.
I WILL FORGET THAT YOU DON'T LEAVE THE TOILET SEAT DOWN.
THESE ARE NOT THE DROIDS YOU'RE LOOKING FOR.
THESE ARE NOT--

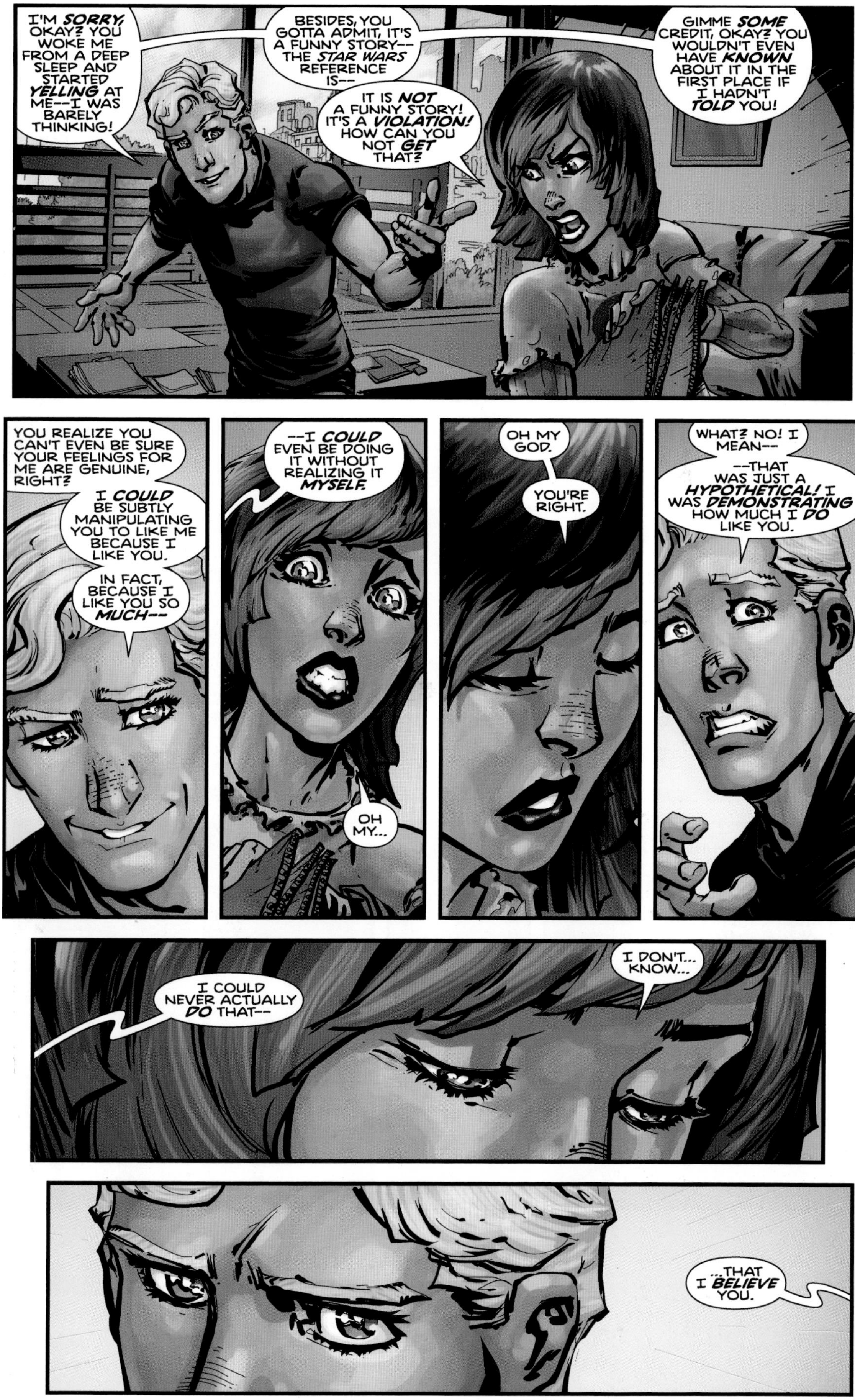
I'M SORRY, OKAY? YOU WOKE ME FROM A DEEP SLEEP AND STARTED YELLING AT ME--I WAS BARELY THINKING!
BESIDES, YOU GOTTA ADMIT, IT'S A FUNNY STORY-- THE STAR WARS REFERENCE IS--
IT IS NOT A FUNNY STORY! IT'S A VIOLATION! HOW CAN YOU NOT GET THAT?
GIMME SOME CREDIT, OKAY? YOU WOULDN'T EVEN HAVE KNOWN ABOUT IT IN THE FIRST PLACE IF I HADN'T TOLD YOU!
YOU REALIZE YOU CAN'T EVEN BE SURE YOUR FEELINGS FOR ME ARE GENUINE, RIGHT?
I COULD BE SUBTLY MANIPULATING YOU TO LIKE ME BECAUSE I LIKE YOU.
IN FACT, BECAUSE I LIKE YOU SO MUCH--
--I COULD EVEN BE DOING IT WITHOUT REALIZING IT MYSELF.
OH MY...
OH MY GOD.
YOU'RE RIGHT.
WHAT? NO! I MEAN--
--THAT WAS JUST A HYPOTHETICAL! I WAS DEMONSTRATING HOW MUCH I DO LIKE YOU.
I COULD NEVER ACTUALLY DO THAT--
I DON'T... KNOW...
...THAT I BELIEVE YOU.

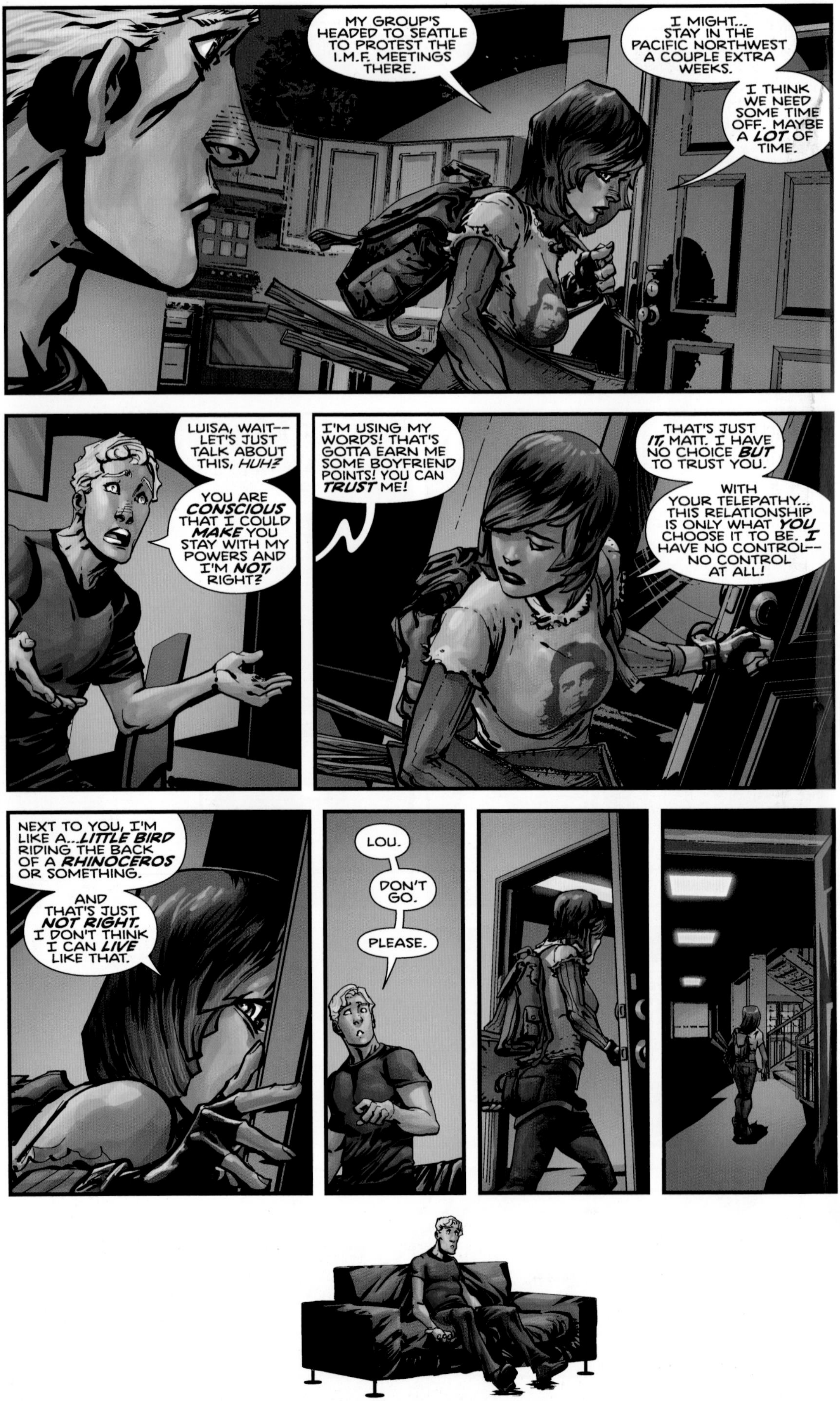
MY GROUP'S HEADED TO SEATTLE TO PROTEST THE I.M.F. MEETINGS THERE.
I MIGHT... STAY IN THE PACIFIC NORTHWEST A COUPLE EXTRA WEEKS.
I THINK WE NEED SOME TIME OFF. MAYBE A LOT OF TIME.
LUISA, WAIT-- LET'S JUST TALK ABOUT THIS, HUH?
YOU ARE CONSCIOUS THAT I COULD MAKE YOU STAY WITH MY POWERS AND I'M NOT, RIGHT?
I'M USING MY WORDS! THAT'S GOTTA EARN ME SOME BOYFRIEND POINTS! YOU CAN TRUST ME!
THAT'S JUST IT, MATT. I HAVE NO CHOICE BUT TO TRUST YOU.
WITH YOUR TELEPATHY... THIS RELATIONSHIP IS ONLY WHAT YOU CHOOSE IT TO BE. I HAVE NO CONTROL-- NO CONTROL AT ALL!
NEXT TO YOU, I'M LIKE A... LITTLE BIRD RIDING THE BACK OF A RHINOCEROS OR SOMETHING.
AND THAT'S JUST NOT RIGHT. I DON'T THINK I CAN LIVE LIKE THAT.
LOU.
DON'T GO.
PLEASE.

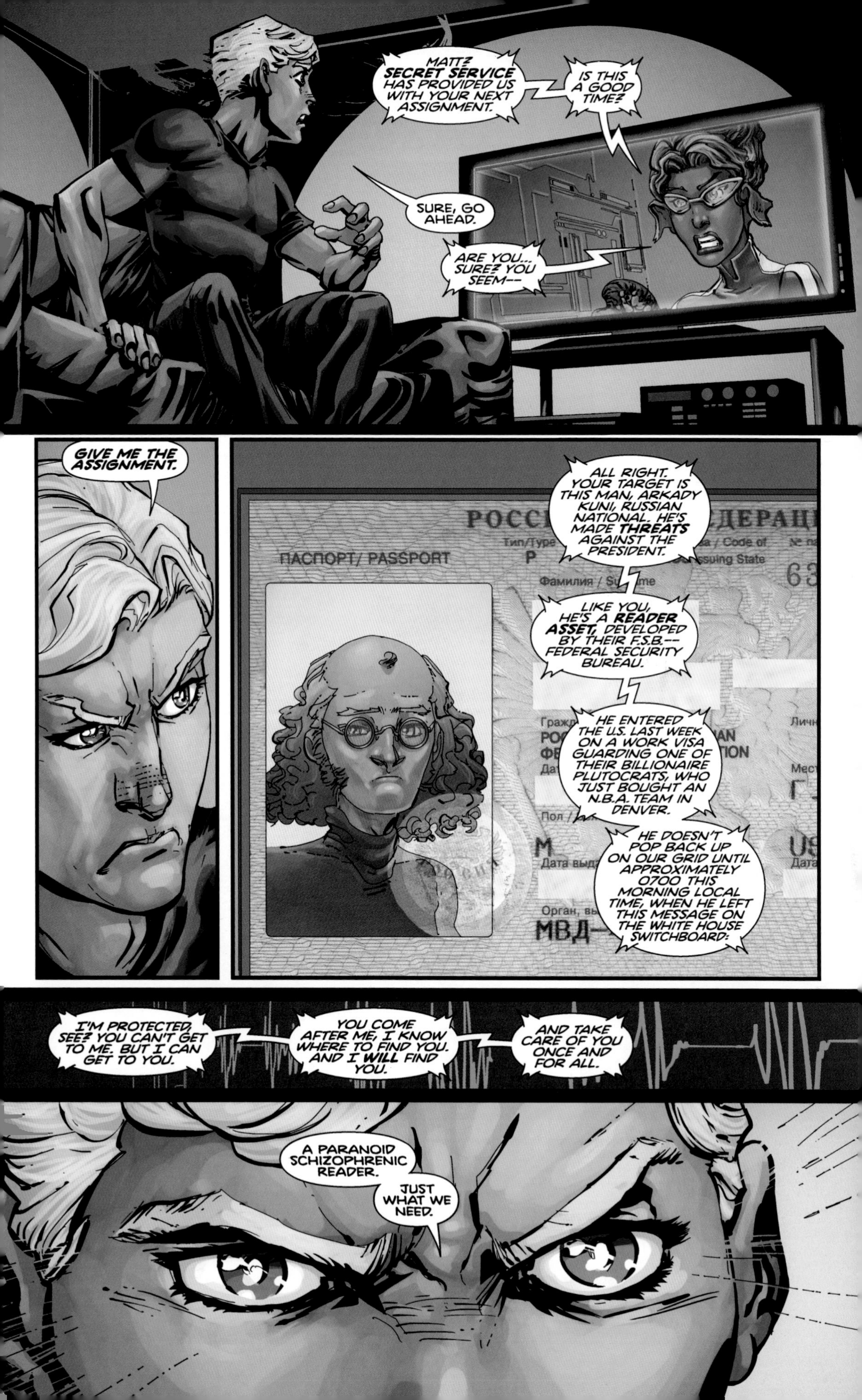
MATT? SECRET SERVICE HAS PROVIDED US WITH YOUR NEXT ASSIGNMENT.
IS THIS A GOOD TIME?
SURE, GO AHEAD.
ARE YOU... SURE? YOU SEEM--
GIVE ME THE ASSIGNMENT.
ALL RIGHT. YOUR TARGET IS THIS MAN, ARKADY KUNI, RUSSIAN NATIONAL. HE'S MADE THREATS AGAINST THE PRESIDENT.
ПАСПОРТ/ PASSPORT
LIKE YOU, HE'S A READER ASSET, DEVELOPED BY THEIR F.S.B.-- FEDERAL SECURITY BUREAU.
HE ENTERED THE U.S. LAST WEEK ON A WORK VISA GUARDING ONE OF THEIR BILLIONAIRE PLUTOCRATS, WHO JUST BOUGHT AN N.B.A. TEAM IN DENVER.
HE DOESN'T POP BACK UP ON OUR GRID UNTIL APPROXIMATELY 0700 THIS MORNING LOCAL TIME, WHEN HE LEFT THIS MESSAGE ON THE WHITE HOUSE SWITCHBOARD:
I'M PROTECTED, SEE? YOU CAN'T GET TO ME. BUT I CAN GET TO YOU.
YOU COME AFTER ME, I KNOW WHERE TO FIND YOU. AND I WILL FIND YOU.
AND TAKE CARE OF YOU ONCE AND FOR ALL.
A PARANOID SCHIZOPHRENIC READER.
JUST WHAT WE NEED.

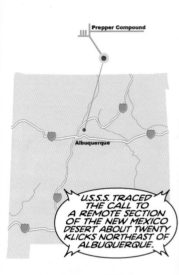

Prepper Compound

Albuquerque

SATELLITE RECONNAISSANCE AND LOCAL LAW ENFORCEMENT CONFIRM THERE'S A COMPOUND OF *"DOOMSDAY PREPPERS"* SQUATTING OUT THERE SINCE POTUS'S REELECTION.

U.S.S.S. TRACED THE CALL TO A REMOTE SECTION OF THE NEW MEXICO DESERT ABOUT TWENTY KLICKS NORTHEAST OF ALBUQUERQUE.

WAITING FOR A *RACE WAR?* OR THE *OIL* TO RUN OUT? OR THE BLACK HELICOPTERS TO START ROUNDING UP N.R.A. MEMBERS?

ALL OF THE ABOVE, FOR ALL I *KNOW.* OR *CARE.*

THIS IS AN *EXTRACTION*-- U.S.S.S. WANTS ARKADY BROUGHT IN *ALIVE* TO D.C. FOR QUESTIONING.

FIND OUT IF HE'S ASSOCIATED WITH THE PREPPERS AND IF SO, *WHY* AND HOW MUCH OF A THREAT THEY POSE.

YOU'LL PROCEED TO NEW MEXICO ON A COMMERCIAL AIRLINE. OUR OLD FRIEND AGENT *FARADAY* WILL LEND OPERATIONAL SUPPORT.

YOU MEAN OPERATIONAL *BABYSITTING,* DON'T YOU?

GEORGINA, WHEN WILL YOU LEARN I'M OLD ENOUGH TO CROSS THE STREET WITH-OUT HOLDING YOUR HAND?

WHEN YOU *PROVE* IT TO ME.

FARADAY WILL HAVE SOME ADDITIONAL *GEAR* BIO-VANCEMENTS DEVELOPED FOR THIS ASSIGNMENT.

WE'RE PRETTY SURE YOU'LL *NEED* IT.

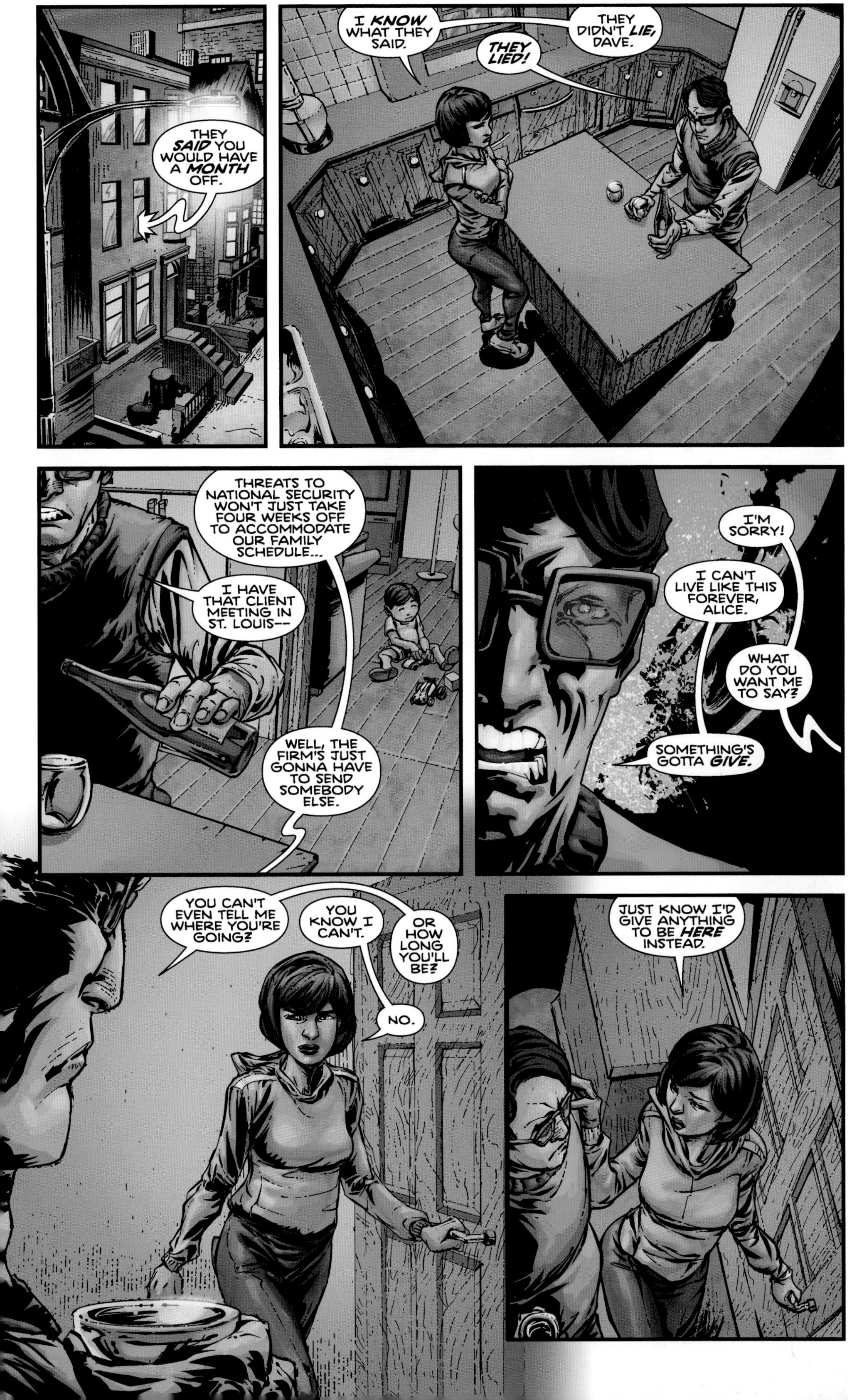
THEY SAID YOU WOULD HAVE A MONTH OFF.
I KNOW WHAT THEY SAID.
THEY DIDN'T LIE, DAVE.
THEY LIED!
THREATS TO NATIONAL SECURITY WON'T JUST TAKE FOUR WEEKS OFF TO ACCOMMODATE OUR FAMILY SCHEDULE...
I HAVE THAT CLIENT MEETING IN ST. LOUIS--
WELL, THE FIRM'S JUST GONNA HAVE TO SEND SOMEBODY ELSE.
I'M SORRY!
I CAN'T LIVE LIKE THIS FOREVER, ALICE.
WHAT DO YOU WANT ME TO SAY?
SOMETHING'S GOTTA GIVE.
YOU CAN'T EVEN TELL ME WHERE YOU'RE GOING?
YOU KNOW I CAN'T.
OR HOW LONG YOU'LL BE?
NO.
JUST KNOW I'D GIVE ANYTHING TO BE HERE INSTEAD.

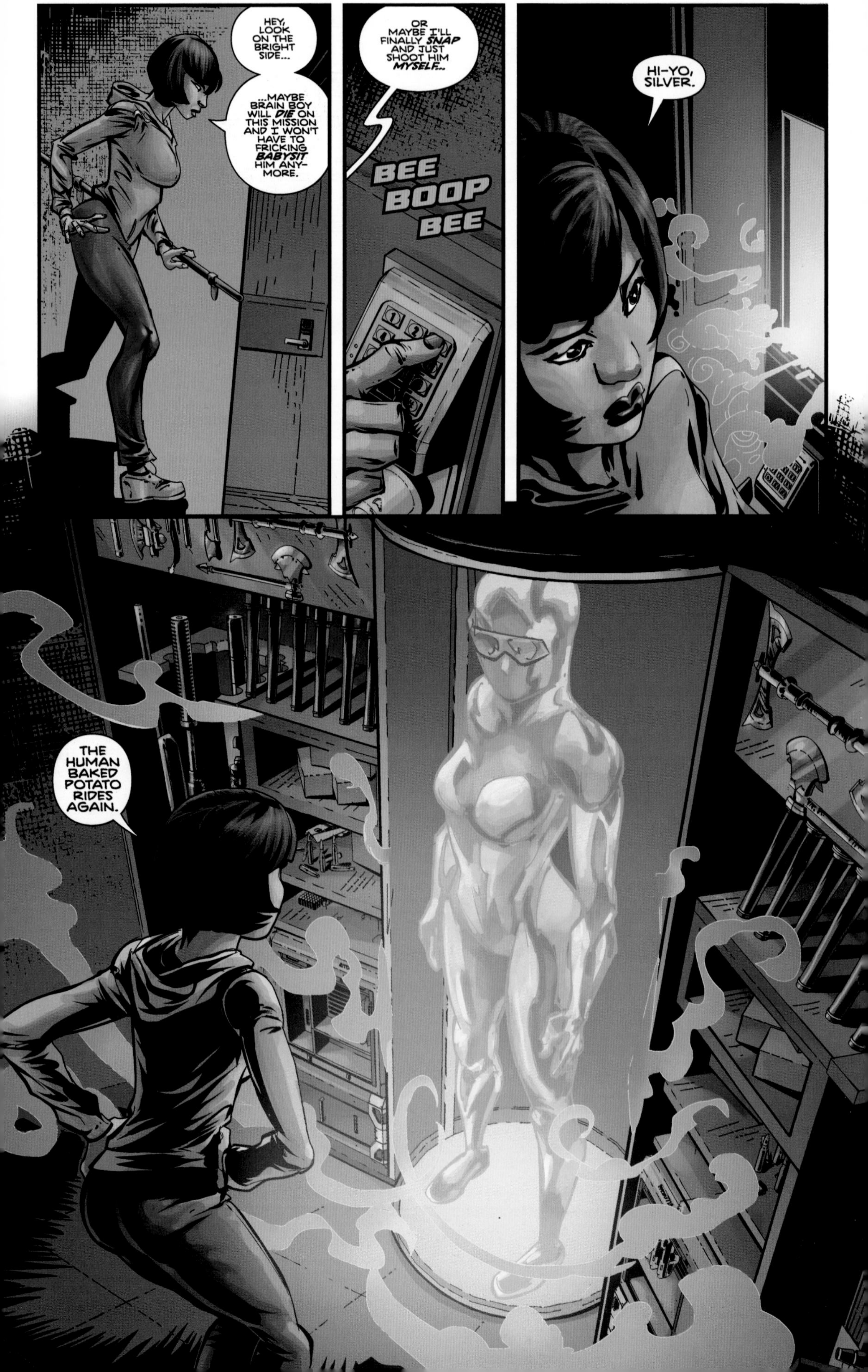
HEY, LOOK ON THE BRIGHT SIDE...
...MAYBE BRAIN BOY WILL DIE ON THIS MISSION AND I WON'T HAVE TO FRICKING BABYSIT HIM ANY-MORE.
OR MAYBE I'LL FINALLY SNAP AND JUST SHOOT HIM MYSELF...
BEE BOOP BEE
HI-YO, SILVER.
THE HUMAN BAKED POTATO RIDES AGAIN.

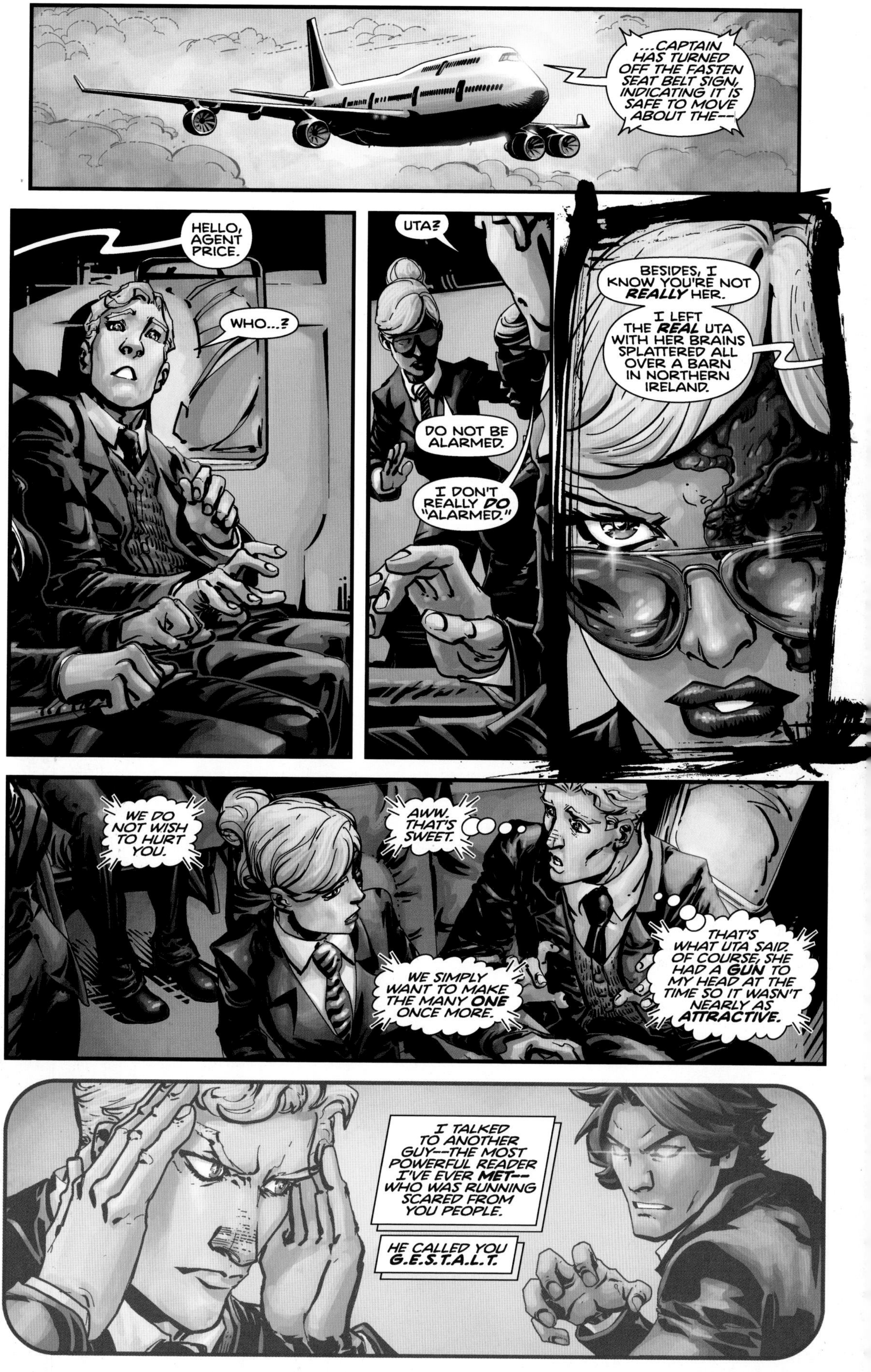
...CAPTAIN HAS TURNED OFF THE FASTEN SEAT BELT SIGN, INDICATING IT IS SAFE TO MOVE ABOUT THE--
HELLO, AGENT PRICE.
WHO...?
UTA?
DO NOT BE ALARMED.
I DON'T REALLY DO "ALARMED."
BESIDES, I KNOW YOU'RE NOT REALLY HER.
I LEFT THE REAL UTA WITH HER BRAINS SPLATTERED ALL OVER A BARN IN NORTHERN IRELAND.
WE DO NOT WISH TO HURT YOU.
AWW. THAT'S SWEET.
WE SIMPLY WANT TO MAKE THE MANY ONE ONCE MORE.
THAT'S WHAT UTA SAID. OF COURSE, SHE HAD A GUN TO MY HEAD AT THE TIME SO IT WASN'T NEARLY AS ATTRACTIVE.
I TALKED TO ANOTHER GUY--THE MOST POWERFUL READER I'VE EVER MET--WHO WAS RUNNING SCARED FROM YOU PEOPLE.
HE CALLED YOU G.E.S.T.A.L.T.

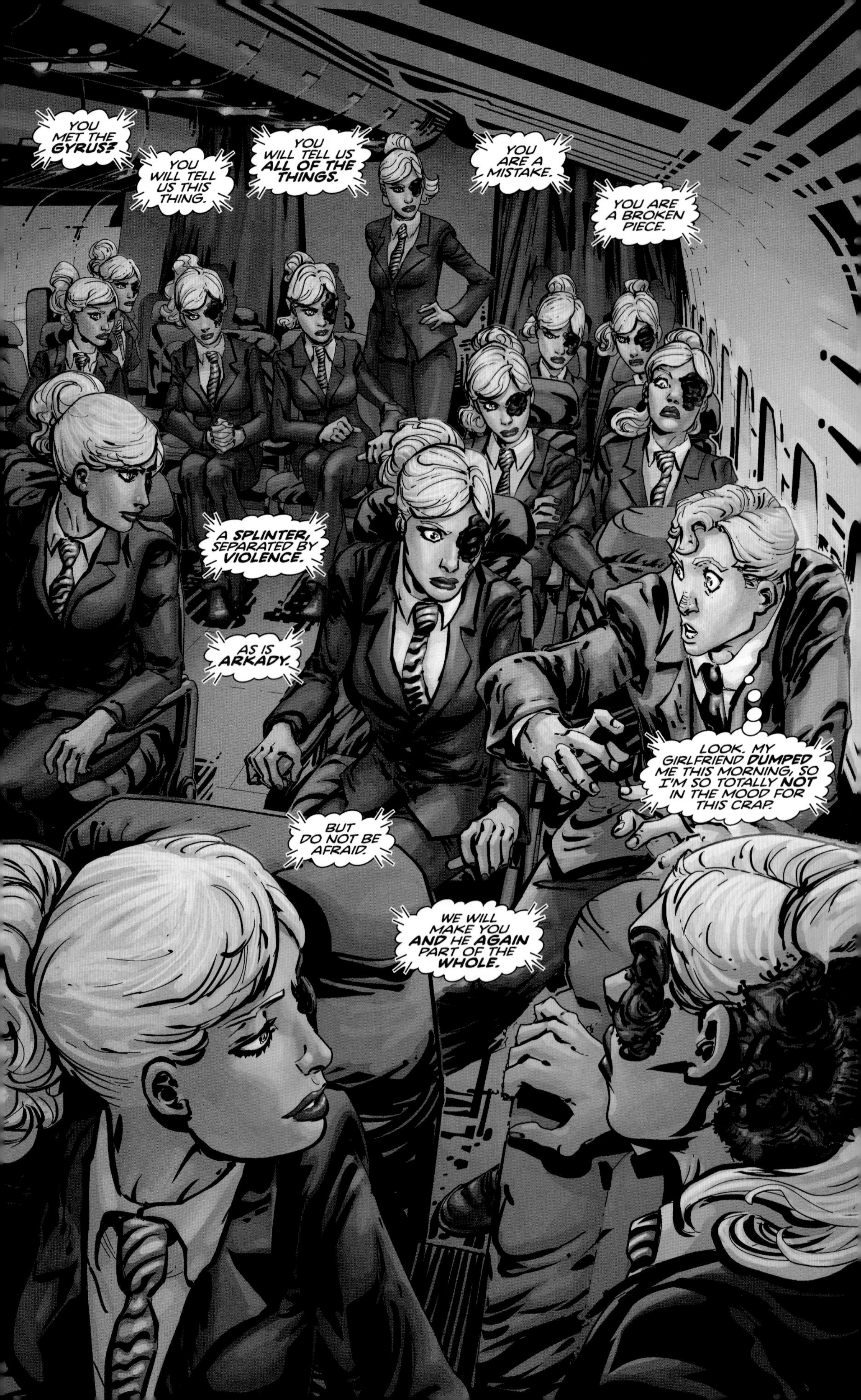
YOU MET THE GYRUS?
YOU WILL TELL US THIS THING.
YOU WILL TELL US ALL OF THE THINGS.
YOU ARE A MISTAKE.
YOU ARE A BROKEN PIECE.
A SPLINTER, SEPARATED BY VIOLENCE.
AS IS ARKADY.
LOOK. MY GIRLFRIEND DUMPED ME THIS MORNING, SO I'M SO TOTALLY NOT IN THE MOOD FOR THIS CRAP.
BUT DO NOT BE AFRAID.
WE WILL MAKE YOU AND HE AGAIN PART OF THE WHOLE.

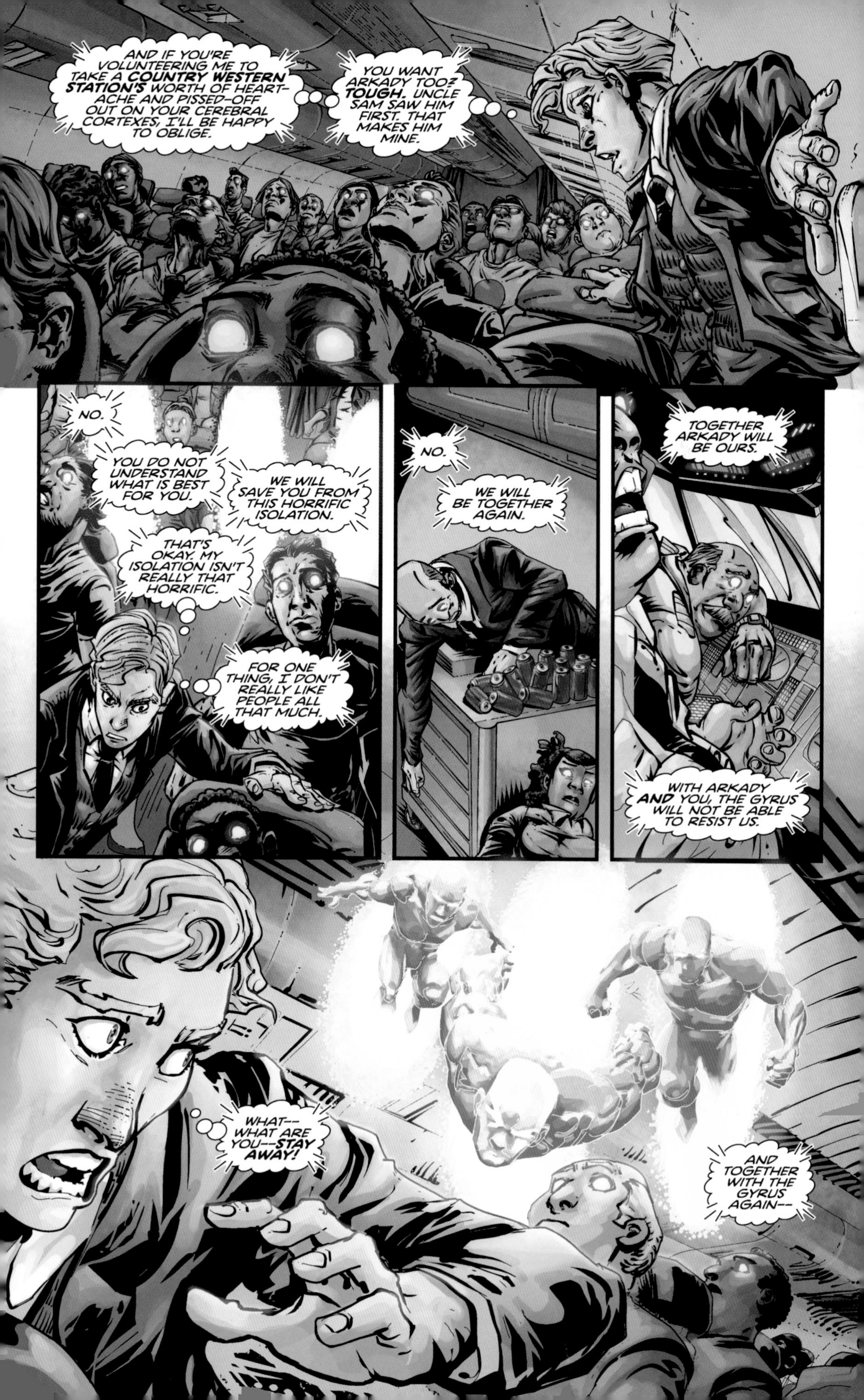
AND IF YOU'RE VOLUNTEERING ME TO TAKE A COUNTRY WESTERN STATION'S WORTH OF HEART-ACHE AND PISSED-OFF OUT ON YOUR CEREBRAL CORTEXES, I'LL BE HAPPY TO OBLIGE.
YOU WANT ARKADY TOO? TOUGH. UNCLE SAM SAW HIM FIRST. THAT MAKES HIM MINE.
NO.
YOU DO NOT UNDERSTAND WHAT IS BEST FOR YOU.
WE WILL SAVE YOU FROM THIS HORRIFIC ISOLATION.
THAT'S OKAY. MY ISOLATION ISN'T REALLY THAT HORRIFIC.
FOR ONE THING, I DON'T REALLY LIKE PEOPLE ALL THAT MUCH.
NO.
WE WILL BE TOGETHER AGAIN.
TOGETHER ARKADY WILL BE OURS.
WITH ARKADY AND YOU, THE GYRUS WILL NOT BE ABLE TO RESIST US.
WHAT-- WHAT ARE YOU--STAY AWAY!
AND TOGETHER WITH THE GYRUS AGAIN--

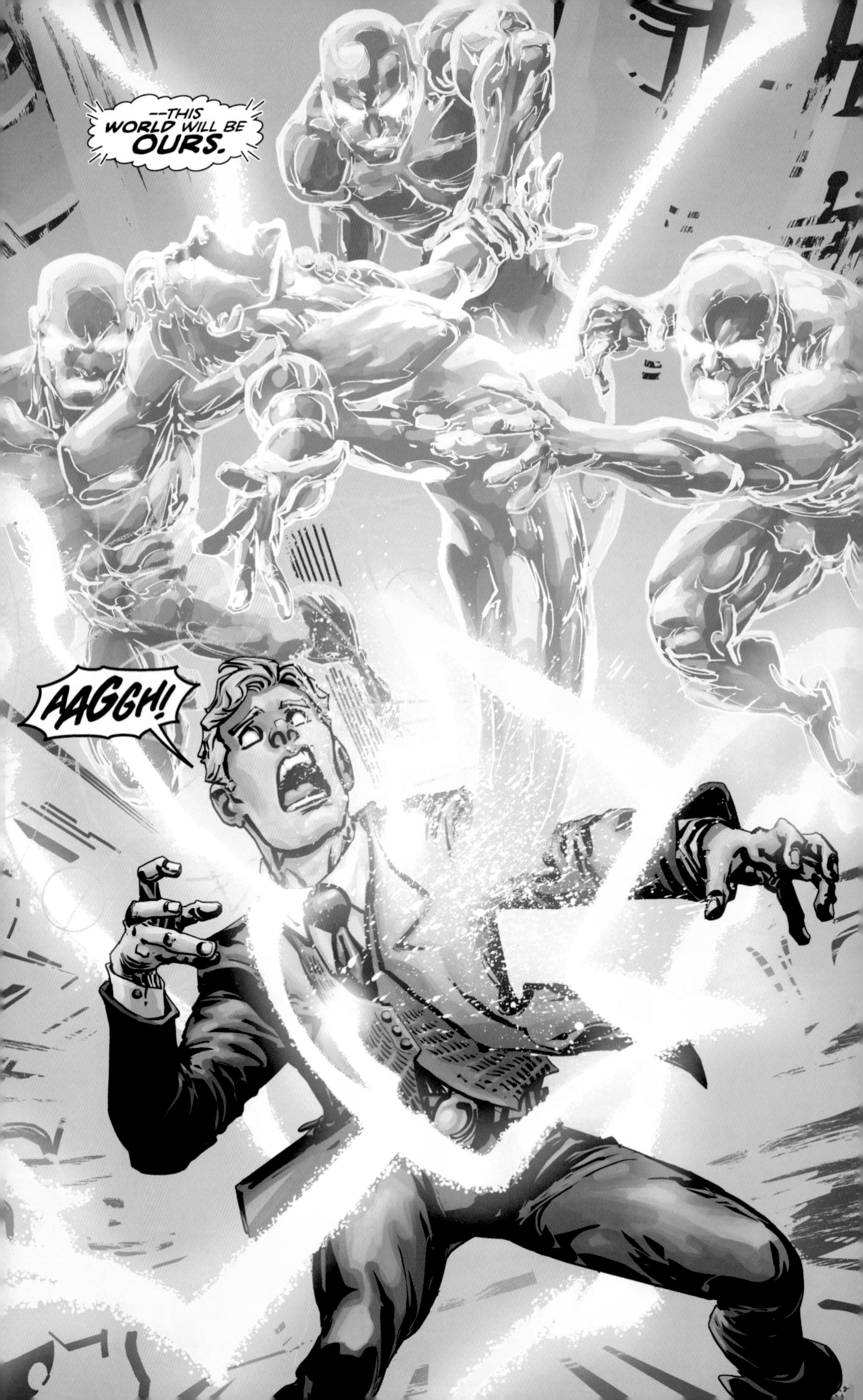
--THIS WORLD WILL BE OURS.
AAGGH!

CHAPTER 2

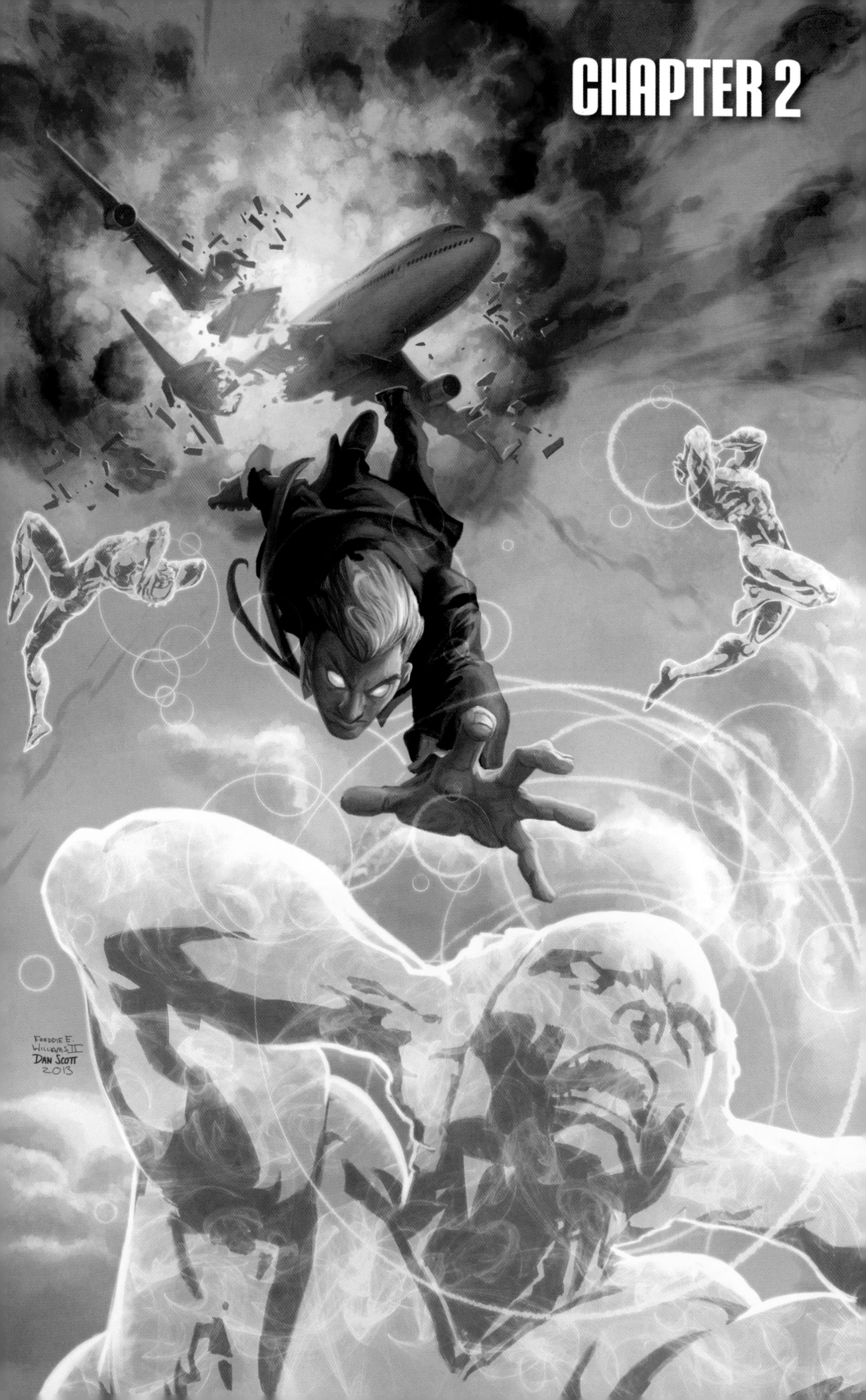
FREDDIE E. WILLIAMS II
DAN SCOTT
2013

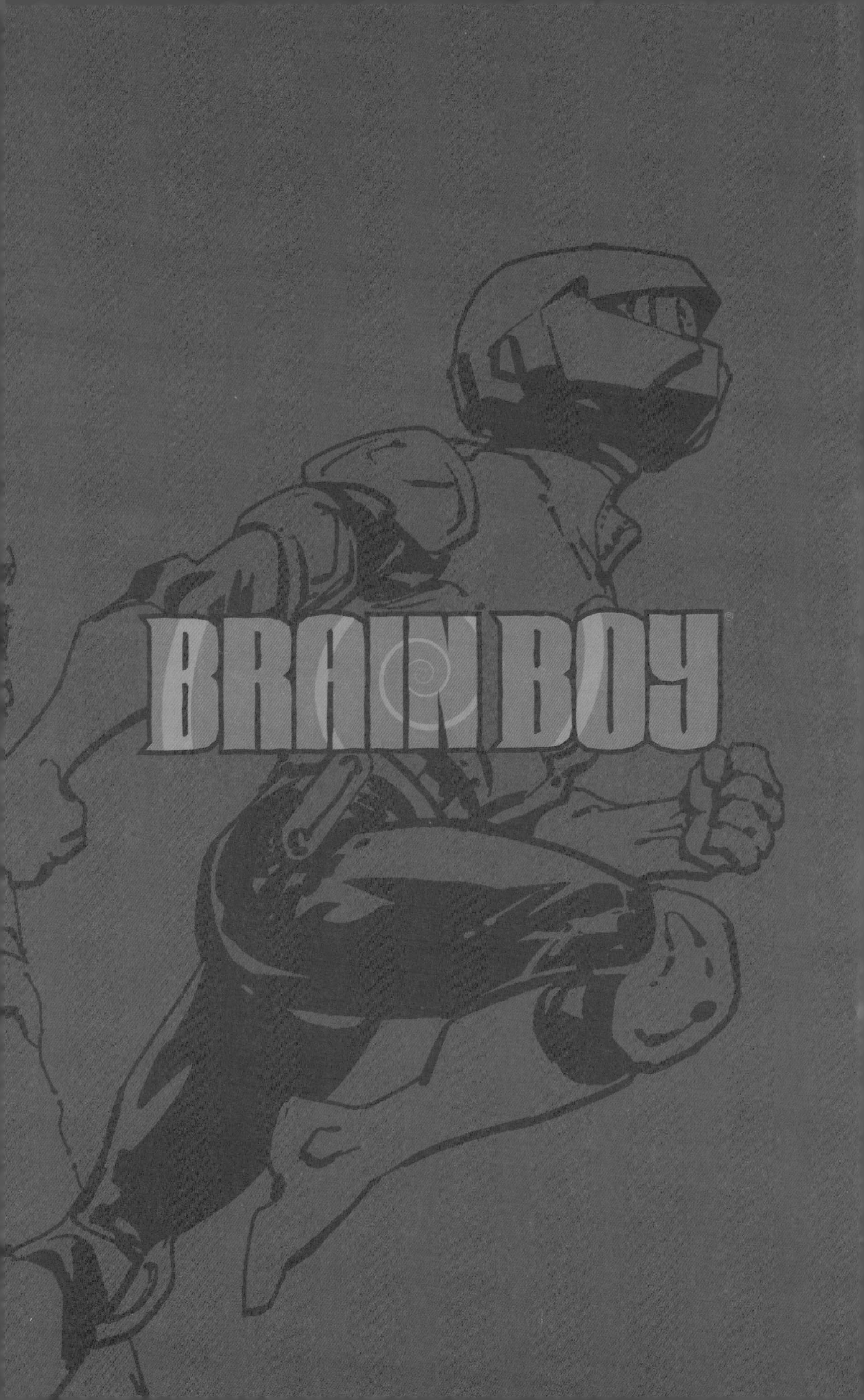
BRAIN BOY

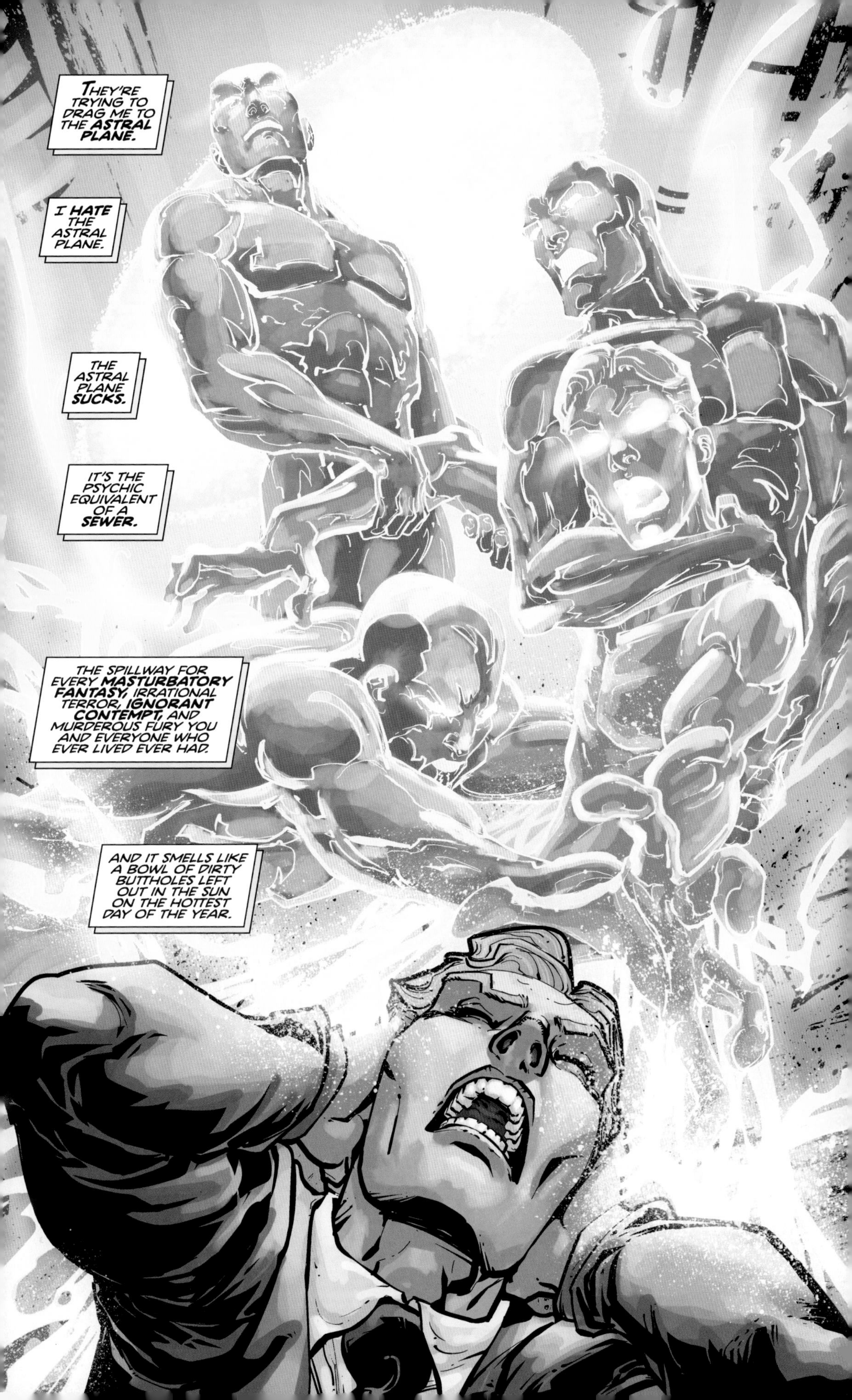
THEY'RE TRYING TO DRAG ME TO THE ASTRAL PLANE.
I HATE THE ASTRAL PLANE.
THE ASTRAL PLANE SUCKS.
IT'S THE PSYCHIC EQUIVALENT OF A SEWER.
THE SPILLWAY FOR EVERY MASTURBATORY FANTASY, IRRATIONAL TERROR, IGNORANT CONTEMPT, AND MURDEROUS FURY YOU AND EVERYONE WHO EVER LIVED EVER HAD.
AND IT SMELLS LIKE A BOWL OF DIRTY BUTTHOLES LEFT OUT IN THE SUN ON THE HOTTEST DAY OF THE YEAR.

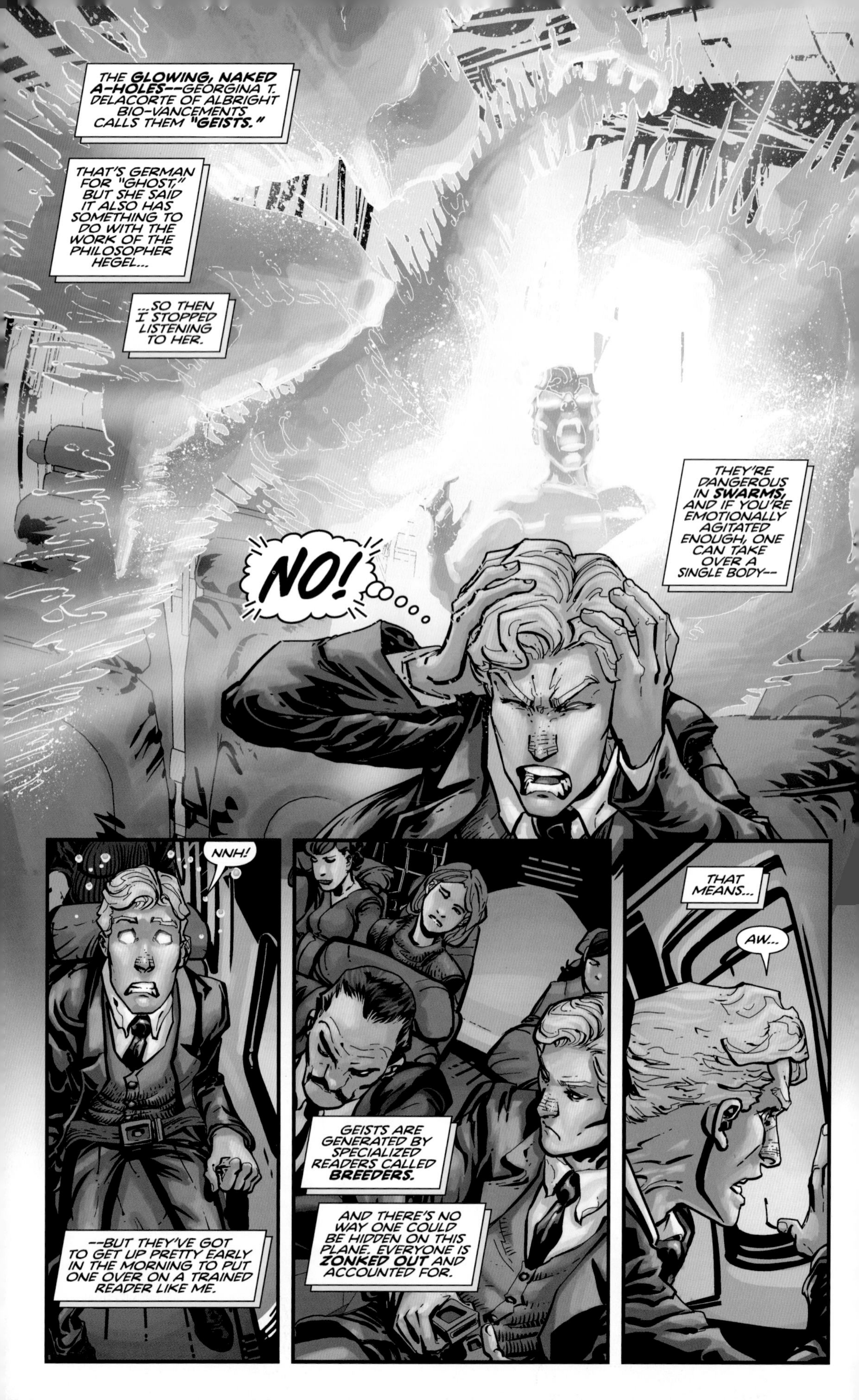
THE GLOWING, NAKED A-HOLES--GEORGINA T. DELACORTE OF ALBRIGHT BIO-VANCEMENTS CALLS THEM "GEISTS."
THAT'S GERMAN FOR "GHOST," BUT SHE SAID IT ALSO HAS SOMETHING TO DO WITH THE WORK OF THE PHILOSOPHER HEGEL...
...SO THEN I STOPPED LISTENING TO HER.
THEY'RE DANGEROUS IN SWARMS, AND IF YOU'RE EMOTIONALLY AGITATED ENOUGH, ONE CAN TAKE OVER A SINGLE BODY--
NO!
NNH!
--BUT THEY'VE GOT TO GET UP PRETTY EARLY IN THE MORNING TO PUT ONE OVER ON A TRAINED READER LIKE ME.
GEISTS ARE GENERATED BY SPECIALIZED READERS CALLED BREEDERS.
AND THERE'S NO WAY ONE COULD BE HIDDEN ON THIS PLANE. EVERYONE IS ZONKED OUT AND ACCOUNTED FOR.
THAT MEANS...
AW...

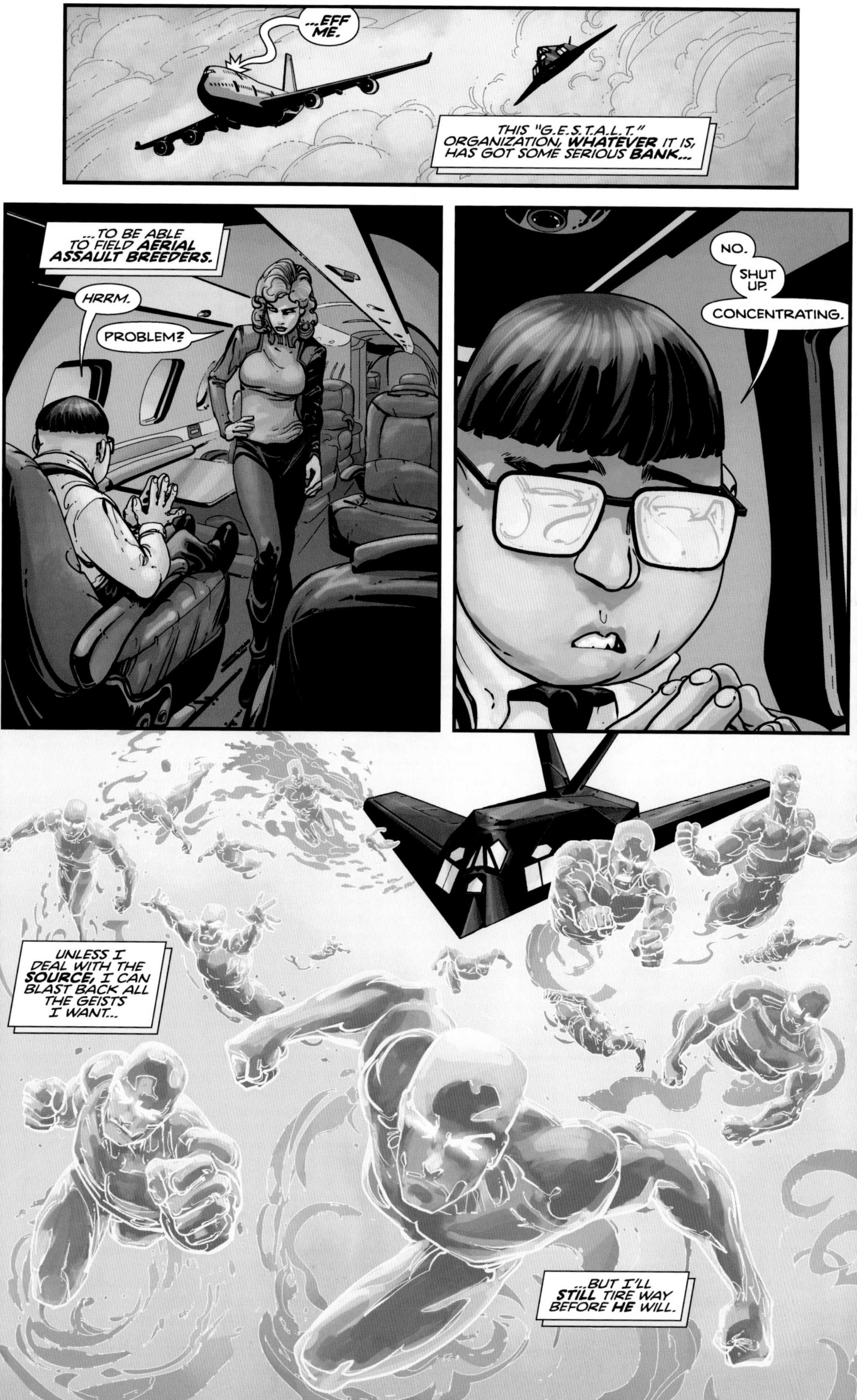
...EFF ME.
THIS "G.E.S.T.A.L.T." ORGANIZATION, WHATEVER IT IS, HAS GOT SOME SERIOUS BANK...
...TO BE ABLE TO FIELD AERIAL ASSAULT BREEDERS.
HRRM.
PROBLEM?
NO.
SHUT UP.
CONCENTRATING.
UNLESS I DEAL WITH THE SOURCE, I CAN BLAST BACK ALL THE GEISTS I WANT...
...BUT I'LL STILL TIRE WAY BEFORE HE WILL.

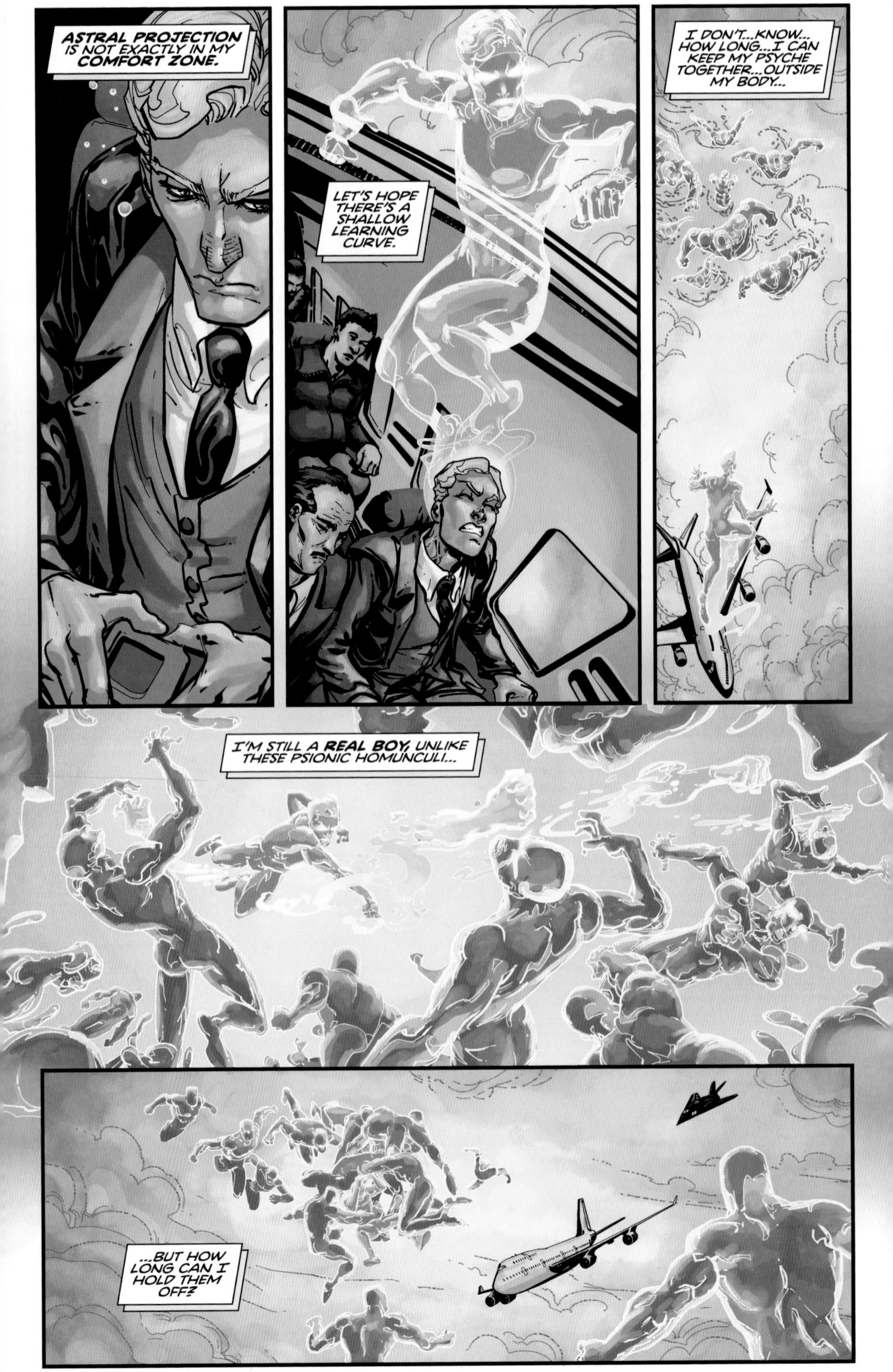
ASTRAL PROJECTION IS NOT EXACTLY IN MY COMFORT ZONE.
LET'S HOPE THERE'S A SHALLOW LEARNING CURVE.
I DON'T...KNOW... HOW LONG...I CAN KEEP MY PSYCHE TOGETHER...OUTSIDE MY BODY...
I'M STILL A REAL BOY, UNLIKE THESE PSIONIC HOMUNCULI...
...BUT HOW LONG CAN I HOLD THEM OFF?

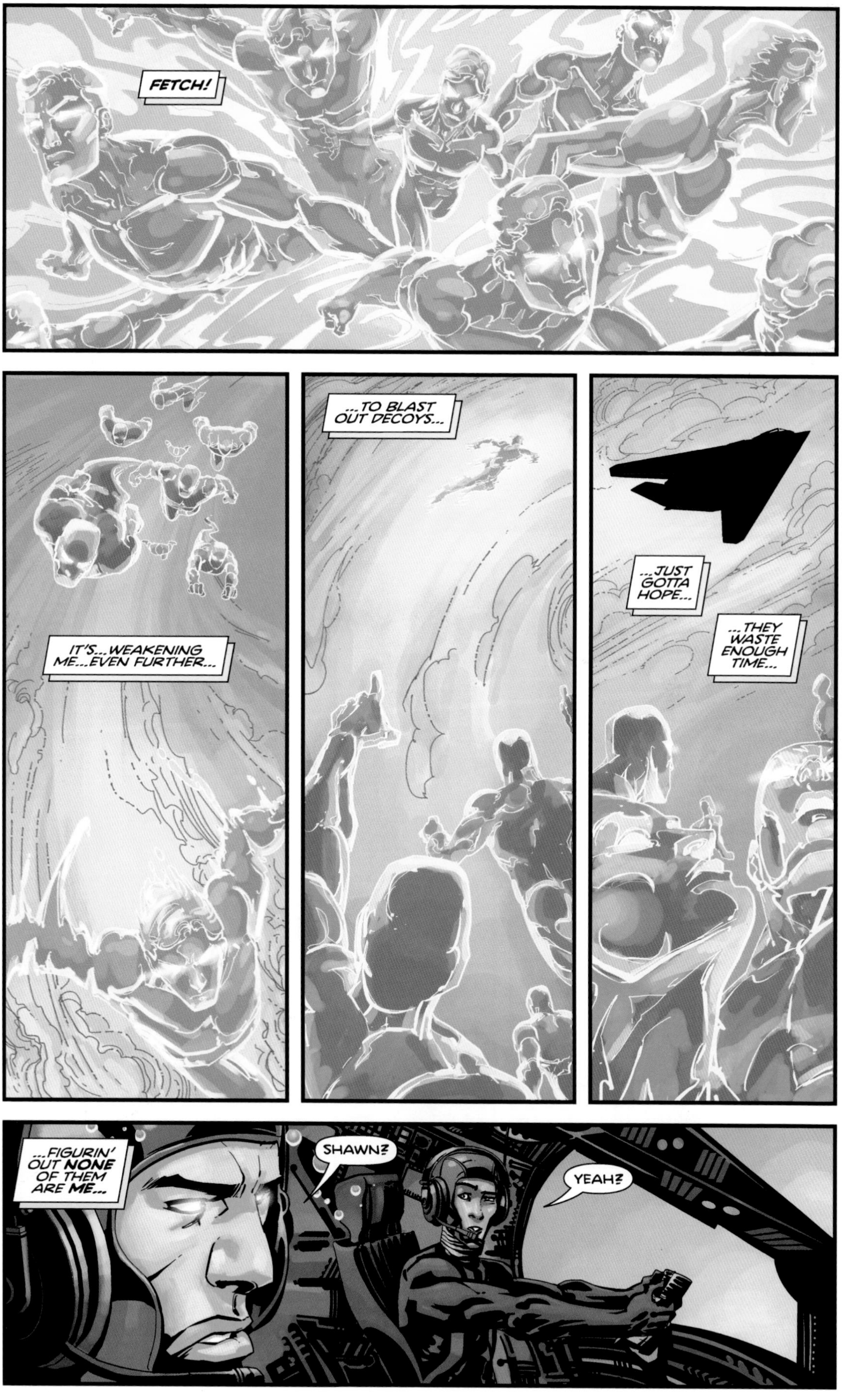
FETCH!
IT'S...WEAKENING ME...EVEN FURTHER...
...TO BLAST OUT DECOYS...
...JUST GOTTA HOPE...
...THEY WASTE ENOUGH TIME...
...FIGURIN' OUT **NONE** OF THEM ARE **ME**...
SHAWN?
YEAH?

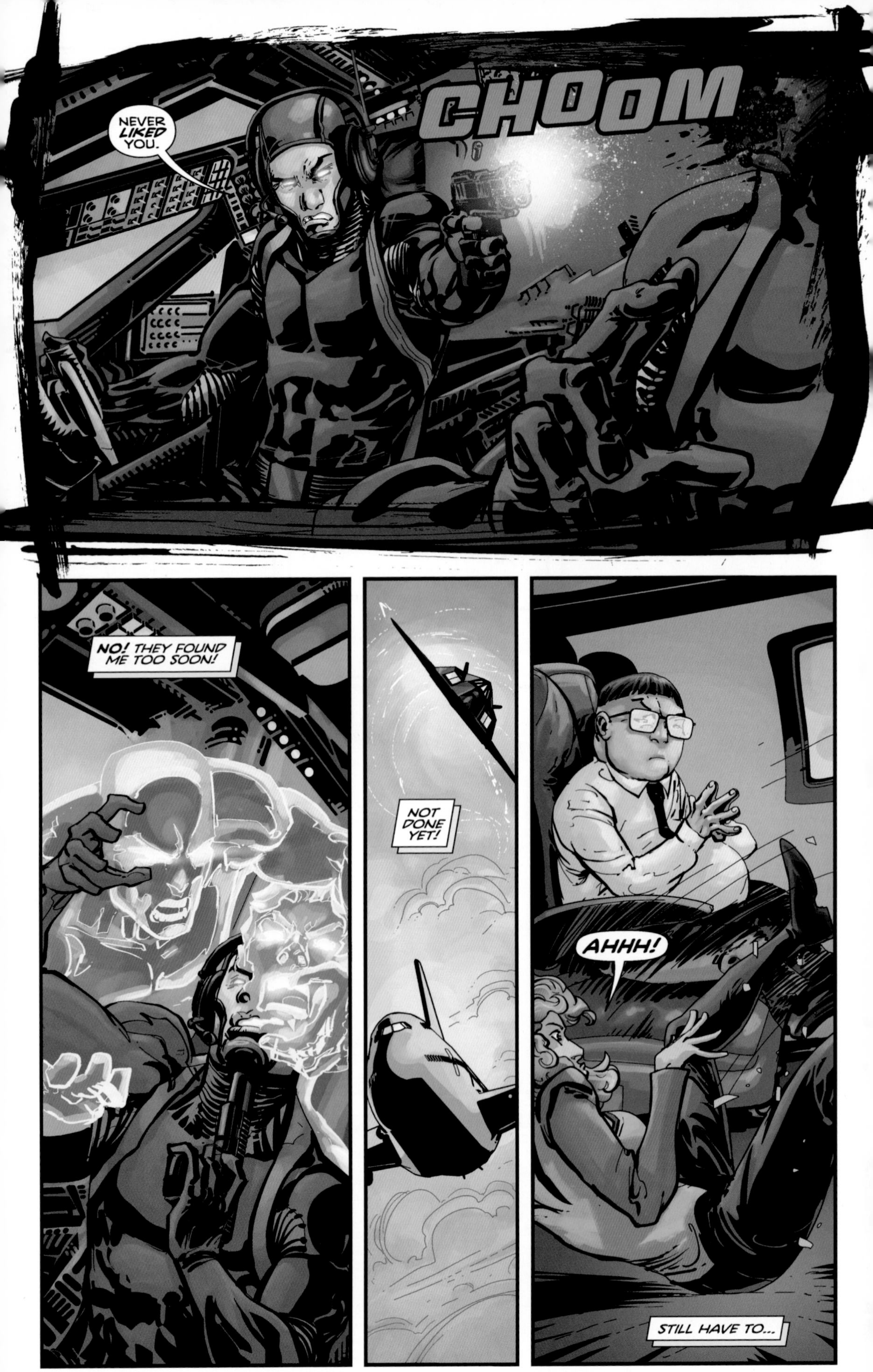
NEVER LIKED YOU.
CHOOM
NO! THEY FOUND ME TOO SOON!
NOT DONE YET!
AHHH!
STILL HAVE TO...

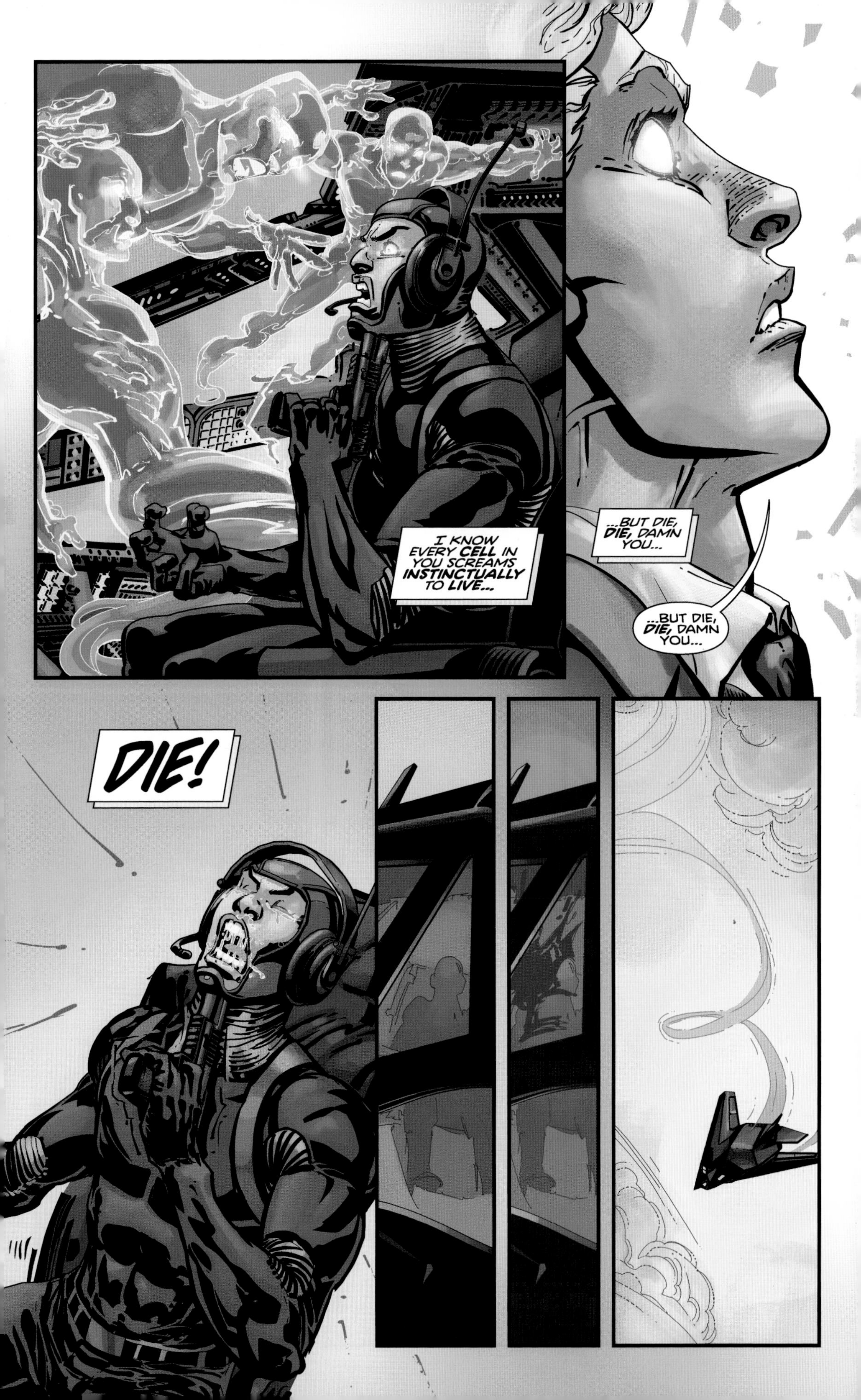

I KNOW EVERY CELL IN YOU SCREAMS INSTINCTUALLY TO LIVE...
...BUT DIE, DIE, DAMN YOU...
...BUT DIE, DIE, DAMN YOU...
DIE!

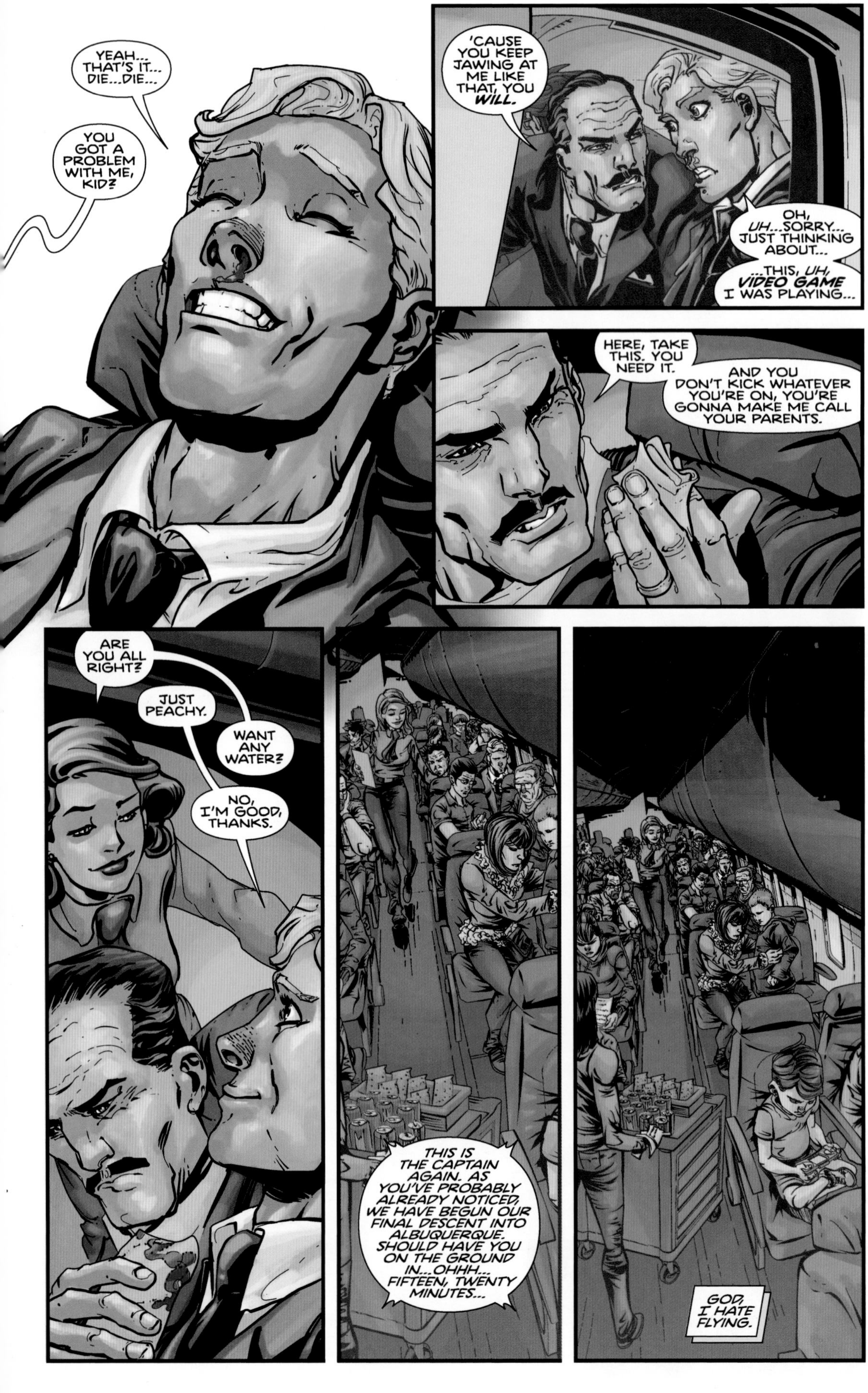
YEAH... THAT'S IT... DIE...DIE...
YOU GOT A PROBLEM WITH ME, KID?
'CAUSE YOU KEEP JAWING AT ME LIKE THAT, YOU WILL.
OH, UH...SORRY... JUST THINKING ABOUT...
...THIS, UH, VIDEO GAME I WAS PLAYING...
HERE, TAKE THIS. YOU NEED IT.
AND YOU DON'T KICK WHATEVER YOU'RE ON, YOU'RE GONNA MAKE ME CALL YOUR PARENTS.
ARE YOU ALL RIGHT?
JUST PEACHY.
WANT ANY WATER?
NO, I'M GOOD, THANKS.
THIS IS THE CAPTAIN AGAIN. AS YOU'VE PROBABLY ALREADY NOTICED, WE HAVE BEGUN OUR FINAL DESCENT INTO ALBUQUERQUE. SHOULD HAVE YOU ON THE GROUND IN...OHHH... FIFTEEN, TWENTY MINUTES...
GOD, I HATE FLYING.

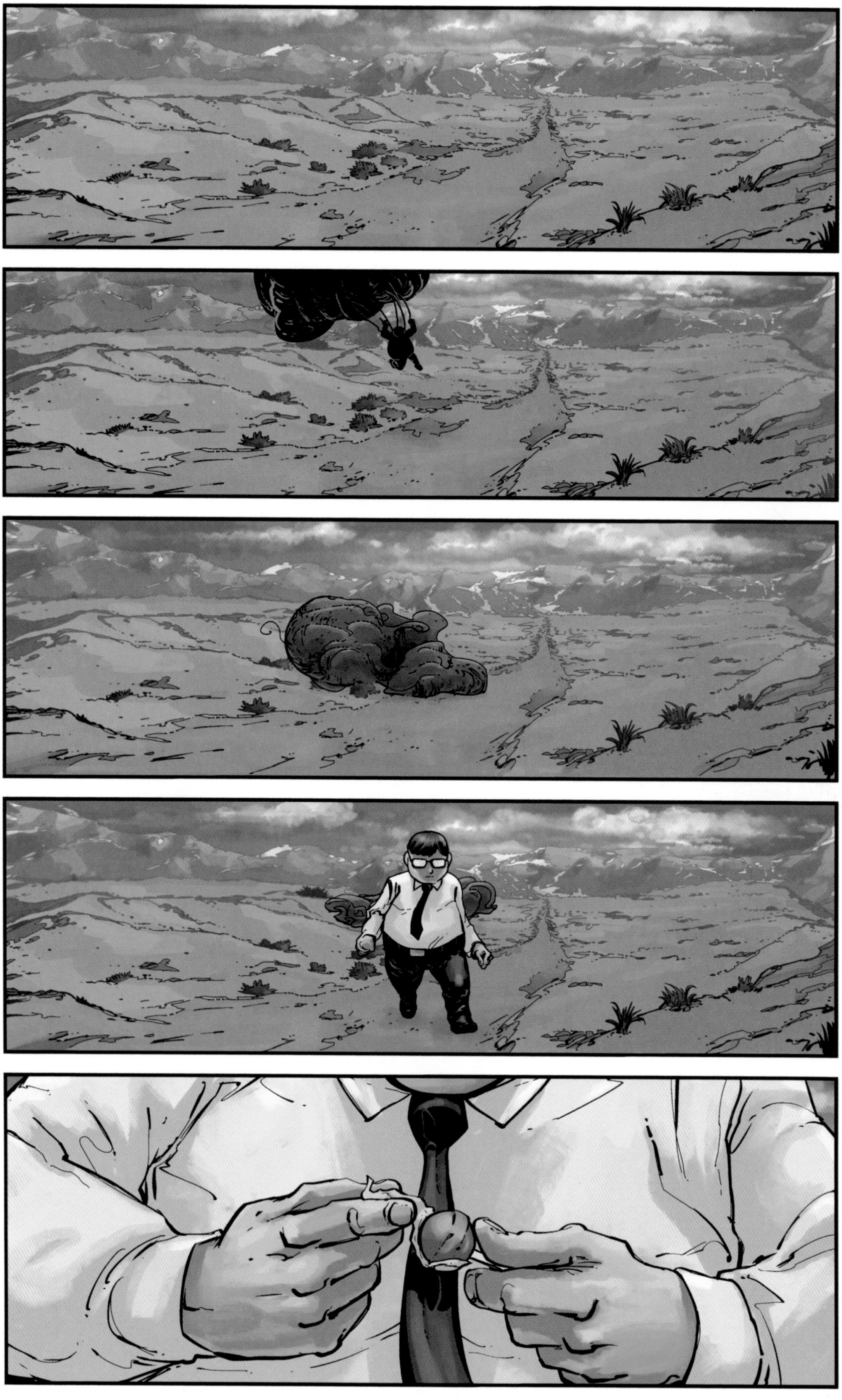

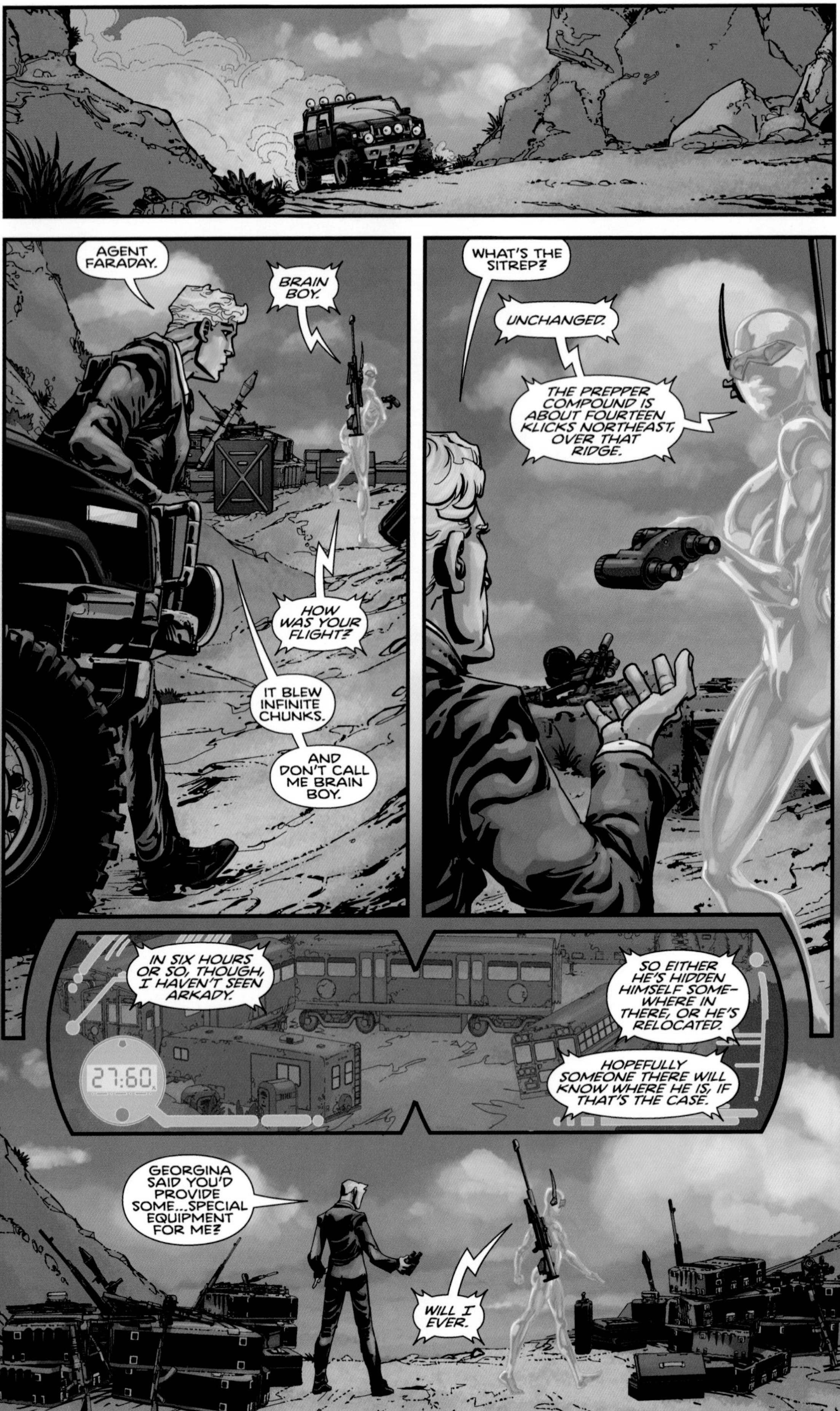
AGENT FARADAY.
BRAIN BOY.
HOW WAS YOUR FLIGHT?
IT BLEW INFINITE CHUNKS.
AND DON'T CALL ME BRAIN BOY.
WHAT'S THE SITREP?
UNCHANGED.
THE PREPPER COMPOUND IS ABOUT FOURTEEN KLICKS NORTHEAST, OVER THAT RIDGE.
IN SIX HOURS OR SO, THOUGH, I HAVEN'T SEEN ARKADY.
SO EITHER HE'S HIDDEN HIMSELF SOME-WHERE IN THERE, OR HE'S RELOCATED.
HOPEFULLY SOMEONE THERE WILL KNOW WHERE HE IS, IF THAT'S THE CASE.
27:60
GEORGINA SAID YOU'D PROVIDE SOME...SPECIAL EQUIPMENT FOR ME?
WILL I EVER.

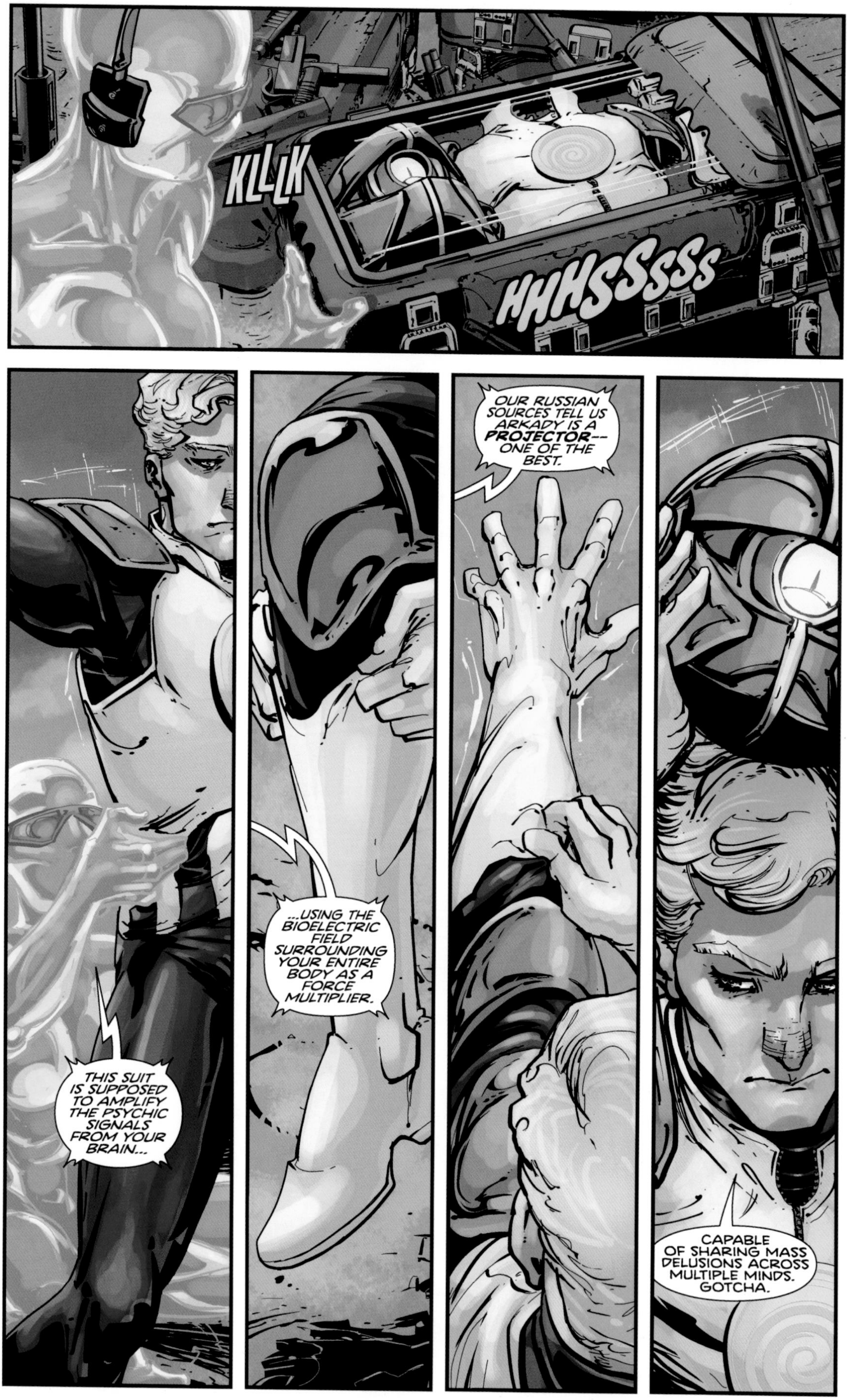
KLLLK
HHHSSSSS
THIS SUIT IS SUPPOSED TO AMPLIFY THE PSYCHIC SIGNALS FROM YOUR BRAIN...
...USING THE BIOELECTRIC FIELD SURROUNDING YOUR ENTIRE BODY AS A FORCE MULTIPLIER.
OUR RUSSIAN SOURCES TELL US ARKADY IS A PROJECTOR-- ONE OF THE BEST.
CAPABLE OF SHARING MASS DELUSIONS ACROSS MULTIPLE MINDS. GOTCHA.

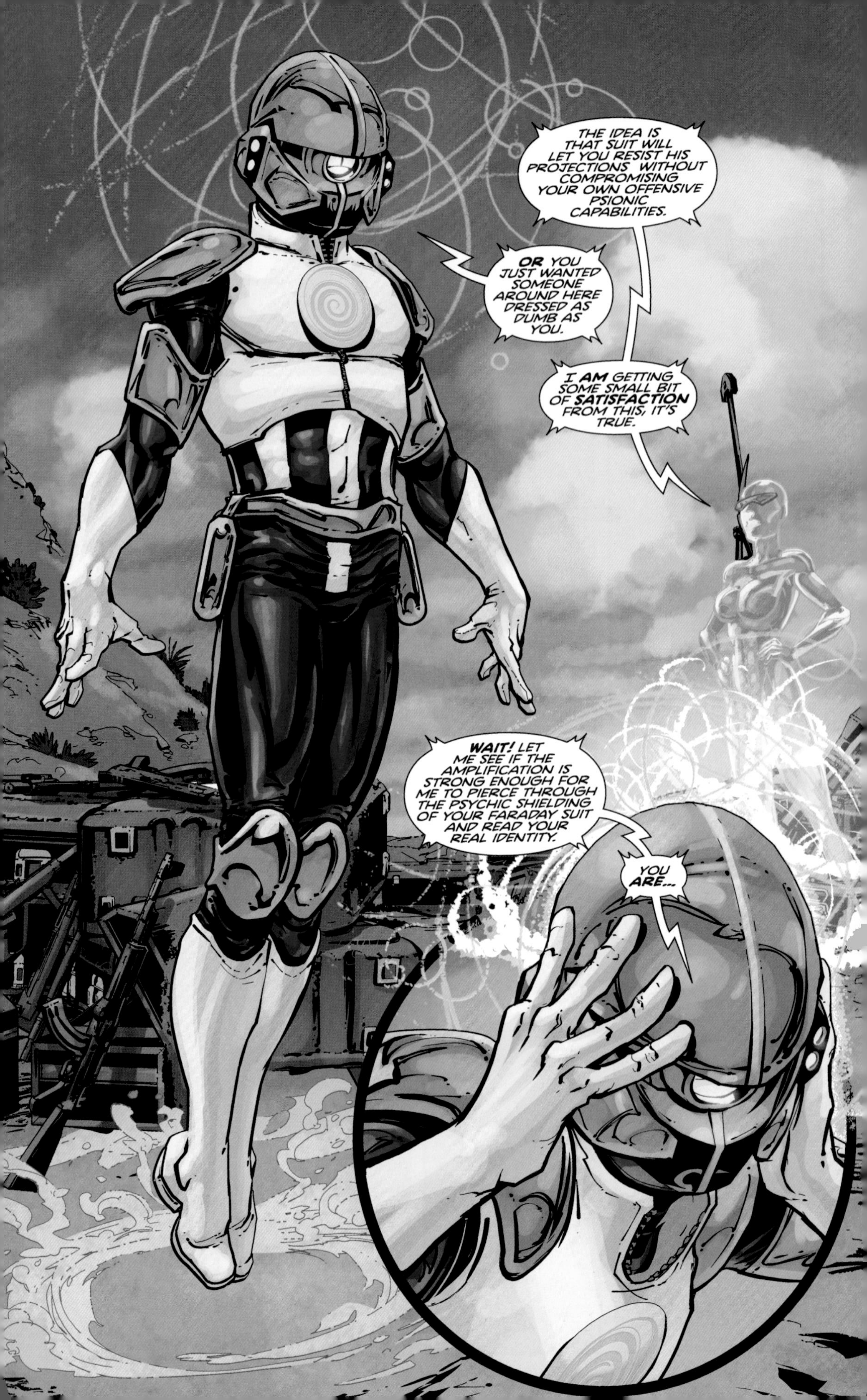
THE IDEA IS THAT SUIT WILL LET YOU RESIST HIS PROJECTIONS WITHOUT COMPROMISING YOUR OWN OFFENSIVE PSIONIC CAPABILITIES.
OR YOU JUST WANTED SOMEONE AROUND HERE DRESSED AS DUMB AS YOU.
I AM GETTING SOME SMALL BIT OF SATISFACTION FROM THIS, IT'S TRUE.
WAIT! LET ME SEE IF THE AMPLIFICATION IS STRONG ENOUGH FOR ME TO PIERCE THROUGH THE PSYCHIC SHIELDING OF YOUR FARADAY SUIT AND READ YOUR REAL IDENTITY.
YOU ARE...

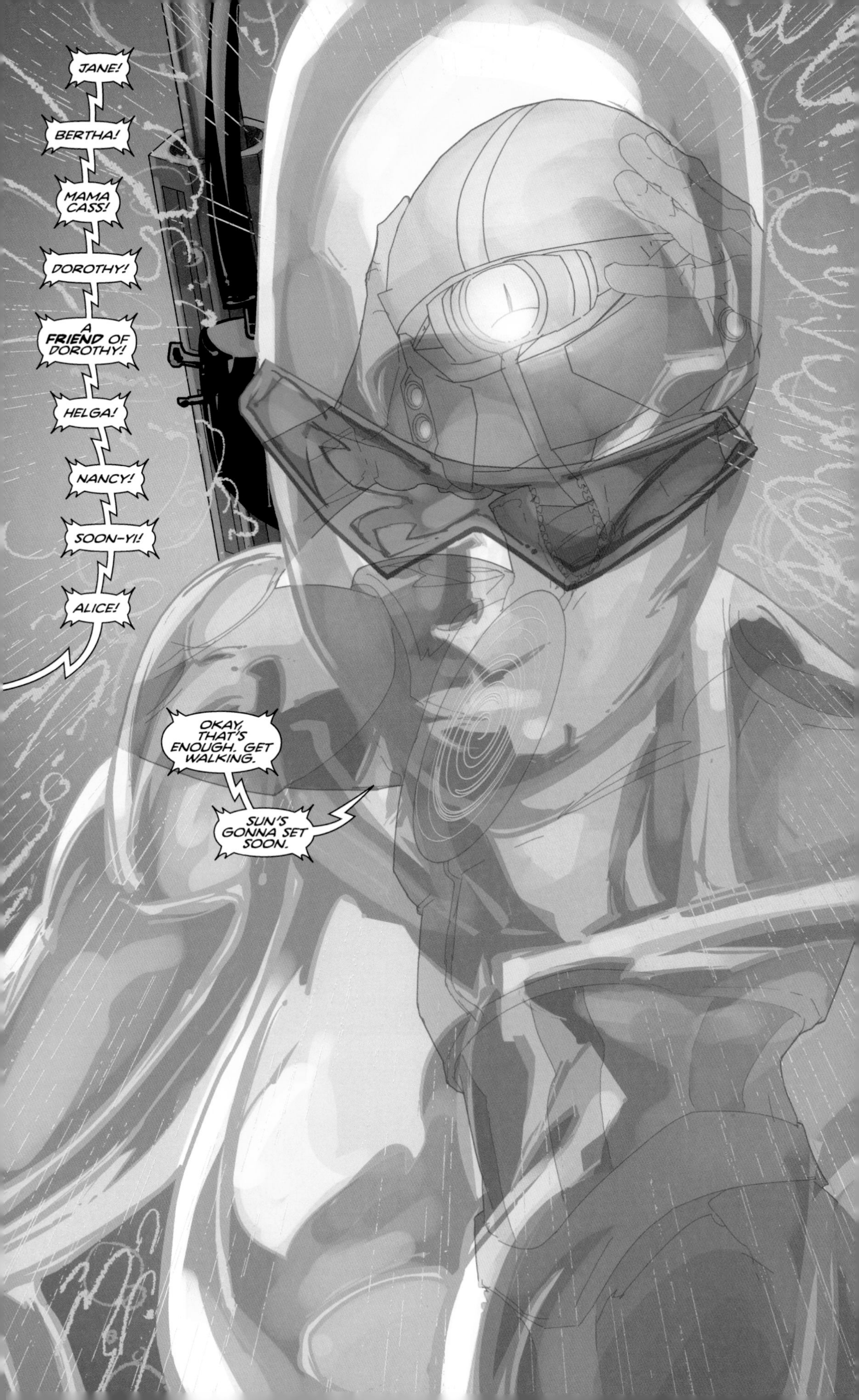
JANE!
BERTHA!
MAMA CASS!
DOROTHY!
A **FRIEND** OF DOROTHY!
HELGA!
NANCY!
SOON-YI!
ALICE!
OKAY, THAT'S ENOUGH. GET WALKING.
SUN'S GONNA SET SOON.

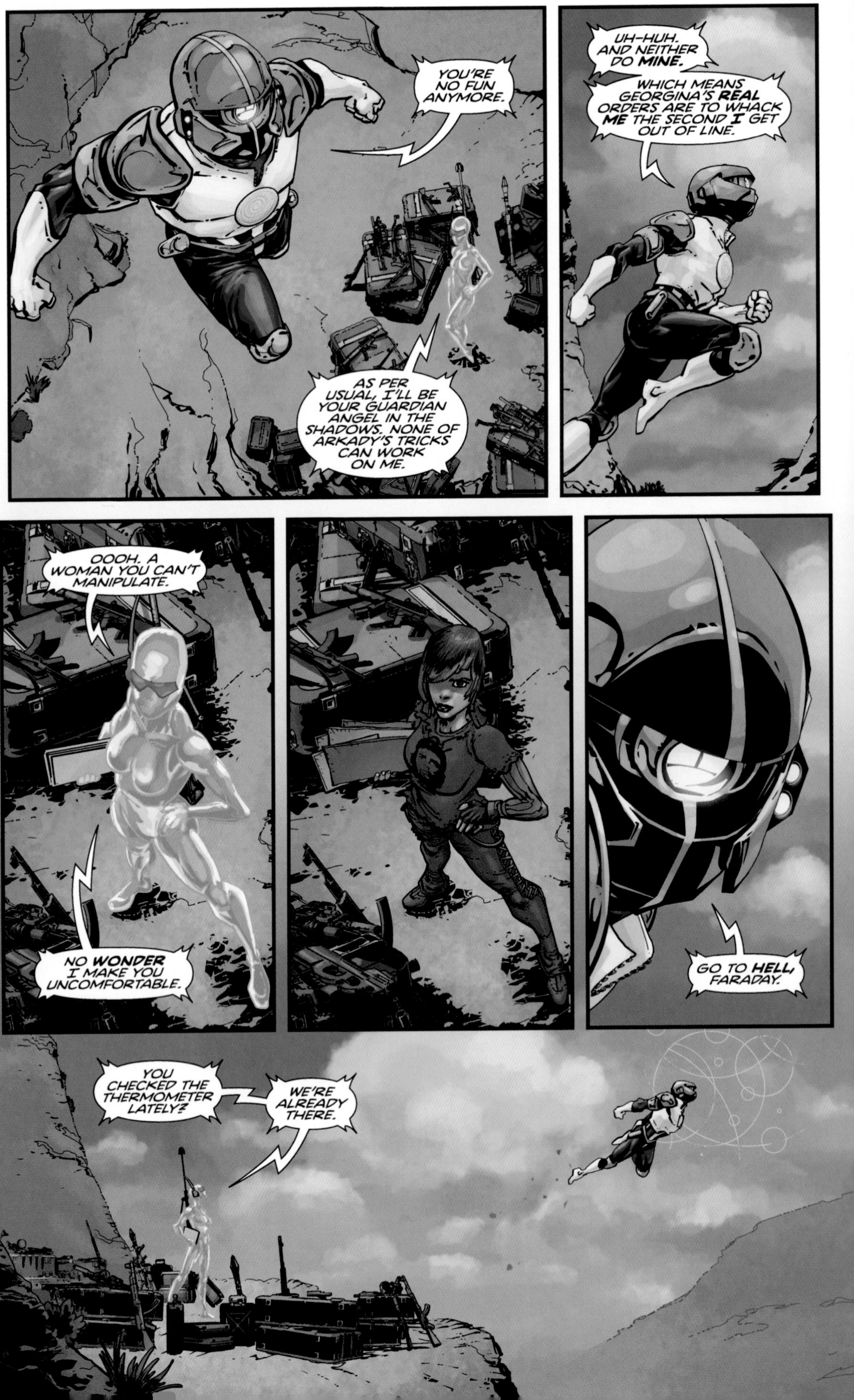
YOU'RE NO FUN ANYMORE.
AS PER USUAL, I'LL BE YOUR GUARDIAN ANGEL IN THE SHADOWS. NONE OF ARKADY'S TRICKS CAN WORK ON ME.
UH-HUH. AND NEITHER DO MINE.
WHICH MEANS GEORGINA'S REAL ORDERS ARE TO WHACK ME THE SECOND I GET OUT OF LINE.
OOOH. A WOMAN YOU CAN'T MANIPULATE.
NO WONDER I MAKE YOU UNCOMFORTABLE.
GO TO HELL, FARADAY.
YOU CHECKED THE THERMOMETER LATELY?
WE'RE ALREADY THERE.

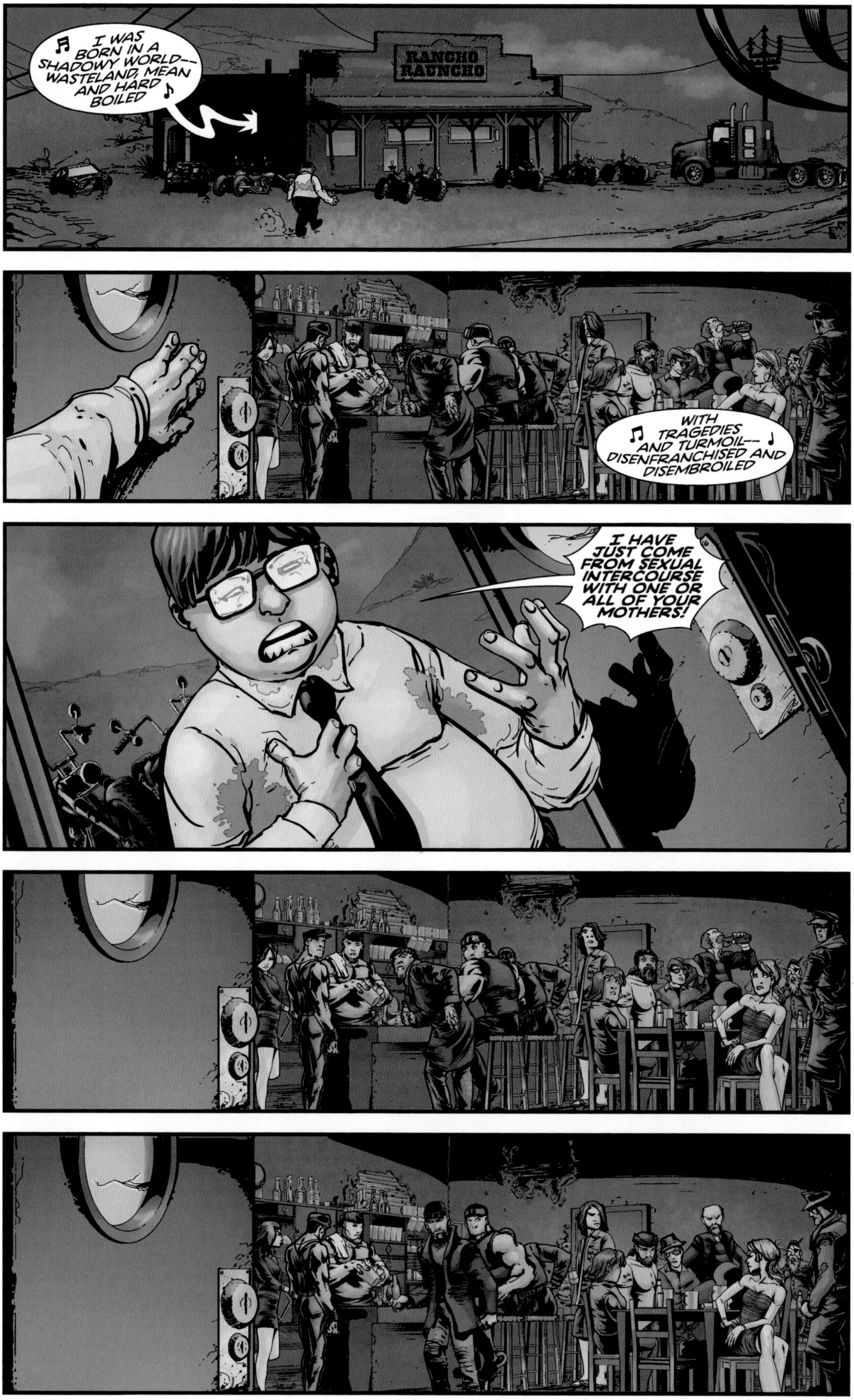
♬ I WAS BORN IN A SHADOWY WORLD-- WASTELAND, MEAN AND HARD BOILED ♪
RANCHO RAUNCHO
♬ WITH TRAGEDIES AND TURMOIL-- ♩ DISENFRANCHISED AND DISEMBROILED
I HAVE JUST COME FROM SEXUAL INTERCOURSE WITH ONE OR ALL OF YOUR MOTHERS!

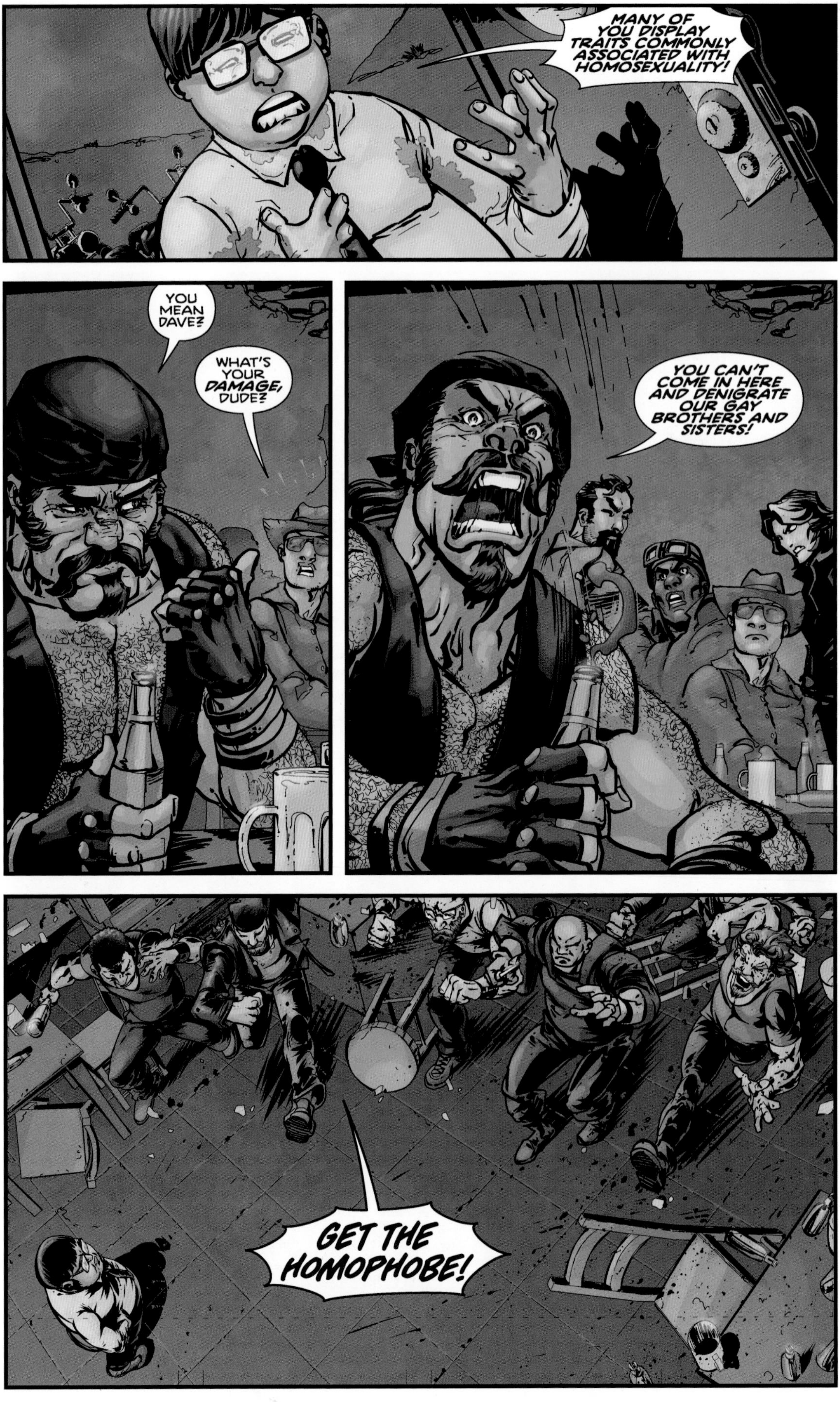
MANY OF YOU DISPLAY TRAITS COMMONLY ASSOCIATED WITH HOMOSEXUALITY!
YOU MEAN DAVE?
WHAT'S YOUR DAMAGE, DUDE?
YOU CAN'T COME IN HERE AND DENIGRATE OUR GAY BROTHERS AND SISTERS!
GET THE HOMOPHOBE!

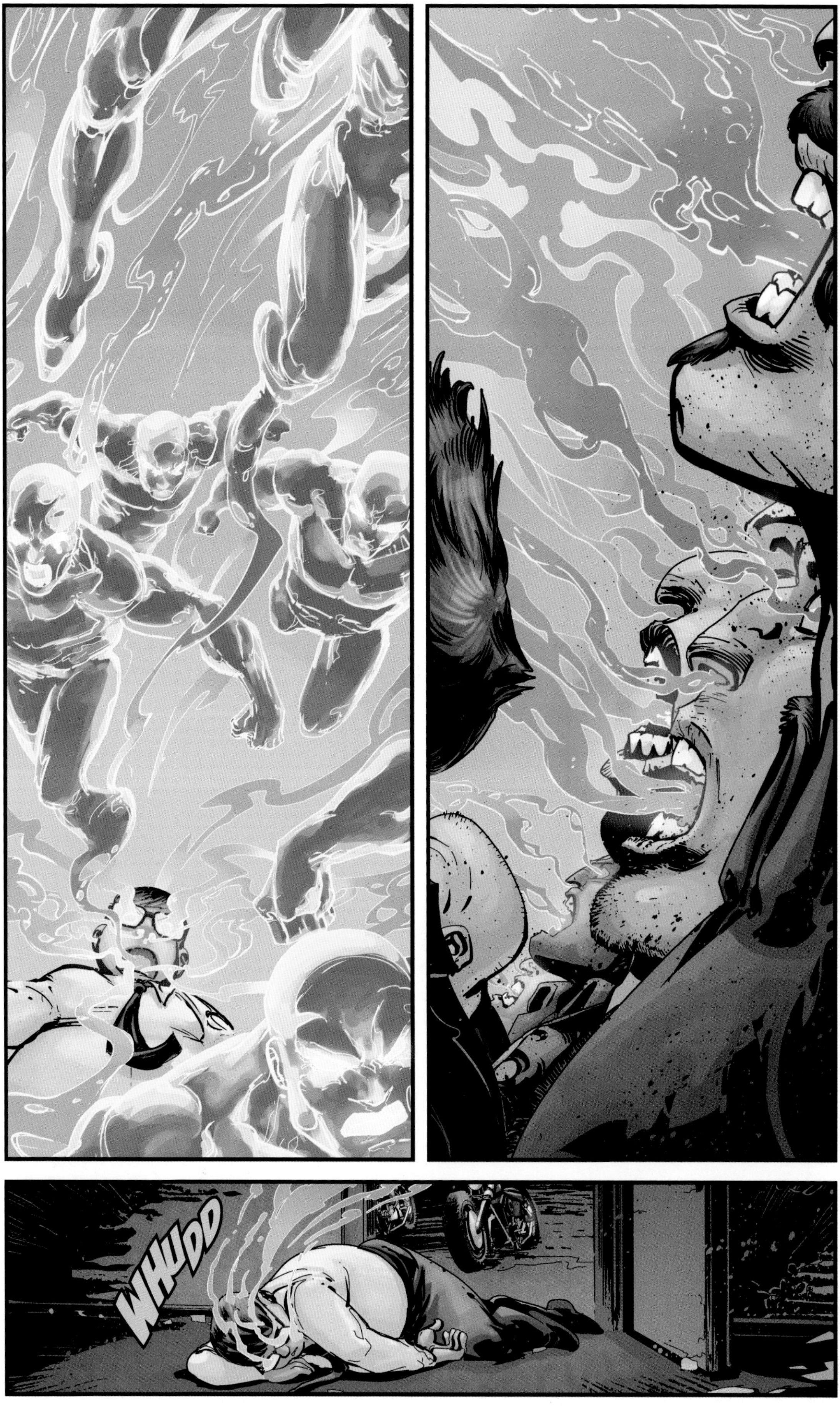
WHUDD

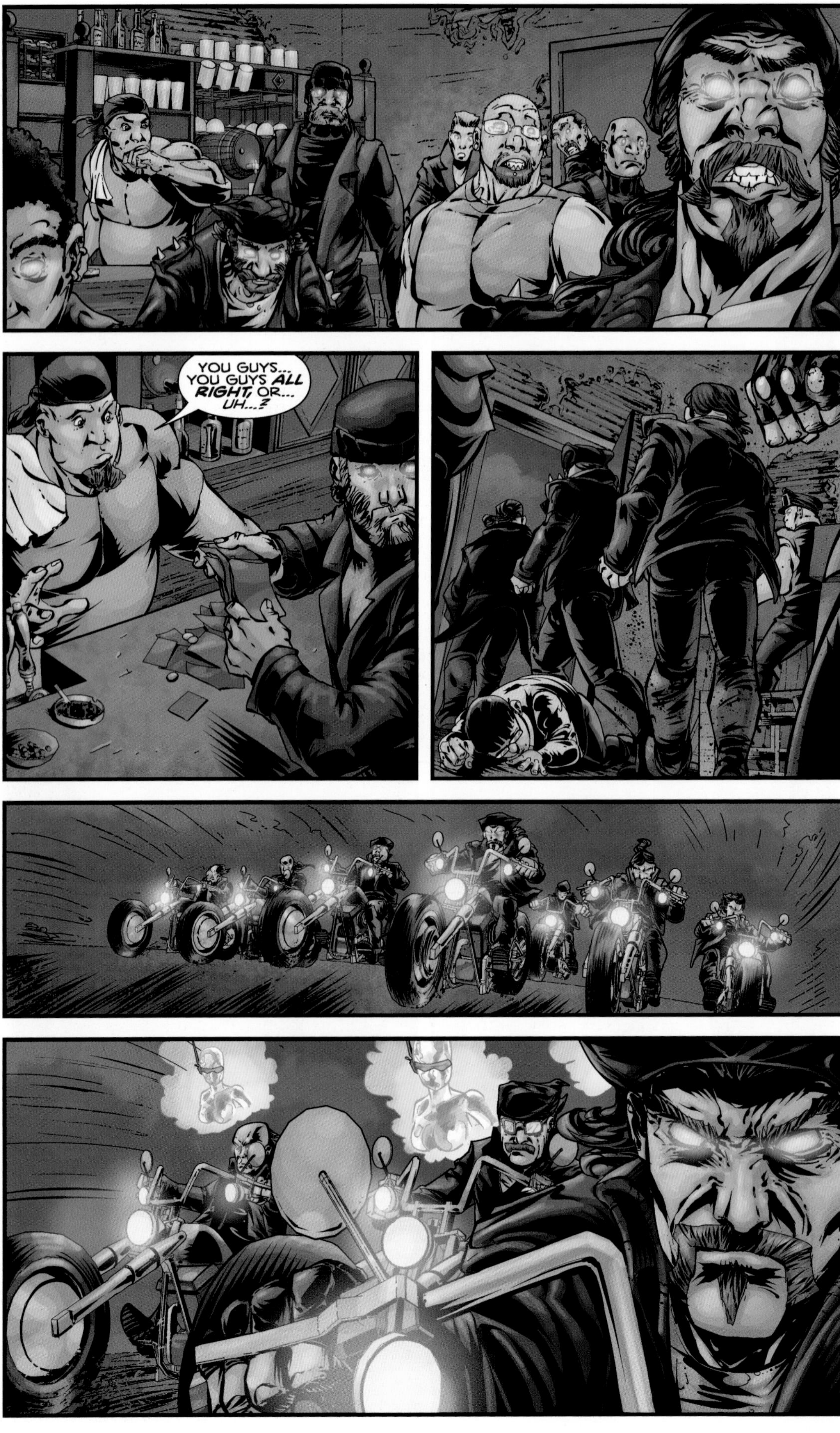
YOU GUYS... YOU GUYS ALL RIGHT, OR... UH...?

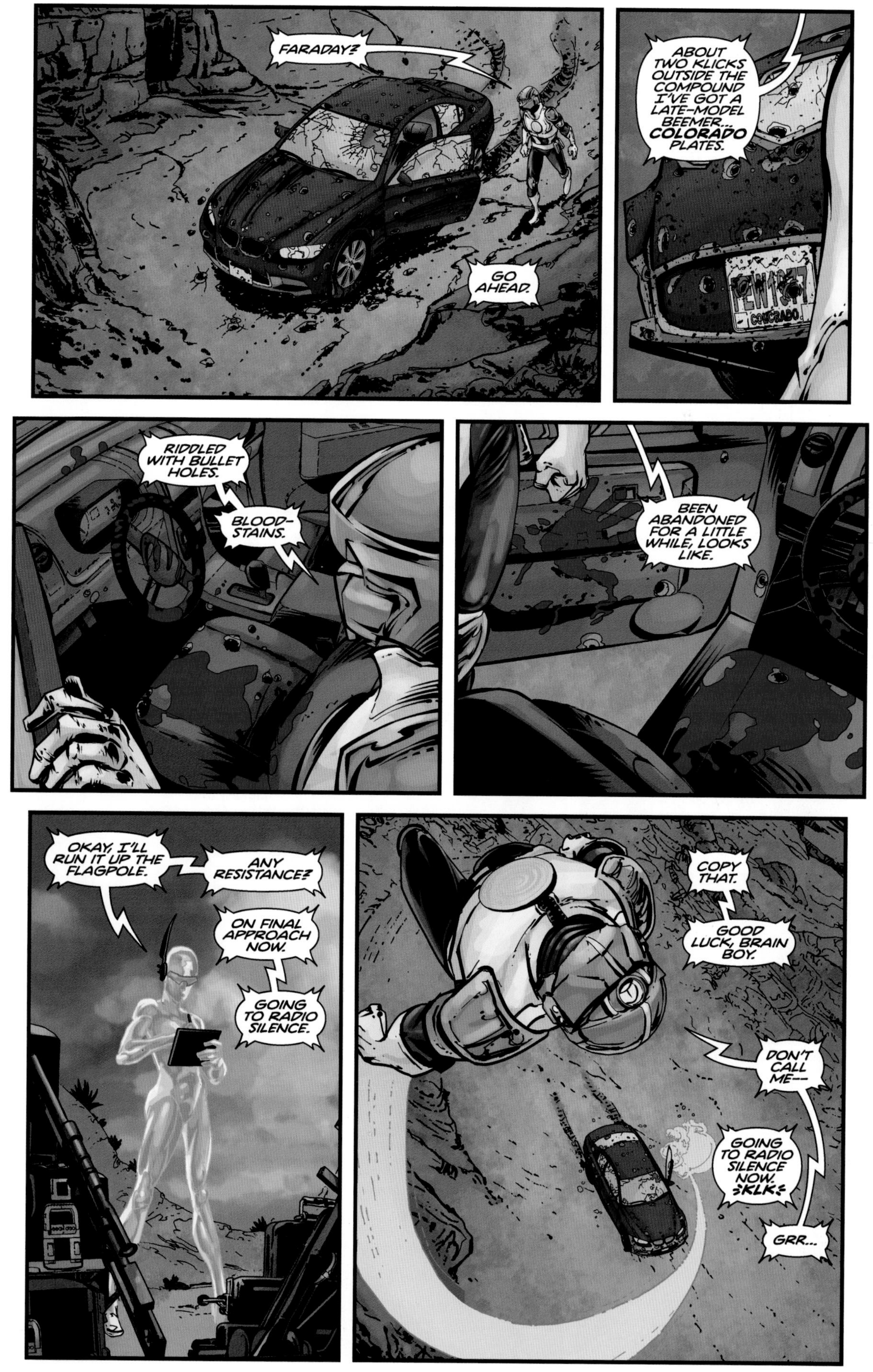
FARADAY?
ABOUT TWO KLICKS OUTSIDE THE COMPOUND I'VE GOT A LATE-MODEL BEEMER... COLORADO PLATES.
GO AHEAD.
COLORADO
RIDDLED WITH BULLET HOLES.
BLOOD-STAINS.
BEEN ABANDONED FOR A LITTLE WHILE, LOOKS LIKE.
OKAY, I'LL RUN IT UP THE FLAGPOLE.
ANY RESISTANCE?
ON FINAL APPROACH NOW.
GOING TO RADIO SILENCE.
COPY THAT.
GOOD LUCK, BRAIN BOY.
DON'T CALL ME--
GOING TO RADIO SILENCE NOW. <KLK>
GRR...

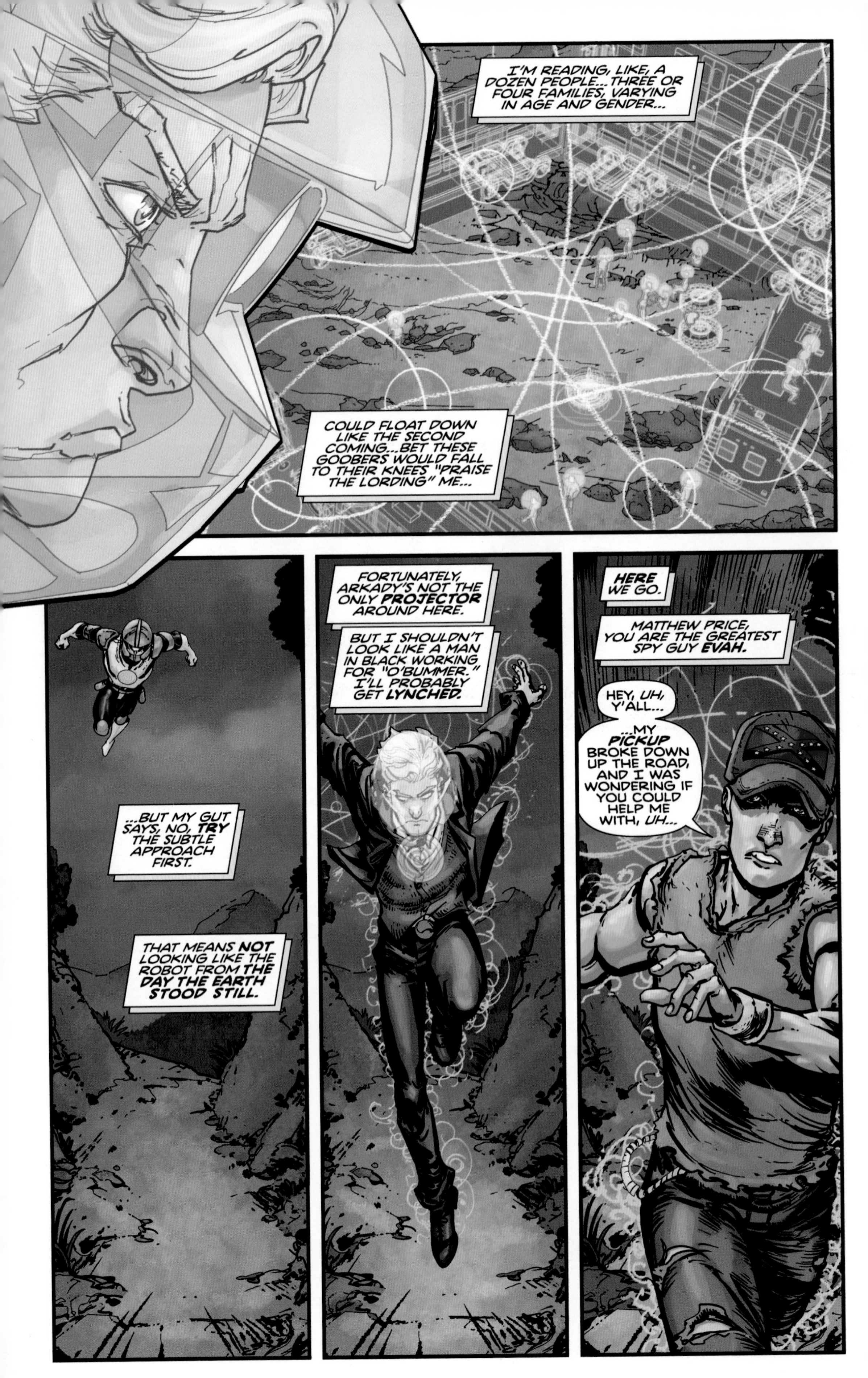
I'M READING, LIKE, A DOZEN PEOPLE... THREE OR FOUR FAMILIES, VARYING IN AGE AND GENDER...
COULD FLOAT DOWN LIKE THE SECOND COMING...BET THESE GOOBERS WOULD FALL TO THEIR KNEES "PRAISE THE LORDING" ME...
...BUT MY GUT SAYS, NO, **TRY** THE SUBTLE APPROACH FIRST.
THAT MEANS **NOT** LOOKING LIKE THE ROBOT FROM **THE DAY THE EARTH STOOD STILL.**
FORTUNATELY, ARKADY'S NOT THE ONLY **PROJECTOR** AROUND HERE.
BUT I SHOULDN'T LOOK LIKE A MAN IN BLACK WORKING FOR "O'BUMMER." I'LL PROBABLY GET **LYNCHED.**
HERE WE GO.
MATTHEW PRICE, YOU ARE THE GREATEST SPY GUY **EVAH.**
HEY, *UH,* Y'ALL...
...MY ***PICKUP*** BROKE DOWN UP THE ROAD, AND I WAS WONDERING IF YOU COULD HELP ME WITH, *UH*...

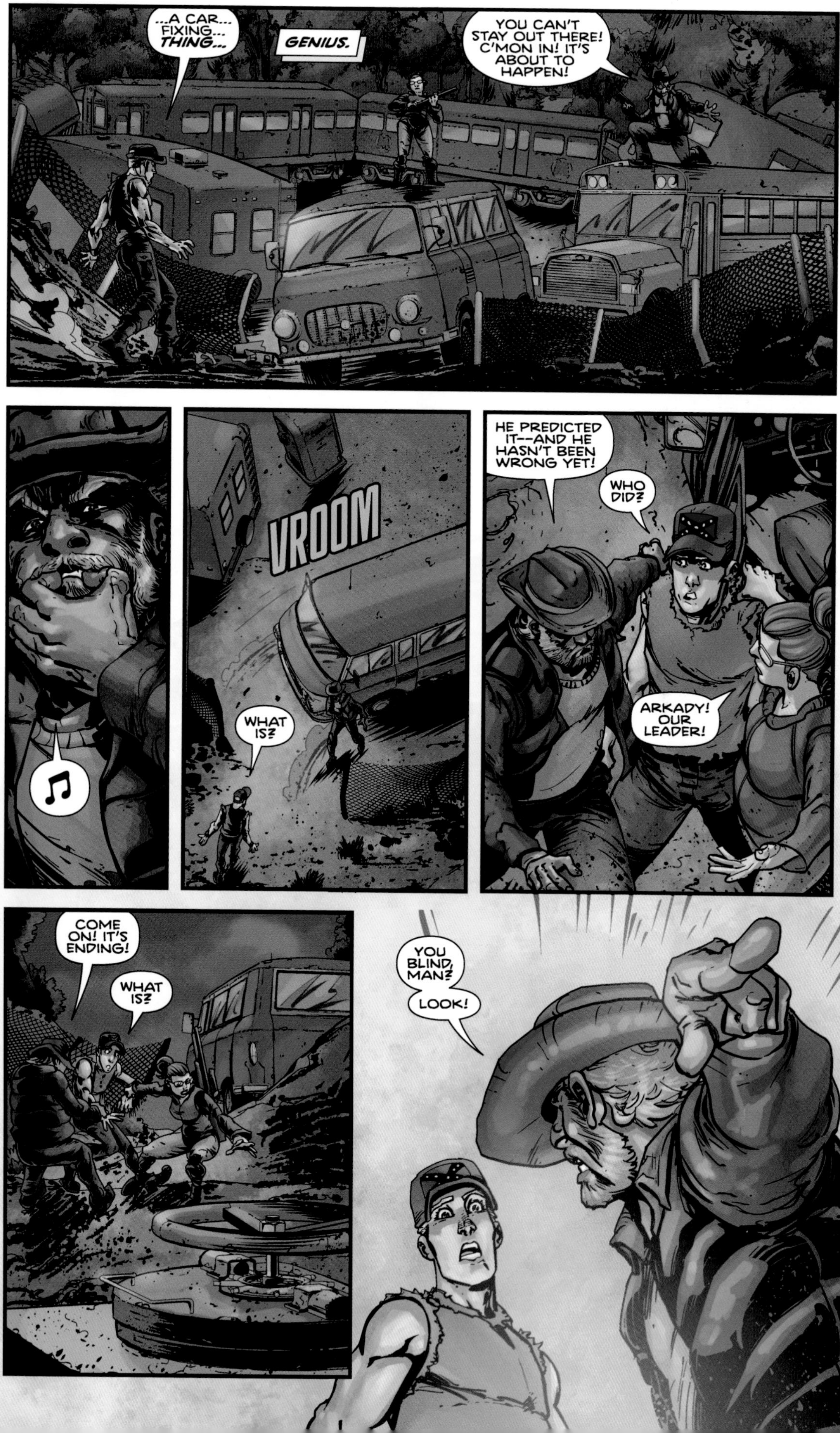
...A CAR... FIXING... THING...
GENIUS.
YOU CAN'T STAY OUT THERE! C'MON IN! IT'S ABOUT TO HAPPEN!
♫
VROOM
WHAT IS?
HE PREDICTED IT--AND HE HASN'T BEEN WRONG YET!
WHO DID?
ARKADY! OUR LEADER!
COME ON! IT'S ENDING!
WHAT IS?
YOU BLIND, MAN?
LOOK!

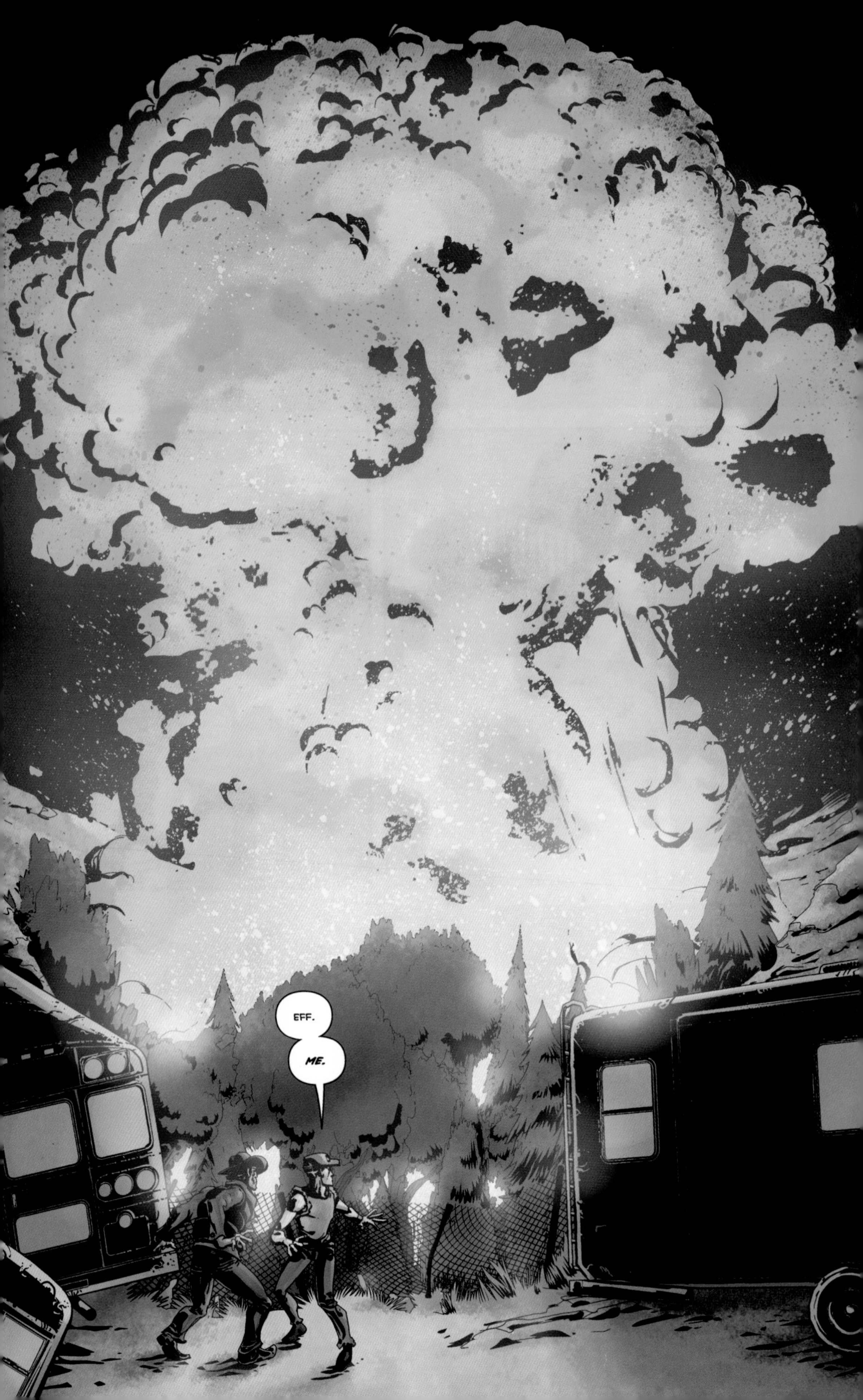
EFF.
ME.

CHAPTER 3

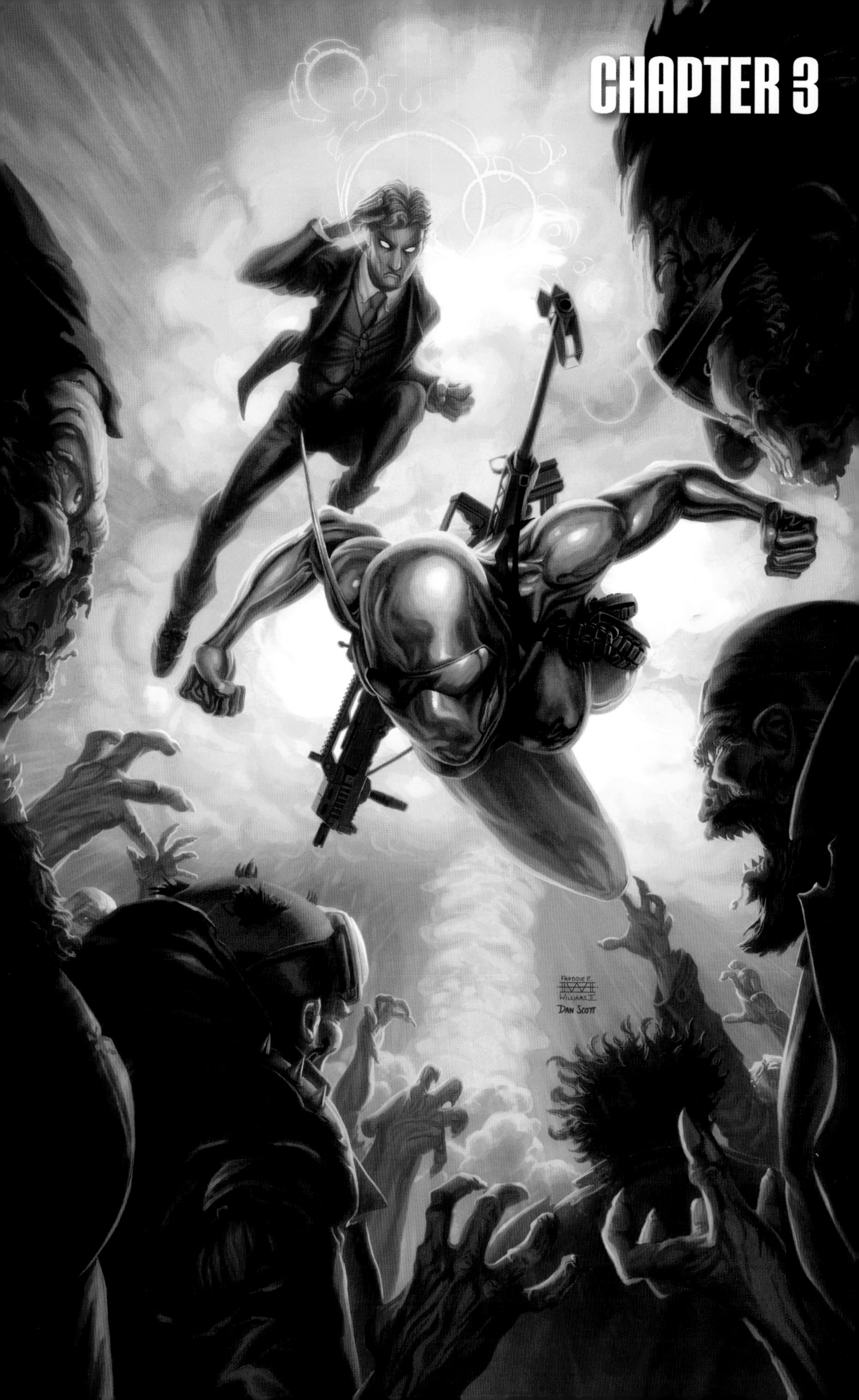
FREDDIE E. WILLIAMS II
DAN SCOTT

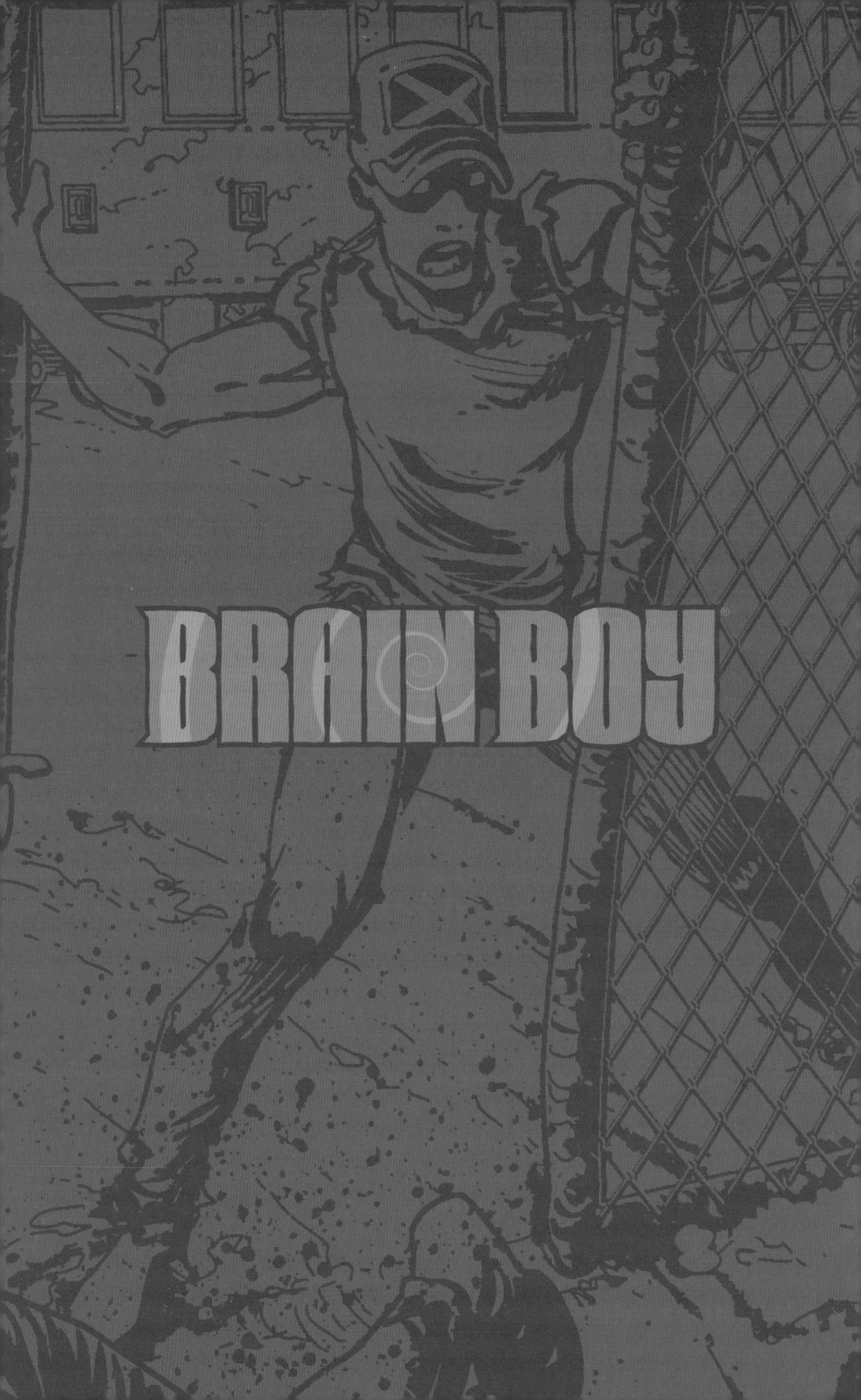
BRAIN BOY

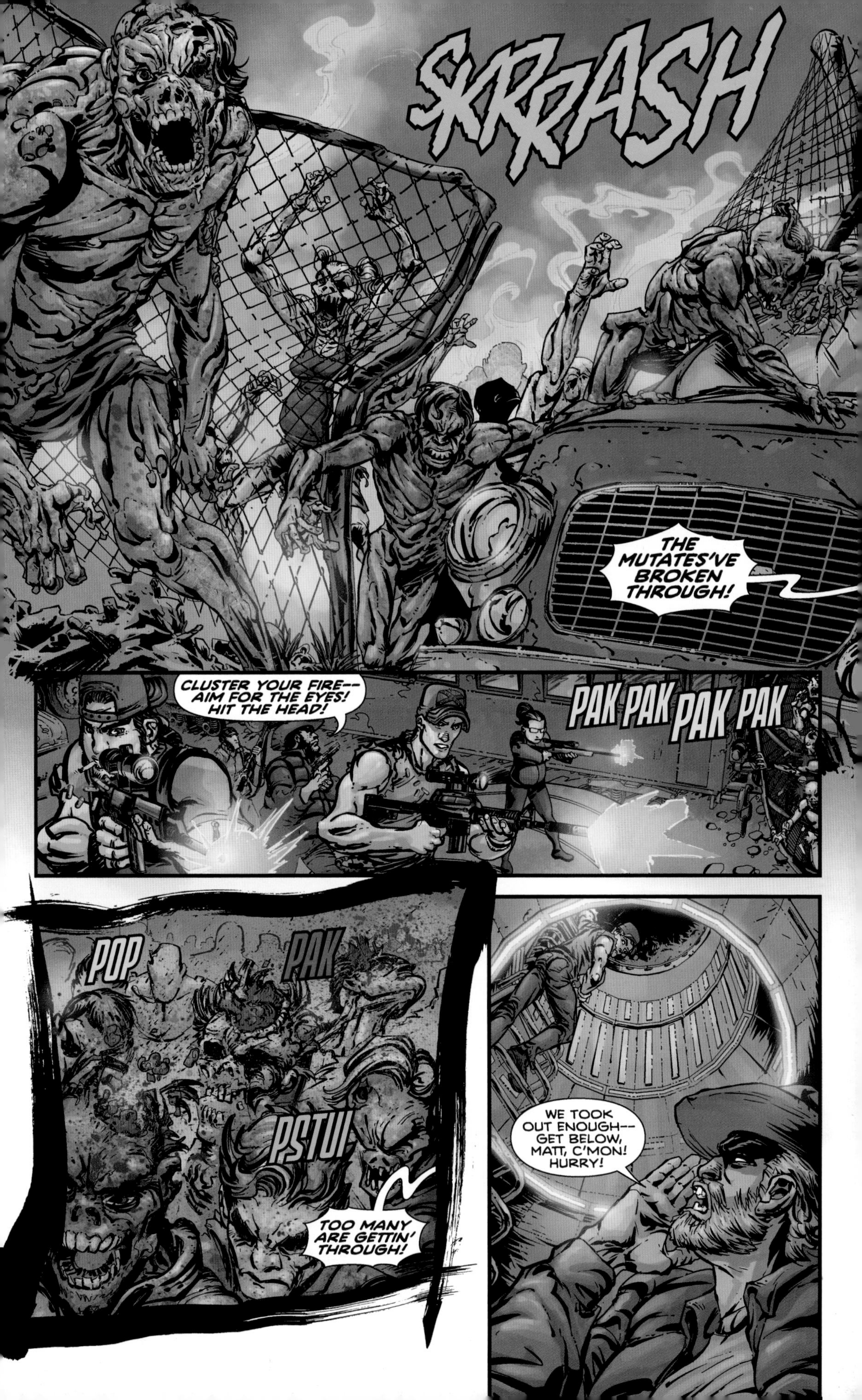
SKRRASH
THE MUTATES'VE BROKEN THROUGH!
CLUSTER YOUR FIRE-- AIM FOR THE EYES! HIT THE HEAD!
PAK PAK PAK PAK
POP
PAK
PSTUI
TOO MANY ARE GETTIN' THROUGH!
WE TOOK OUT ENOUGH-- GET BELOW, MATT, C'MON! HURRY!

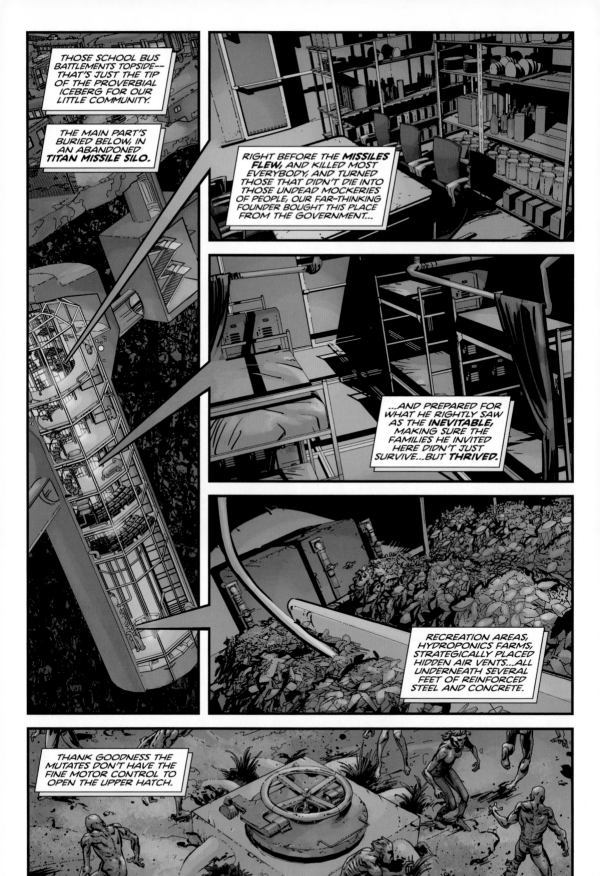

THOSE SCHOOL BUS BATTLEMENTS TOPSIDE-- THAT'S JUST THE TIP OF THE PROVERBIAL ICEBERG FOR OUR LITTLE COMMUNITY.

THE MAIN PART'S BURIED BELOW, IN AN ABANDONED TITAN MISSILE SILO.

RIGHT BEFORE THE MISSILES FLEW, AND KILLED MOST EVERYBODY, AND TURNED THOSE THAT DIDN'T DIE INTO THOSE UNDEAD MOCKERIES OF PEOPLE, OUR FAR-THINKING FOUNDER BOUGHT THIS PLACE FROM THE GOVERNMENT...

...AND PREPARED FOR WHAT HE RIGHTLY SAW AS THE INEVITABLE, MAKING SURE THE FAMILIES HE INVITED HERE DIDN'T JUST SURVIVE...BUT THRIVED.

RECREATION AREAS, HYDROPONICS FARMS, STRATEGICALLY PLACED HIDDEN AIR VENTS...ALL UNDERNEATH SEVERAL FEET OF REINFORCED STEEL AND CONCRETE.

THANK GOODNESS THE MUTATES DON'T HAVE THE FINE MOTOR CONTROL TO OPEN THE UPPER HATCH.

WITH NO OBVIOUS FOOD IN FRONT OF THEIR FACES, THEY'LL FORGET ALL ABOUT US BY NIGHTFALL AND WANDER AWAY.

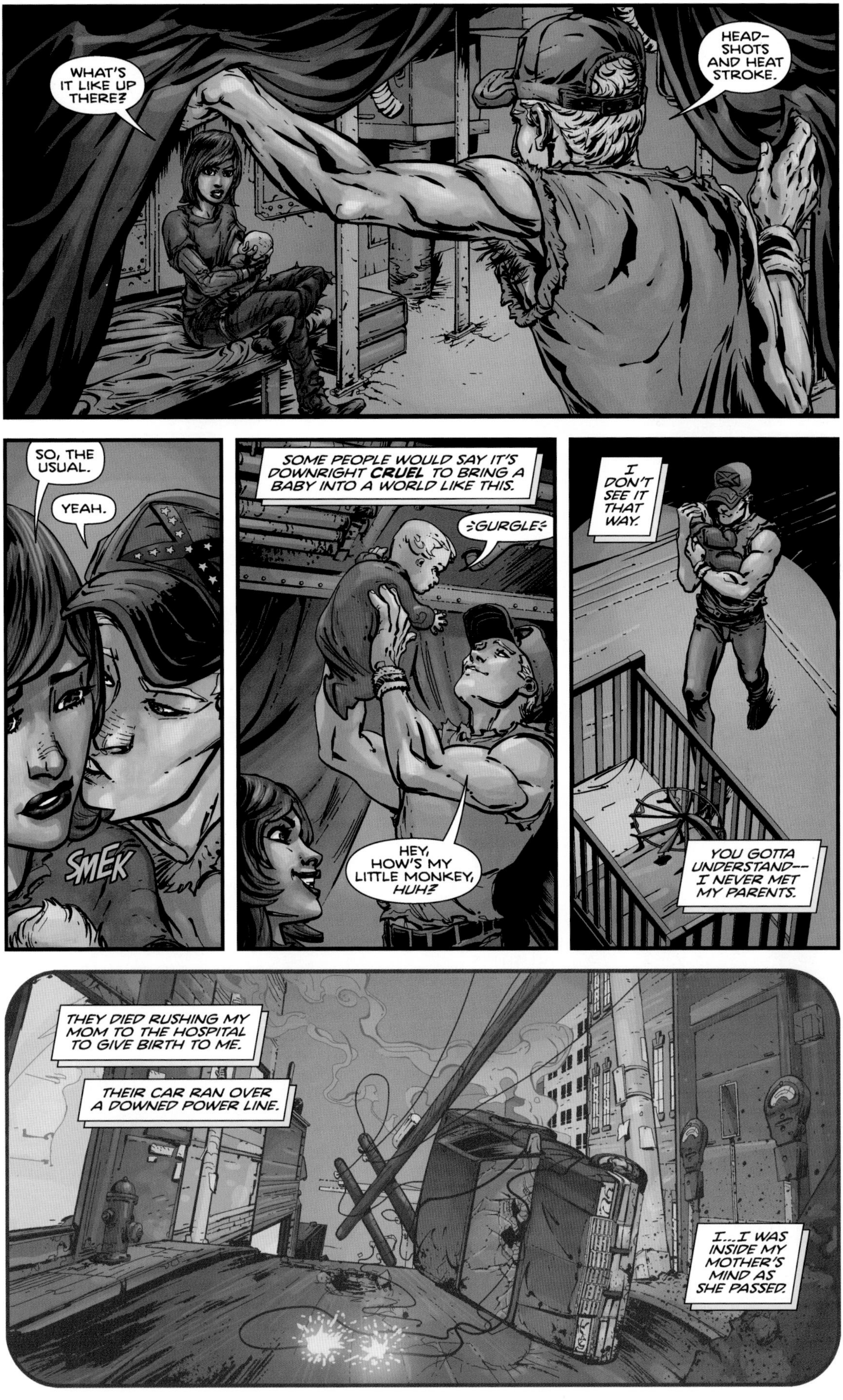
WHAT'S IT LIKE UP THERE?
HEAD-SHOTS AND HEAT STROKE.
SO, THE USUAL.
YEAH.
SMEK
SOME PEOPLE WOULD SAY IT'S DOWNRIGHT CRUEL TO BRING A BABY INTO A WORLD LIKE THIS.
GURGLE
HEY, HOW'S MY LITTLE MONKEY, HUH?
I DON'T SEE IT THAT WAY.
YOU GOTTA UNDERSTAND-- I NEVER MET MY PARENTS.
THEY DIED RUSHING MY MOM TO THE HOSPITAL TO GIVE BIRTH TO ME.
THEIR CAR RAN OVER A DOWNED POWER LINE.
I...I WAS INSIDE MY MOTHER'S MIND AS SHE PASSED.

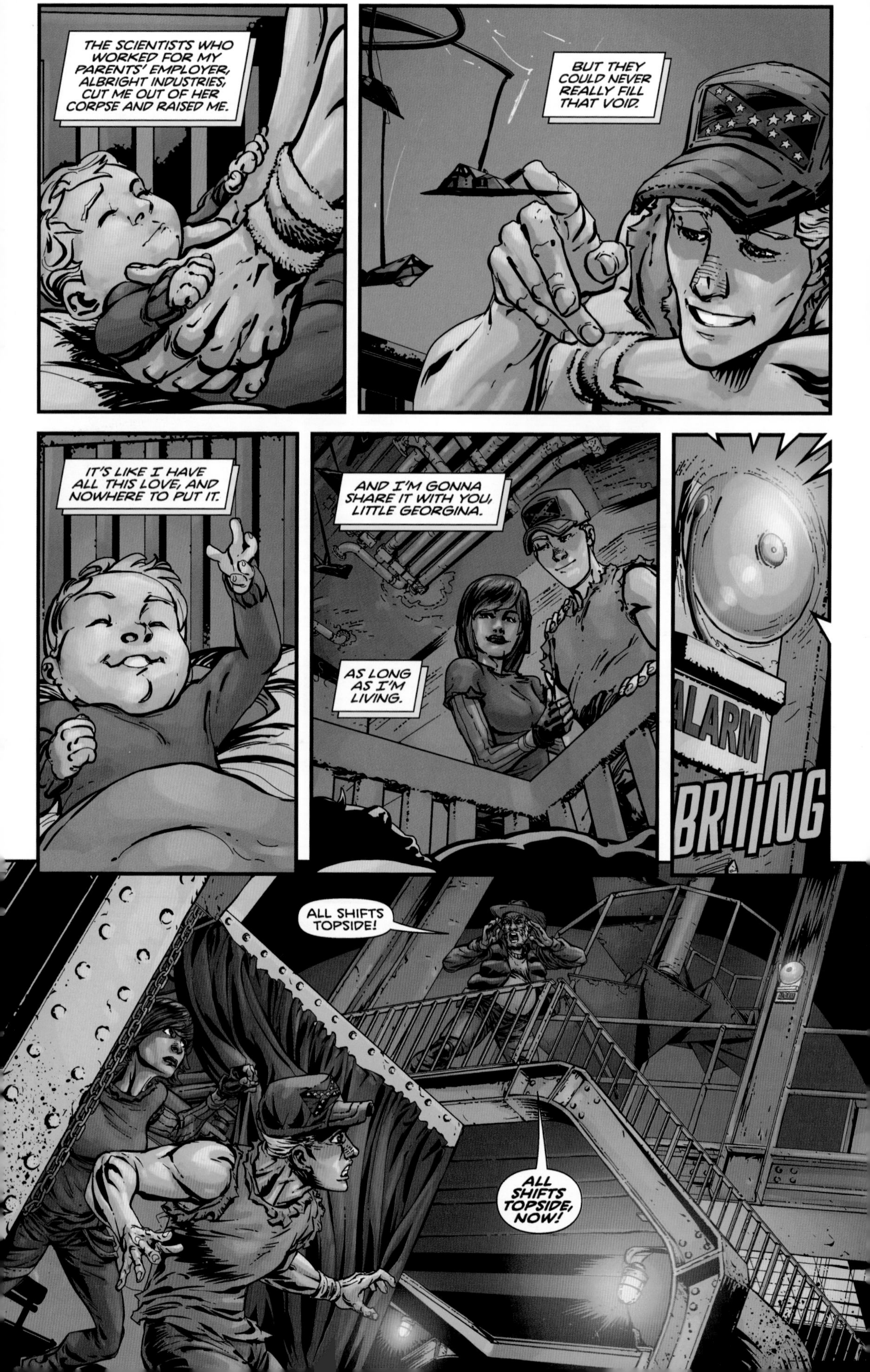
THE SCIENTISTS WHO WORKED FOR MY PARENTS' EMPLOYER, ALBRIGHT INDUSTRIES, CUT ME OUT OF HER CORPSE AND RAISED ME.
BUT THEY COULD NEVER REALLY FILL THAT VOID.
IT'S LIKE I HAVE ALL THIS LOVE, AND NOWHERE TO PUT IT.
AND I'M GONNA SHARE IT WITH YOU, LITTLE GEORGINA.
AS LONG AS I'M LIVING.
ALARM
BRIIIING
ALL SHIFTS TOPSIDE!
ALL SHIFTS TOPSIDE, NOW!

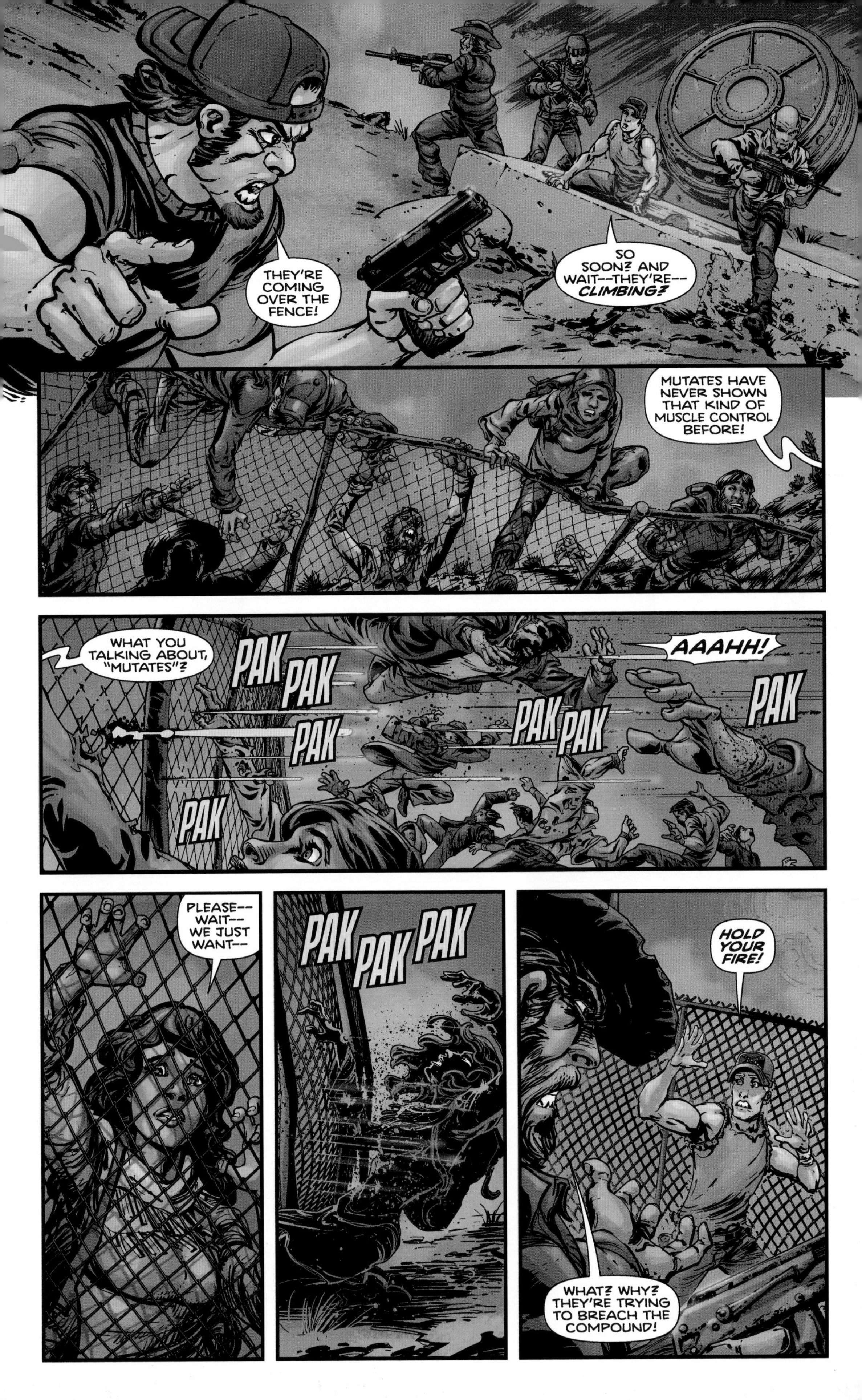
THEY'RE COMING OVER THE FENCE!
SO SOON? AND WAIT--THEY'RE-- CLIMBING?
MUTATES HAVE NEVER SHOWN THAT KIND OF MUSCLE CONTROL BEFORE!
WHAT YOU TALKING ABOUT, "MUTATES"?
PAK PAK
AAAHH!
PAK
PAK PAK
PAK
PAK
PLEASE-- WAIT-- WE JUST WANT--
PAK PAK PAK
HOLD YOUR FIRE!
WHAT? WHY? THEY'RE TRYING TO BREACH THE COMPOUND!

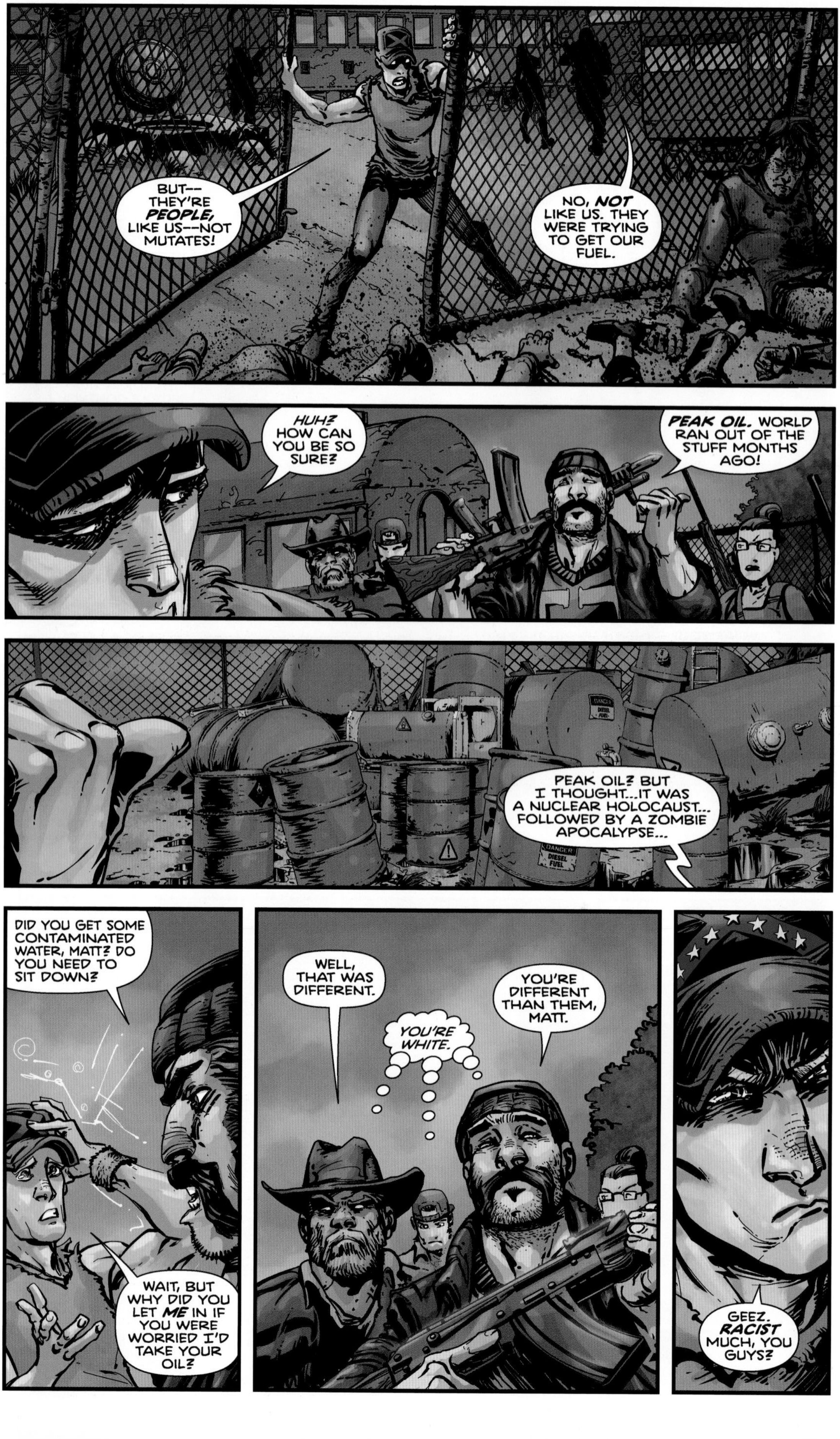
BUT-- THEY'RE *PEOPLE,* LIKE US--NOT MUTATES!
NO, *NOT* LIKE US. THEY WERE TRYING TO GET OUR FUEL.
HUH? HOW CAN YOU BE SO SURE?
PEAK OIL. WORLD RAN OUT OF THE STUFF MONTHS AGO!
DANGER DIESEL FUEL
PEAK OIL? BUT I THOUGHT...IT WAS A NUCLEAR HOLOCAUST... FOLLOWED BY A ZOMBIE APOCALYPSE...
DANGER DIESEL FUEL
DID YOU GET SOME CONTAMINATED WATER, MATT? DO YOU NEED TO SIT DOWN?
WAIT, BUT WHY DID YOU LET *ME* IN IF YOU WERE WORRIED I'D TAKE YOUR OIL?
WELL, THAT WAS DIFFERENT.
YOU'RE WHITE.
YOU'RE DIFFERENT THAN THEM, MATT.
GEEZ. *RACIST* MUCH, YOU GUYS?

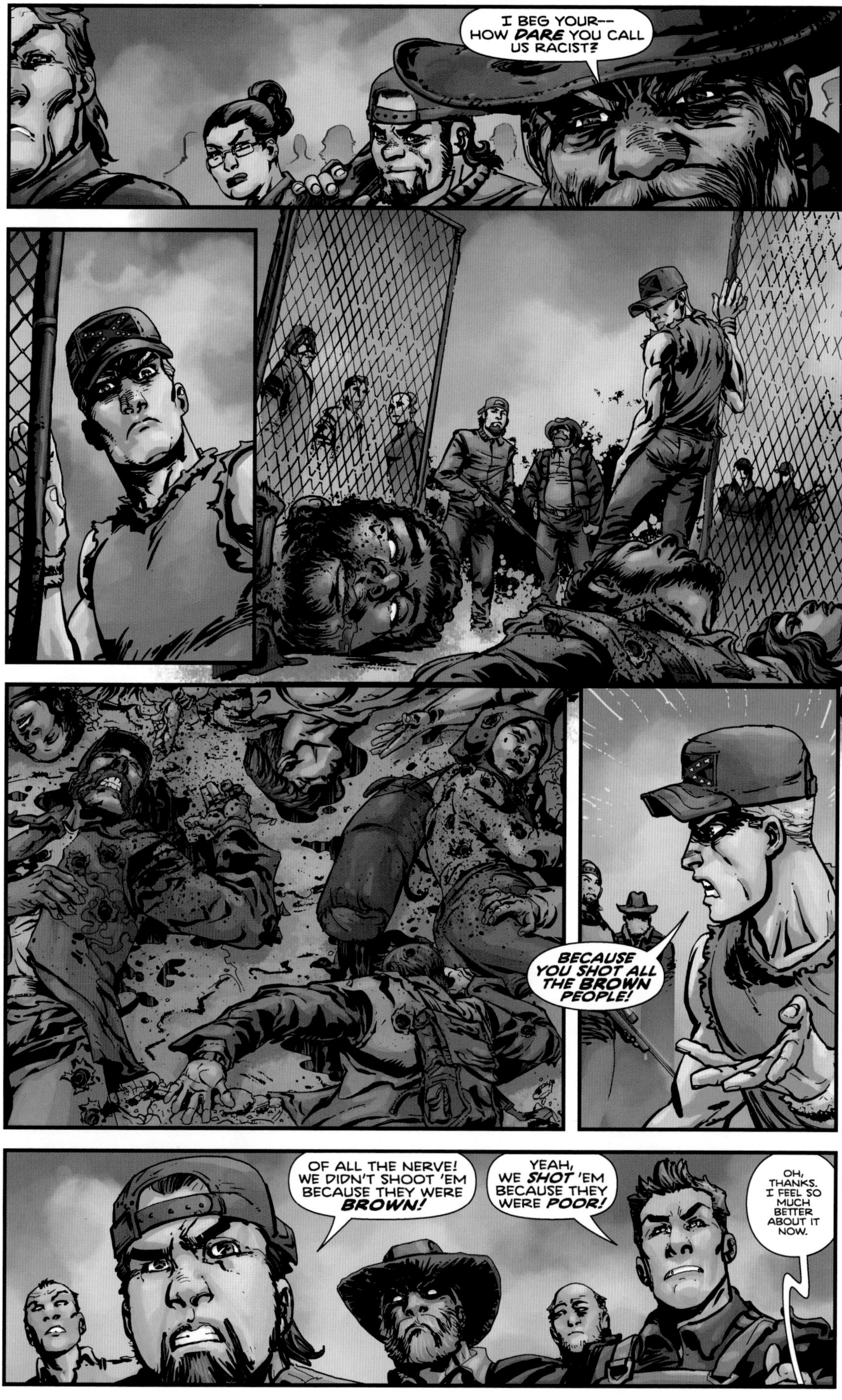
I BEG YOUR-- HOW DARE YOU CALL US RACIST?
BECAUSE YOU SHOT ALL THE BROWN PEOPLE!
OF ALL THE NERVE! WE DIDN'T SHOOT 'EM BECAUSE THEY WERE BROWN!
YEAH, WE SHOT 'EM BECAUSE THEY WERE POOR!
OH, THANKS. I FEEL SO MUCH BETTER ABOUT IT NOW.

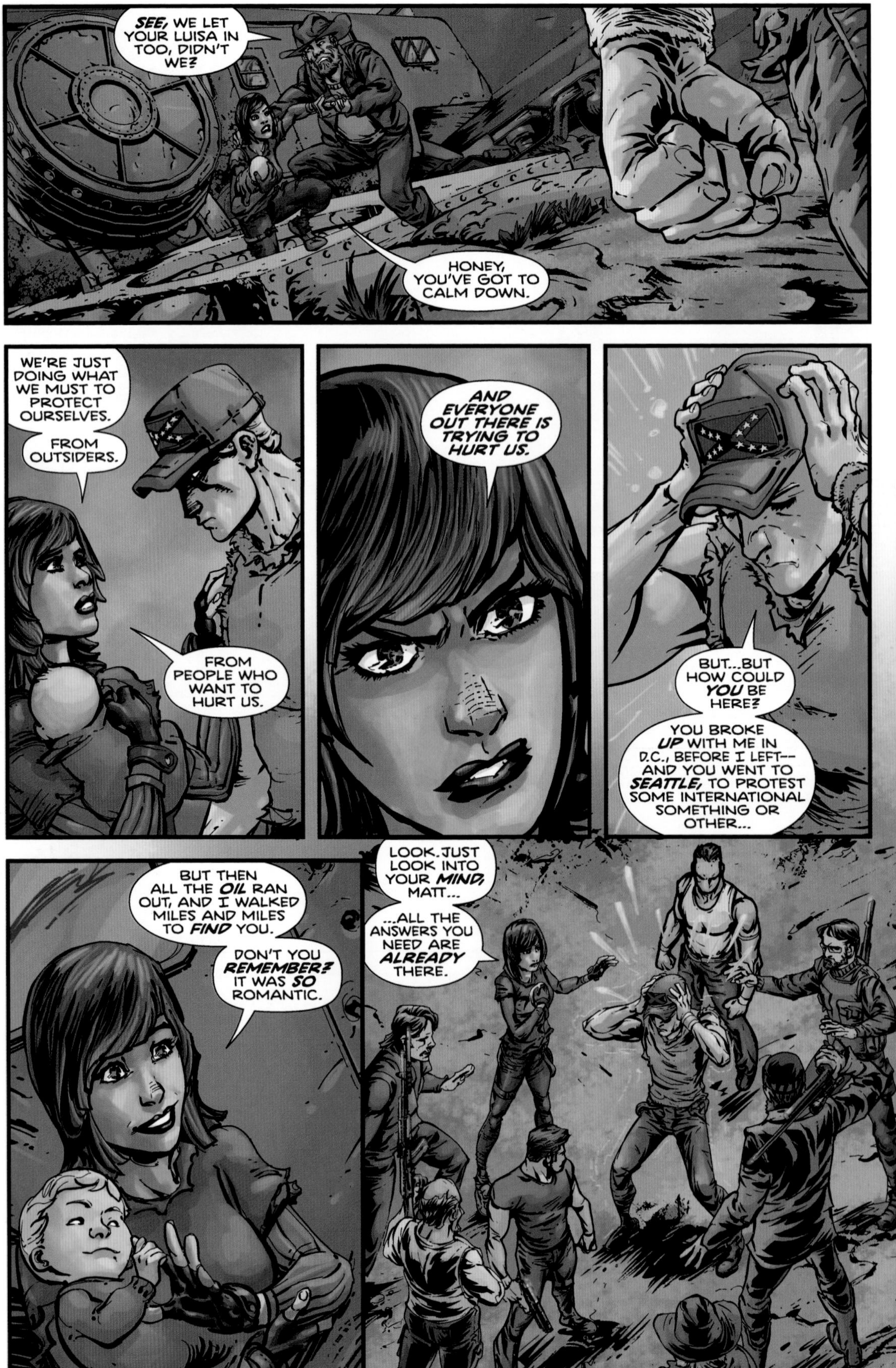
SEE, WE LET YOUR LUISA IN TOO, DIDN'T WE?
HONEY, YOU'VE GOT TO CALM DOWN.
WE'RE JUST DOING WHAT WE MUST TO PROTECT OURSELVES.
FROM OUTSIDERS.
FROM PEOPLE WHO WANT TO HURT US.
AND EVERYONE OUT THERE IS TRYING TO HURT US.
BUT...BUT HOW COULD YOU BE HERE?
YOU BROKE UP WITH ME IN D.C., BEFORE I LEFT-- AND YOU WENT TO SEATTLE, TO PROTEST SOME INTERNATIONAL SOMETHING OR OTHER...
BUT THEN ALL THE OIL RAN OUT, AND I WALKED MILES AND MILES TO FIND YOU.
DON'T YOU REMEMBER? IT WAS SO ROMANTIC.
LOOK. JUST LOOK INTO YOUR MIND, MATT...
...ALL THE ANSWERS YOU NEED ARE ALREADY THERE.

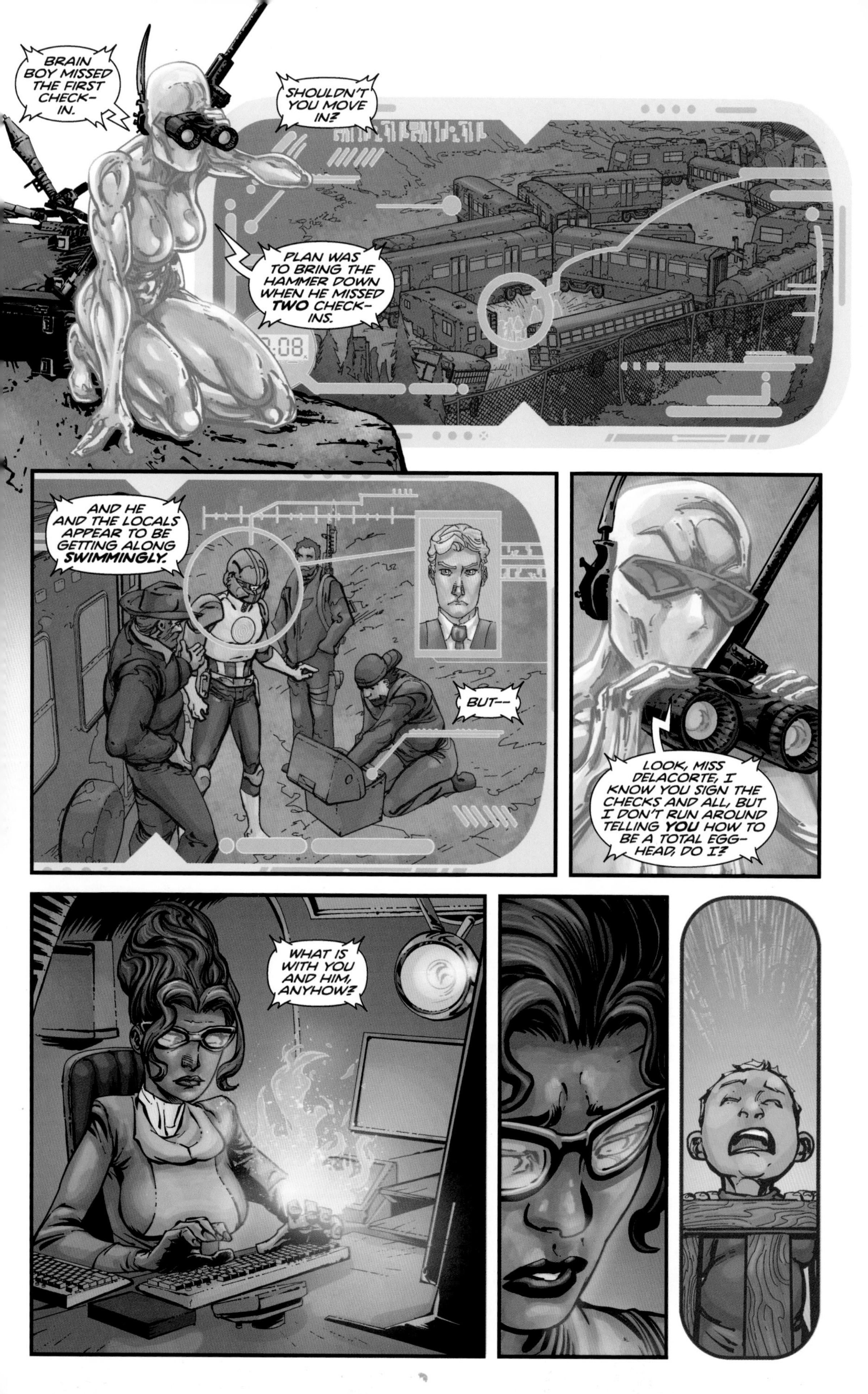
BRAIN BOY MISSED THE FIRST CHECK-IN.
SHOULDN'T YOU MOVE IN?
PLAN WAS TO BRING THE HAMMER DOWN WHEN HE MISSED TWO CHECK-INS.
AND HE AND THE LOCALS APPEAR TO BE GETTING ALONG SWIMMINGLY.
BUT--
LOOK, MISS DELACORTE, I KNOW YOU SIGN THE CHECKS AND ALL, BUT I DON'T RUN AROUND TELLING YOU HOW TO BE A TOTAL EGG-HEAD, DO I?
WHAT IS WITH YOU AND HIM, ANYHOW?

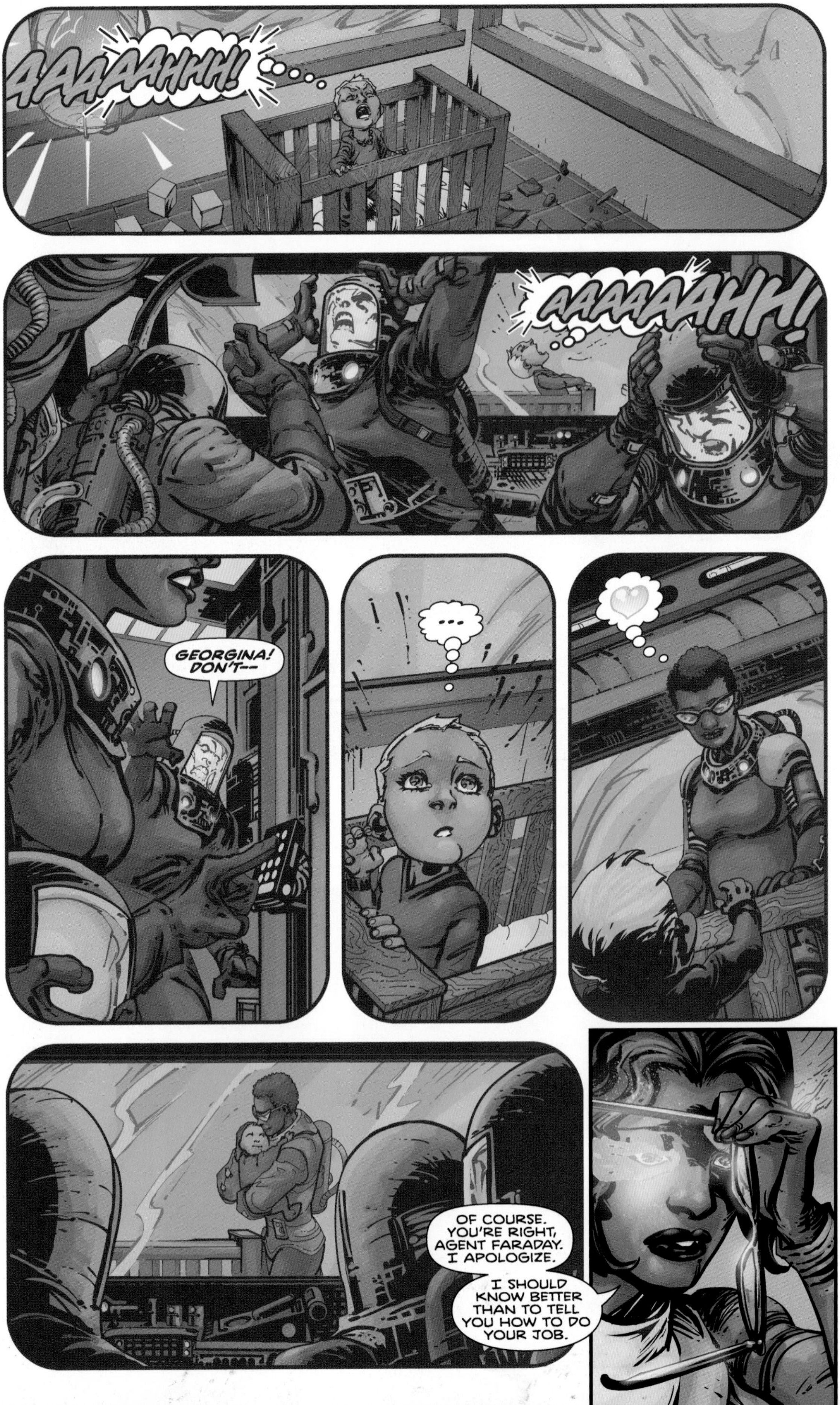
AAAAAHHH!
AAAAAAHH!
GEORGINA! DON'T--
...
OF COURSE. YOU'RE RIGHT, AGENT FARADAY. I APOLOGIZE.
I SHOULD KNOW BETTER THAN TO TELL YOU HOW TO DO YOUR JOB.

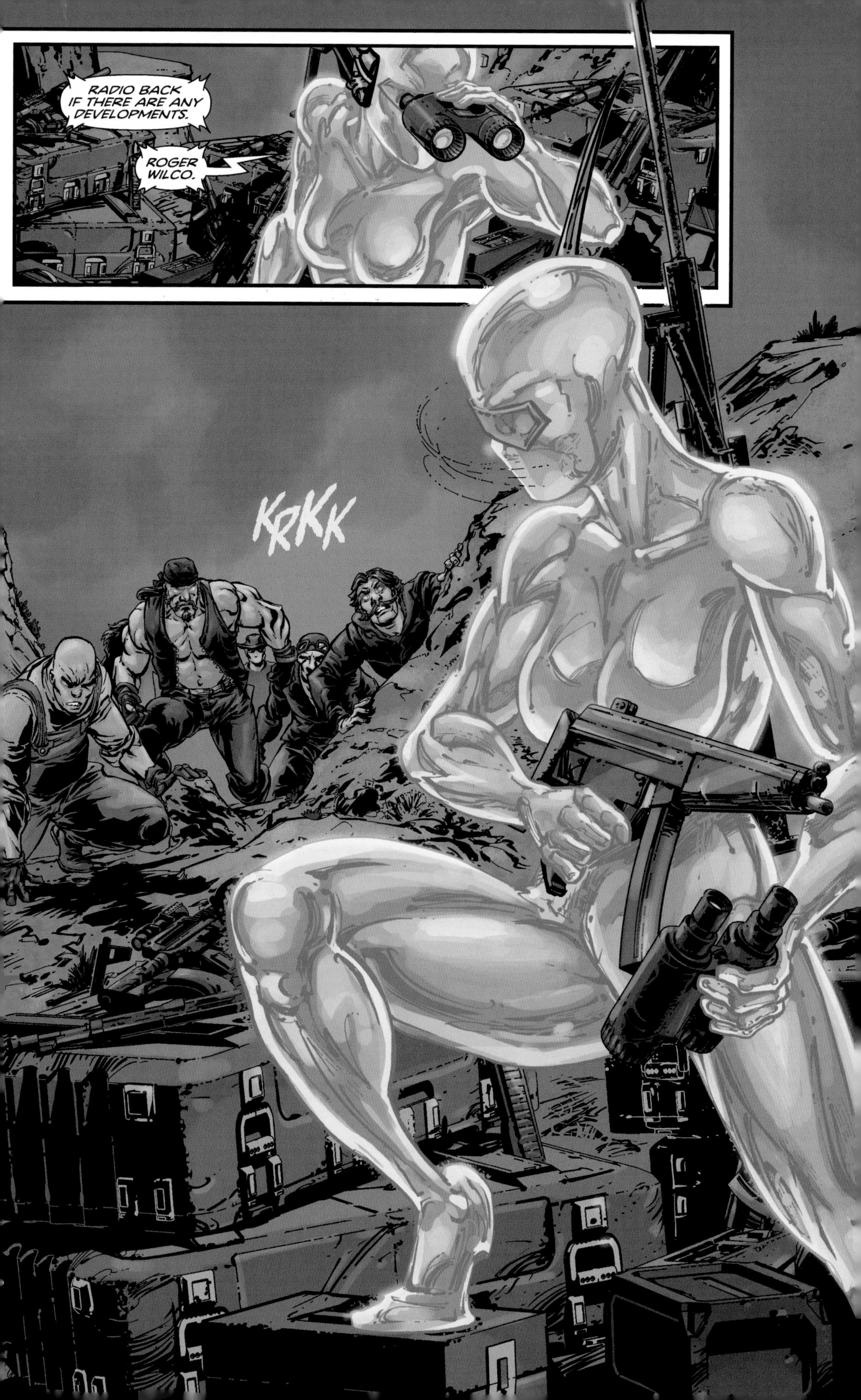
RADIO BACK IF THERE ARE ANY DEVELOPMENTS.
ROGER WILCO.
KRKK

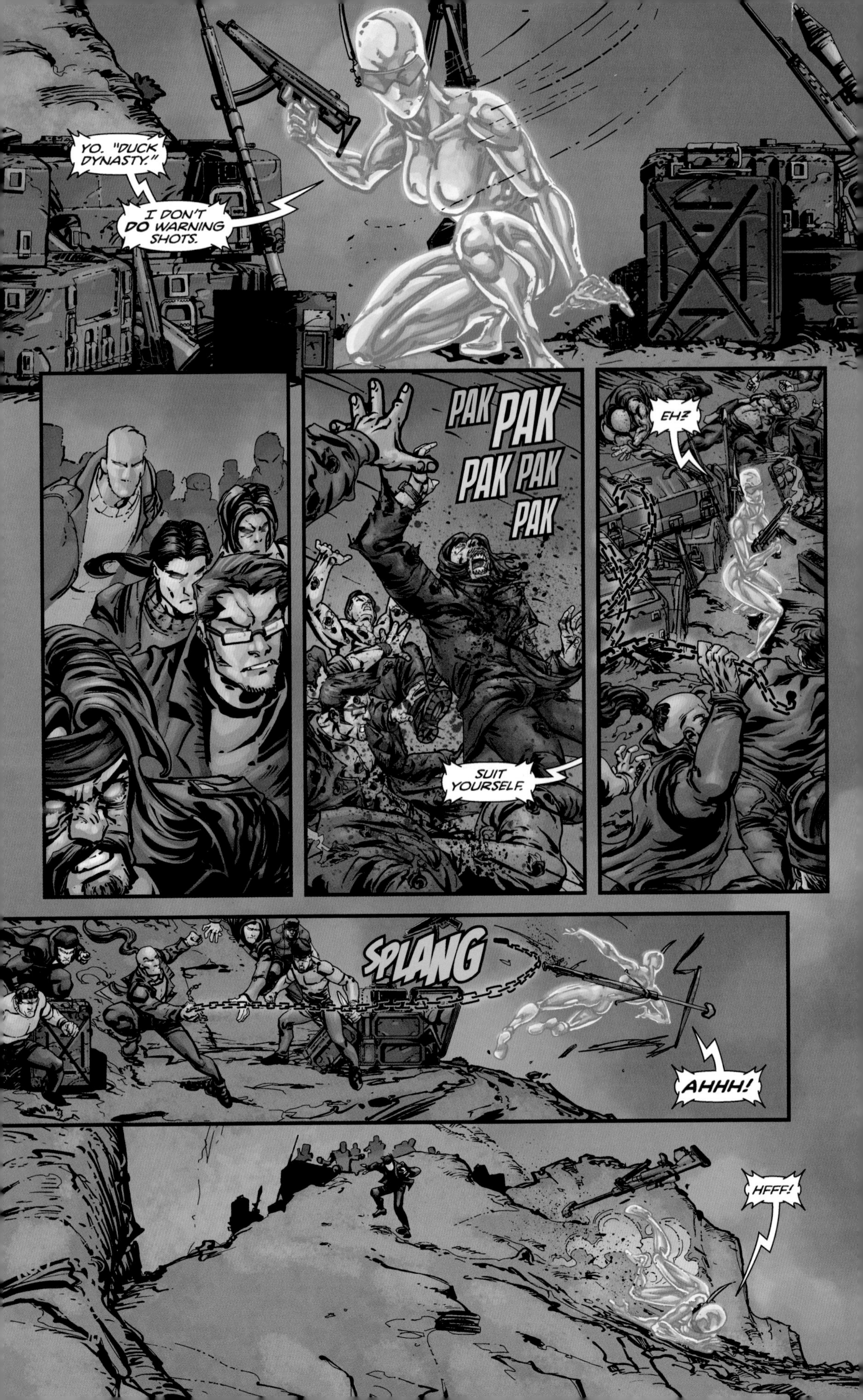
YO. "DUCK DYNASTY."
I DON'T DO WARNING SHOTS.
PAK PAK PAK PAK PAK
SUIT YOURSELF.
EH?
SPLANG
AHHH!
HFFF!

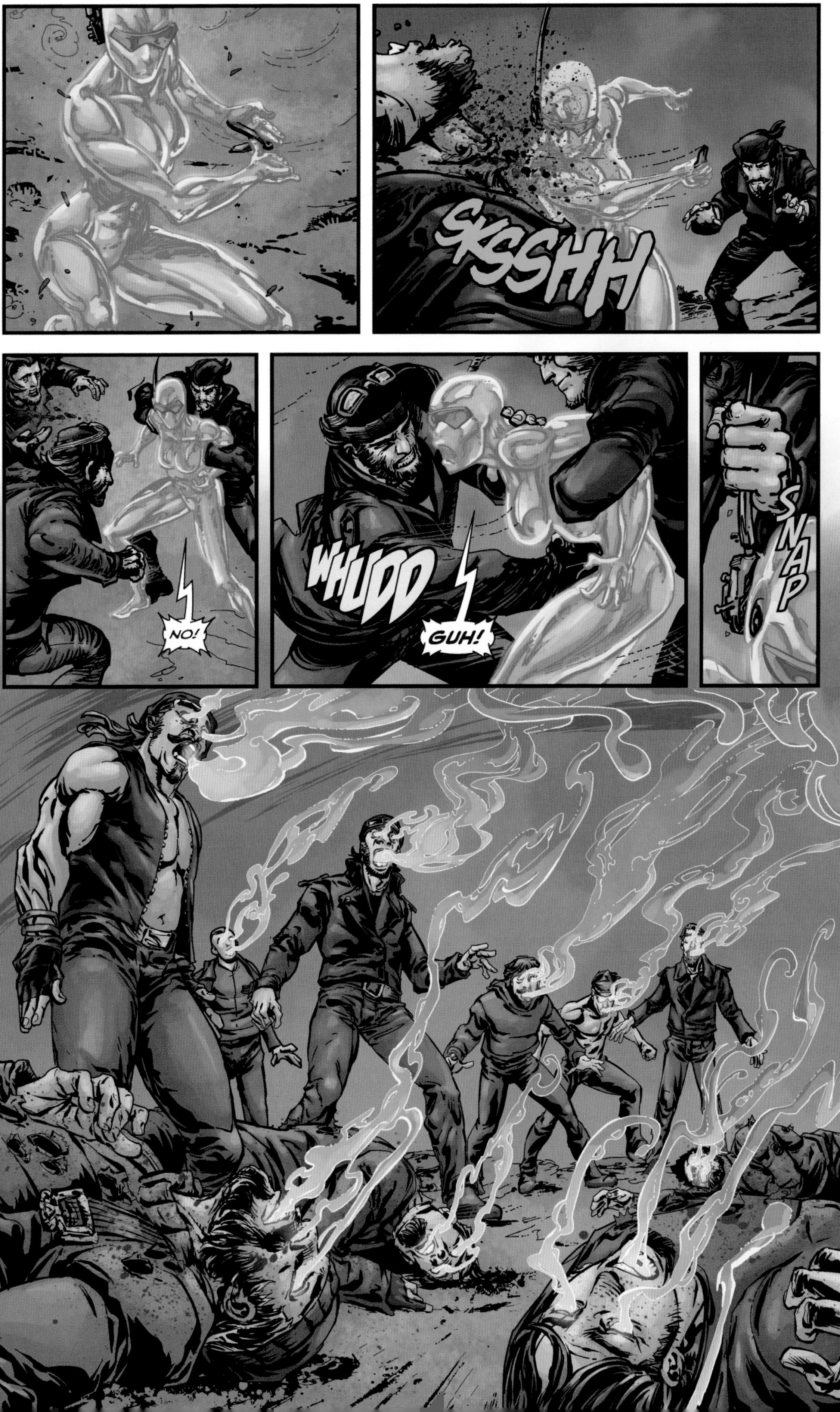
SKSSHH
NO!
WHUDD
GUH!
SNAP

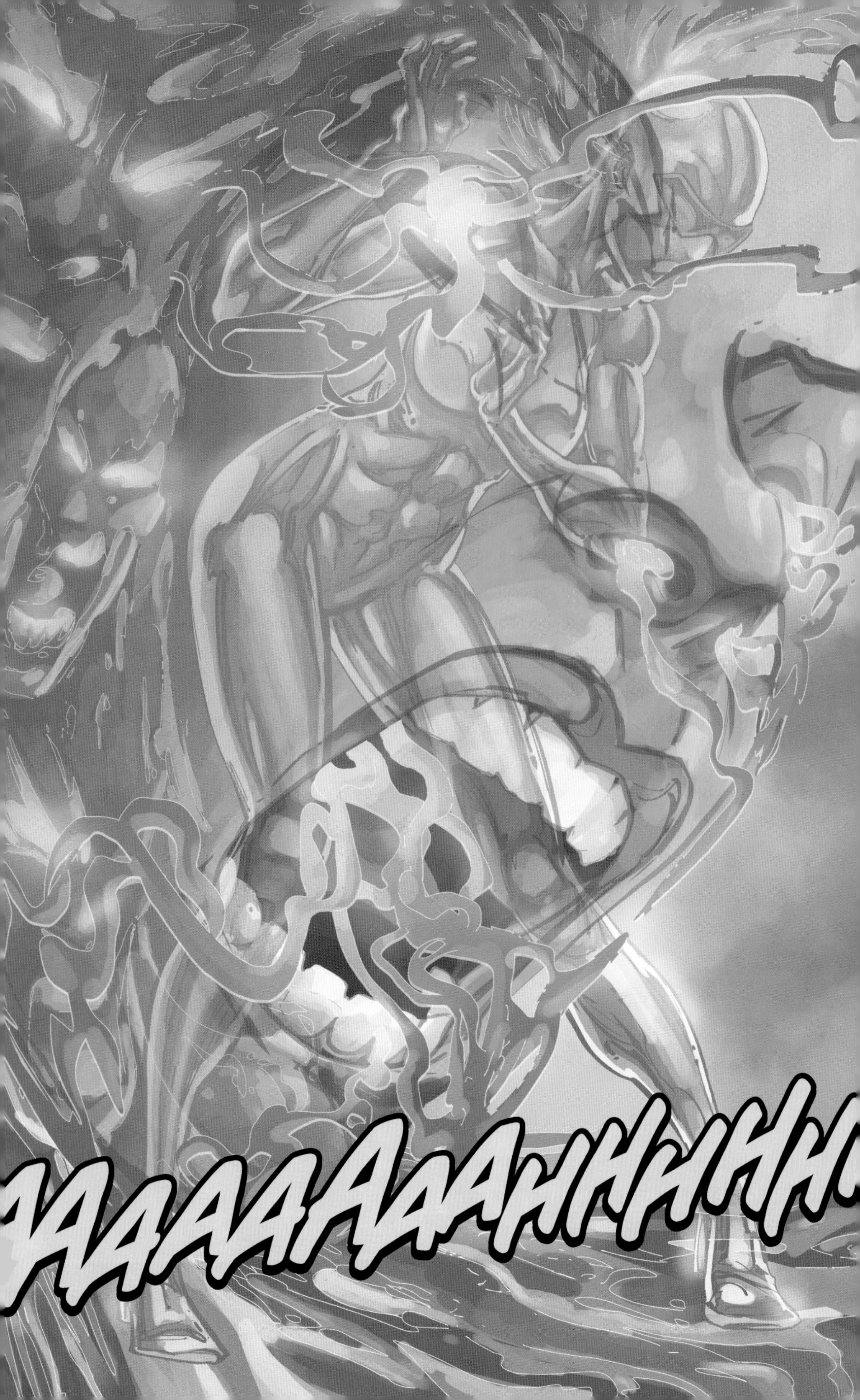
AAAAAAAHHHHH

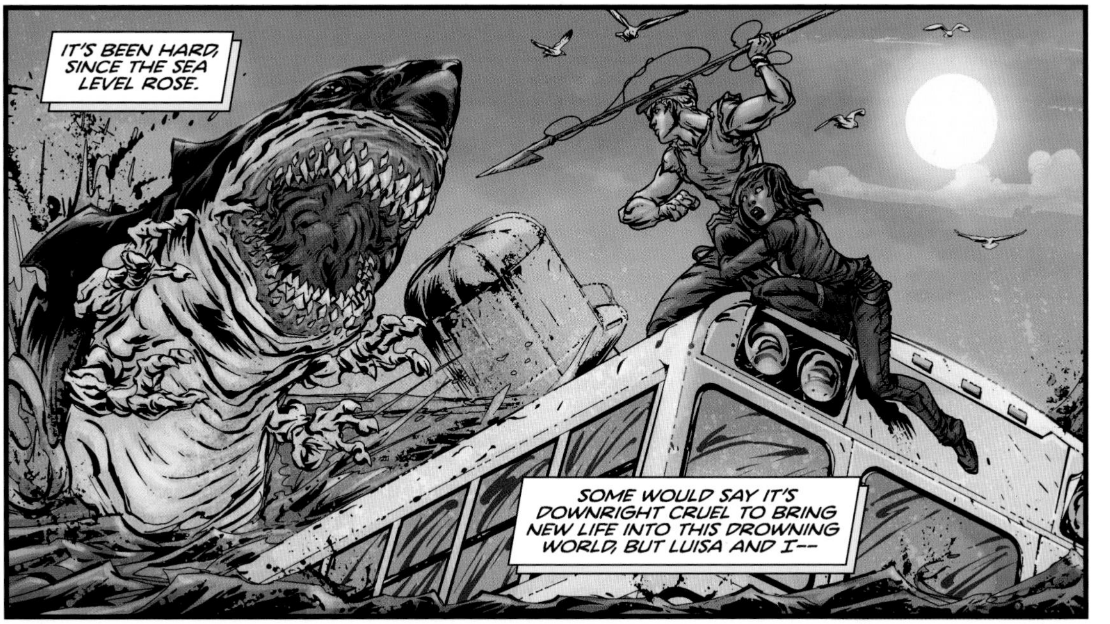
IT'S BEEN HARD, SINCE THE SEA LEVEL ROSE.
SOME WOULD SAY IT'S DOWNRIGHT CRUEL TO BRING NEW LIFE INTO THIS DROWNING WORLD, BUT LUISA AND I--

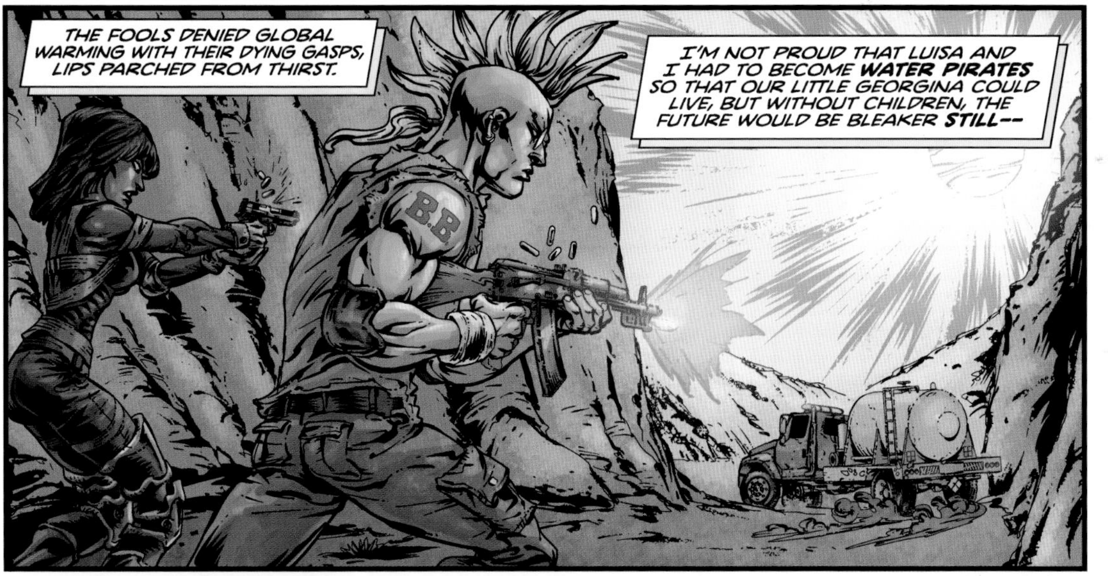
THE FOOLS DENIED GLOBAL WARMING WITH THEIR DYING GASPS, LIPS PARCHED FROM THIRST.
I'M NOT PROUD THAT LUISA AND I HAD TO BECOME **WATER PIRATES** SO THAT OUR LITTLE GEORGINA COULD LIVE, BUT WITHOUT CHILDREN, THE FUTURE WOULD BE BLEAKER **STILL--**

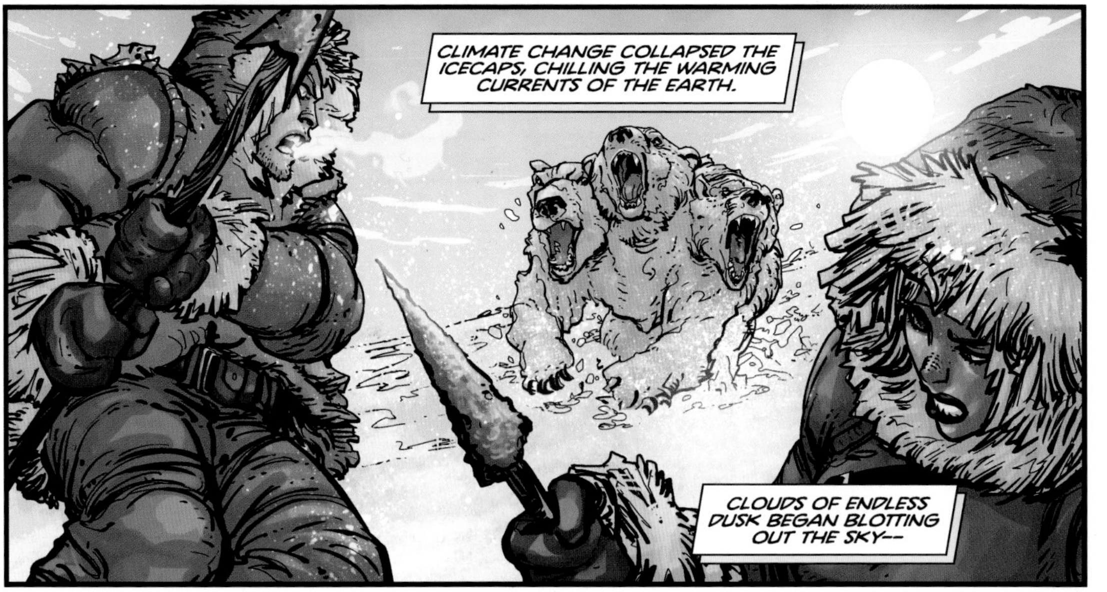
CLIMATE CHANGE COLLAPSED THE ICECAPS, CHILLING THE WARMING CURRENTS OF THE EARTH.
CLOUDS OF ENDLESS DUSK BEGAN BLOTTING OUT THE SKY--

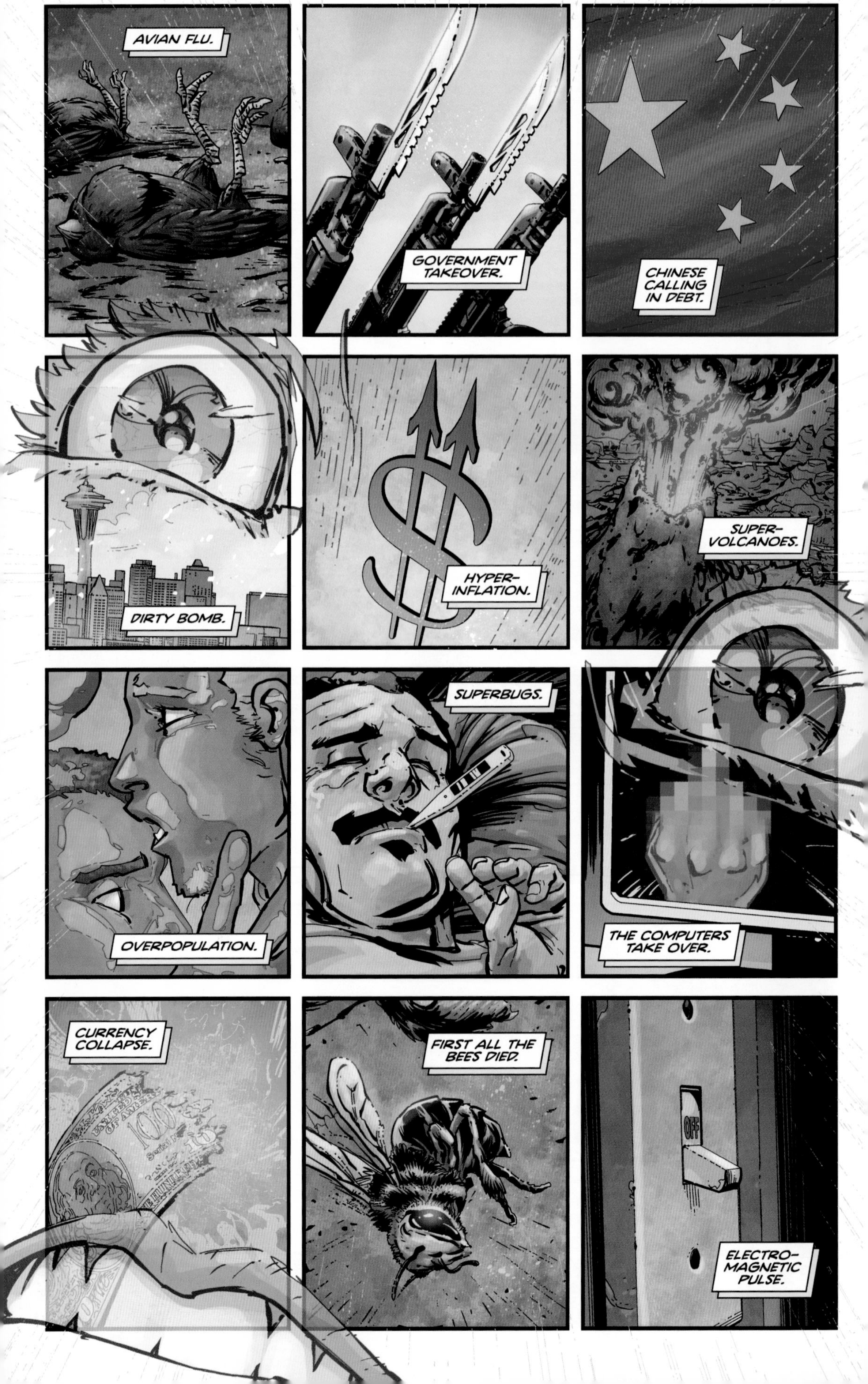
AVIAN FLU.
GOVERNMENT TAKEOVER.
CHINESE CALLING IN DEBT.
DIRTY BOMB.
HYPER-INFLATION.
SUPER-VOLCANOES.
OVERPOPULATION.
SUPERBUGS.
THE COMPUTERS TAKE OVER.
CURRENCY COLLAPSE.
FIRST ALL THE BEES DIED.
OFF
ELECTRO-MAGNETIC PULSE.

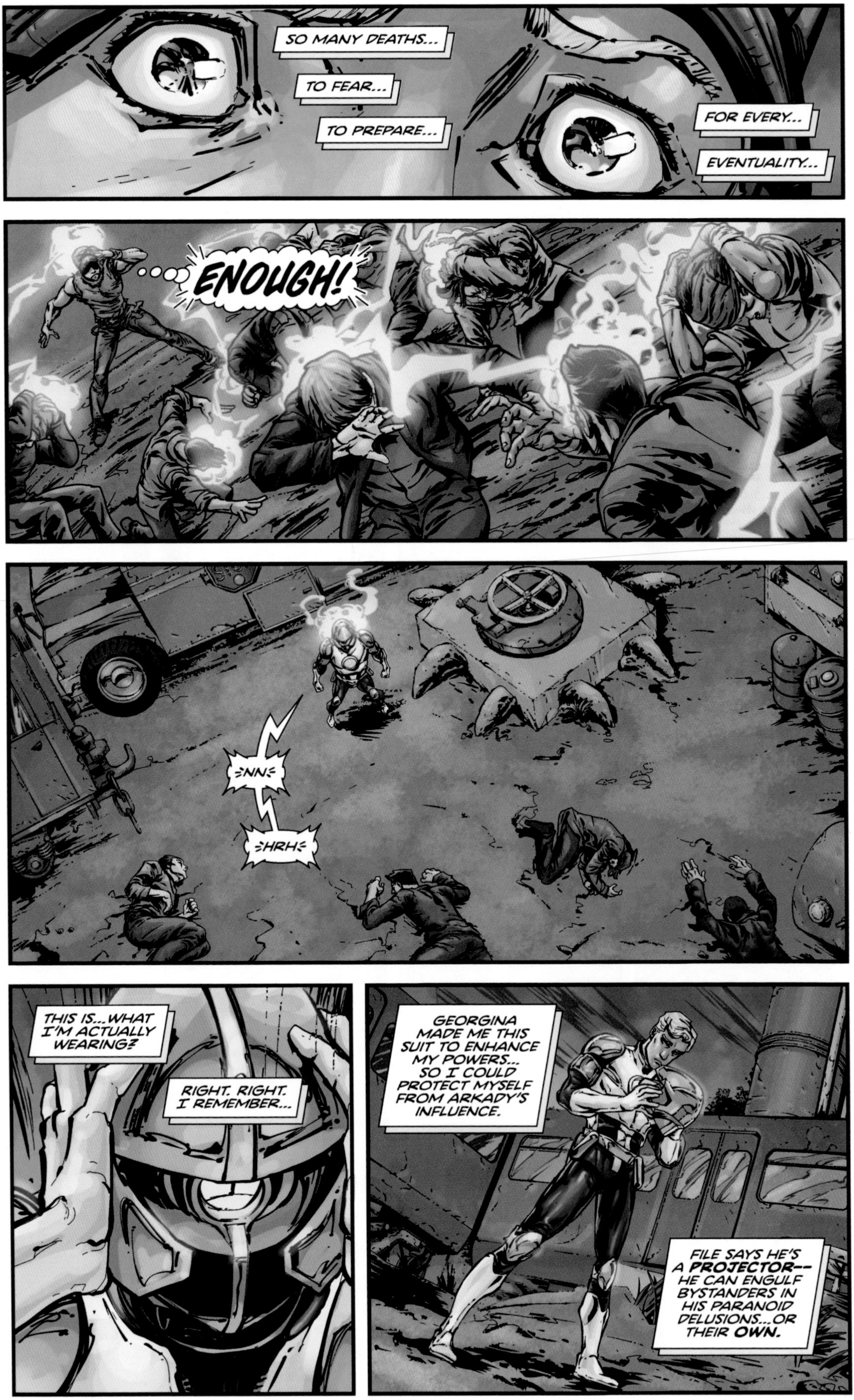
SO MANY DEATHS...
TO FEAR...
TO PREPARE...
FOR EVERY...
EVENTUALITY...
ENOUGH!
NN
HRH
THIS IS...WHAT I'M ACTUALLY WEARING?
RIGHT. RIGHT. I REMEMBER...
GEORGINA MADE ME THIS SUIT TO ENHANCE MY POWERS... SO I COULD PROTECT MYSELF FROM ARKADY'S INFLUENCE.
FILE SAYS HE'S A PROJECTOR-- HE CAN ENGULF BYSTANDERS IN HIS PARANOID DELUSIONS...OR THEIR OWN.

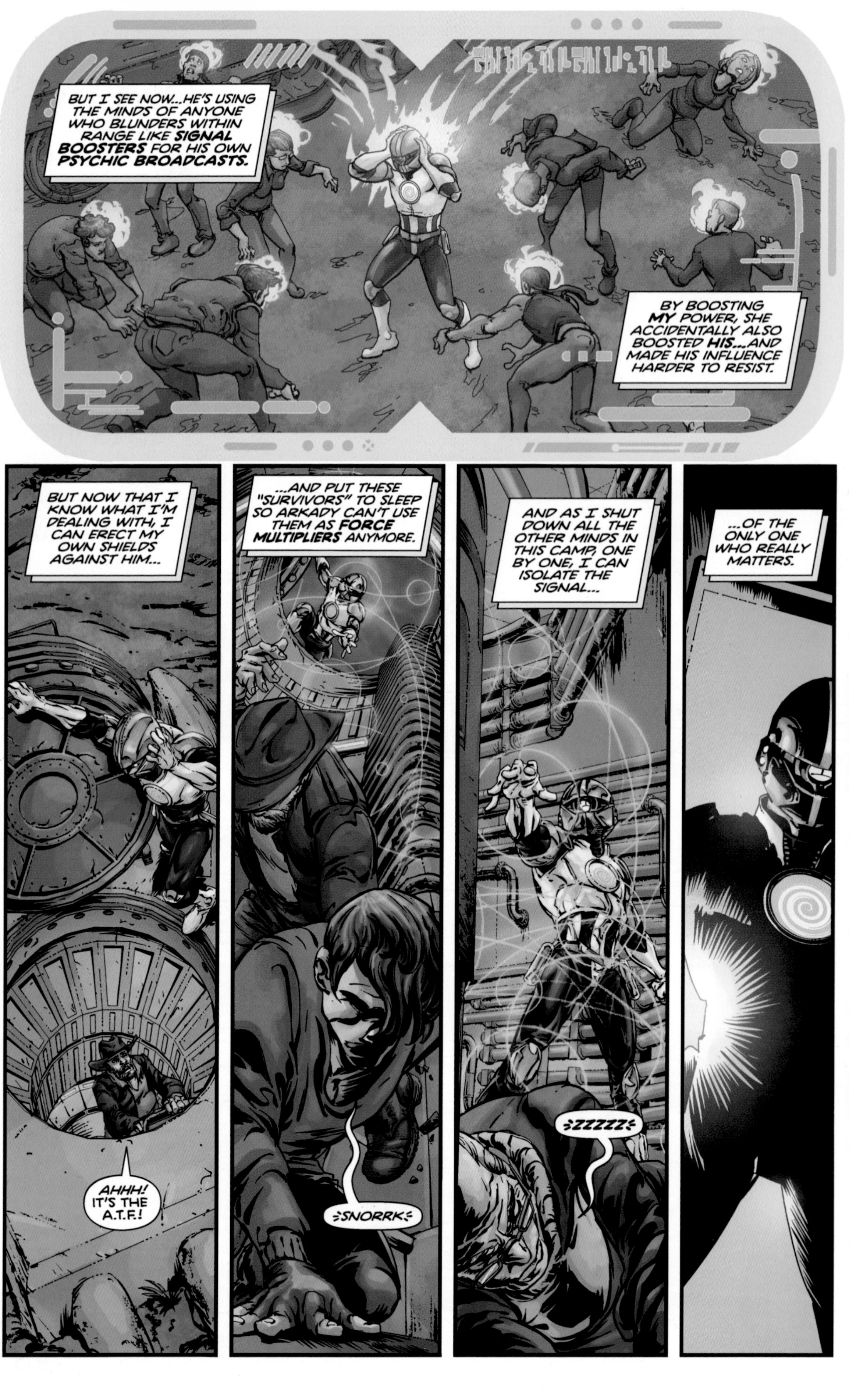
BUT I SEE NOW...HE'S USING THE MINDS OF ANYONE WHO BLUNDERS WITHIN RANGE LIKE SIGNAL BOOSTERS FOR HIS OWN PSYCHIC BROADCASTS.
BY BOOSTING MY POWER, SHE ACCIDENTALLY ALSO BOOSTED HIS...AND MADE HIS INFLUENCE HARDER TO RESIST.
BUT NOW THAT I KNOW WHAT I'M DEALING WITH, I CAN ERECT MY OWN SHIELDS AGAINST HIM...
AHHH! IT'S THE A.T.F.!
...AND PUT THESE "SURVIVORS" TO SLEEP SO ARKADY CAN'T USE THEM AS FORCE MULTIPLIERS ANYMORE.
SNORRK
AND AS I SHUT DOWN ALL THE OTHER MINDS IN THIS CAMP, ONE BY ONE, I CAN ISOLATE THE SIGNAL...
ZZZZZ
...OF THE ONLY ONE WHO REALLY MATTERS.

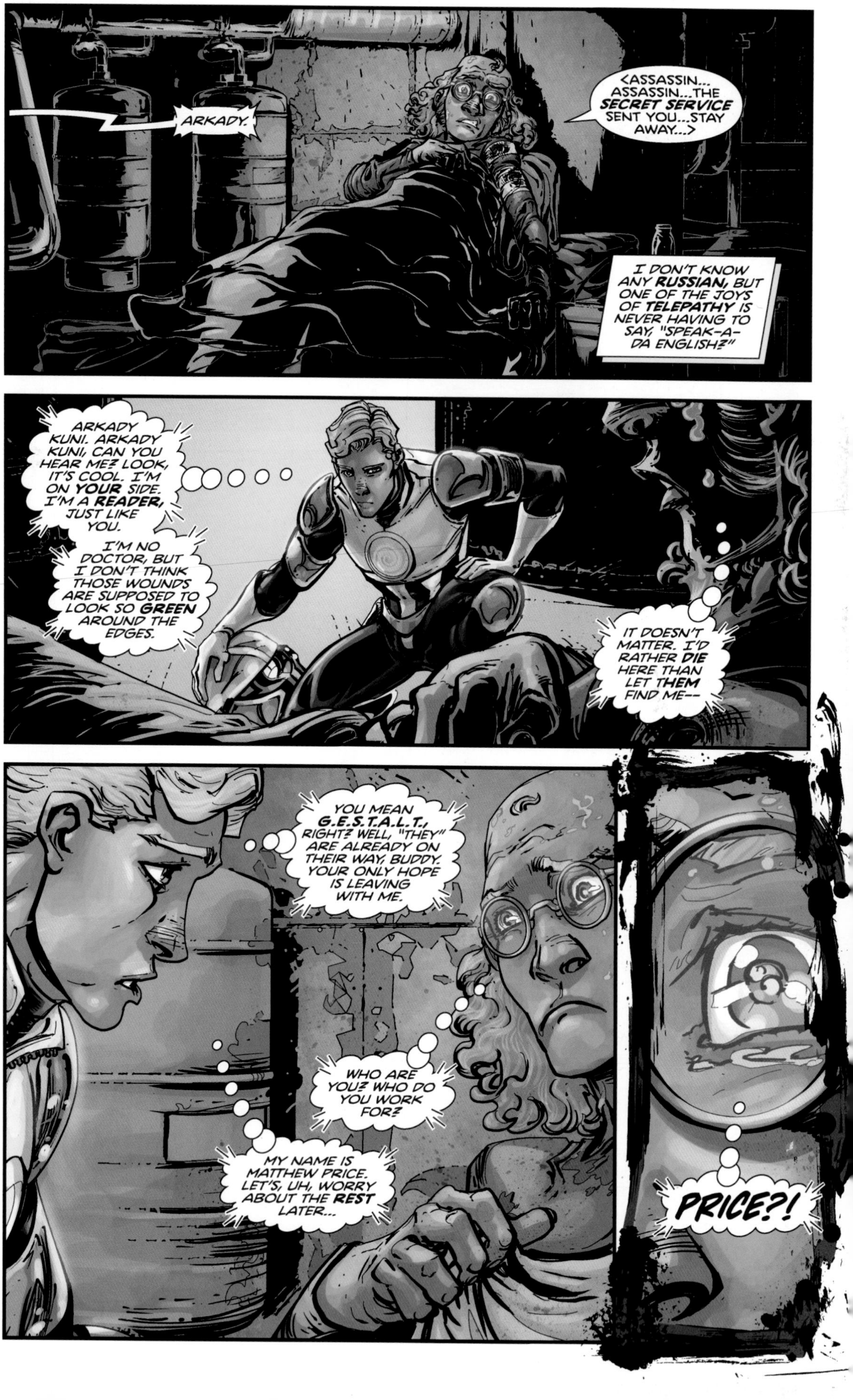
ARKADY.
<ASSASSIN... ASSASSIN...THE SECRET SERVICE SENT YOU...STAY AWAY...>
I DON'T KNOW ANY RUSSIAN, BUT ONE OF THE JOYS OF TELEPATHY IS NEVER HAVING TO SAY, "SPEAK-A-DA ENGLISH?"
ARKADY KUNI. ARKADY KUNI, CAN YOU HEAR ME? LOOK, IT'S COOL. I'M ON YOUR SIDE. I'M A READER, JUST LIKE YOU.
I'M NO DOCTOR, BUT I DON'T THINK THOSE WOUNDS ARE SUPPOSED TO LOOK SO GREEN AROUND THE EDGES.
IT DOESN'T MATTER. I'D RATHER DIE HERE THAN LET THEM FIND ME--
YOU MEAN G.E.S.T.A.L.T., RIGHT? WELL, "THEY" ARE ALREADY ON THEIR WAY, BUDDY. YOUR ONLY HOPE IS LEAVING WITH ME.
WHO ARE YOU? WHO DO YOU WORK FOR?
MY NAME IS MATTHEW PRICE. LET'S, UH, WORRY ABOUT THE REST LATER...
PRICE?!

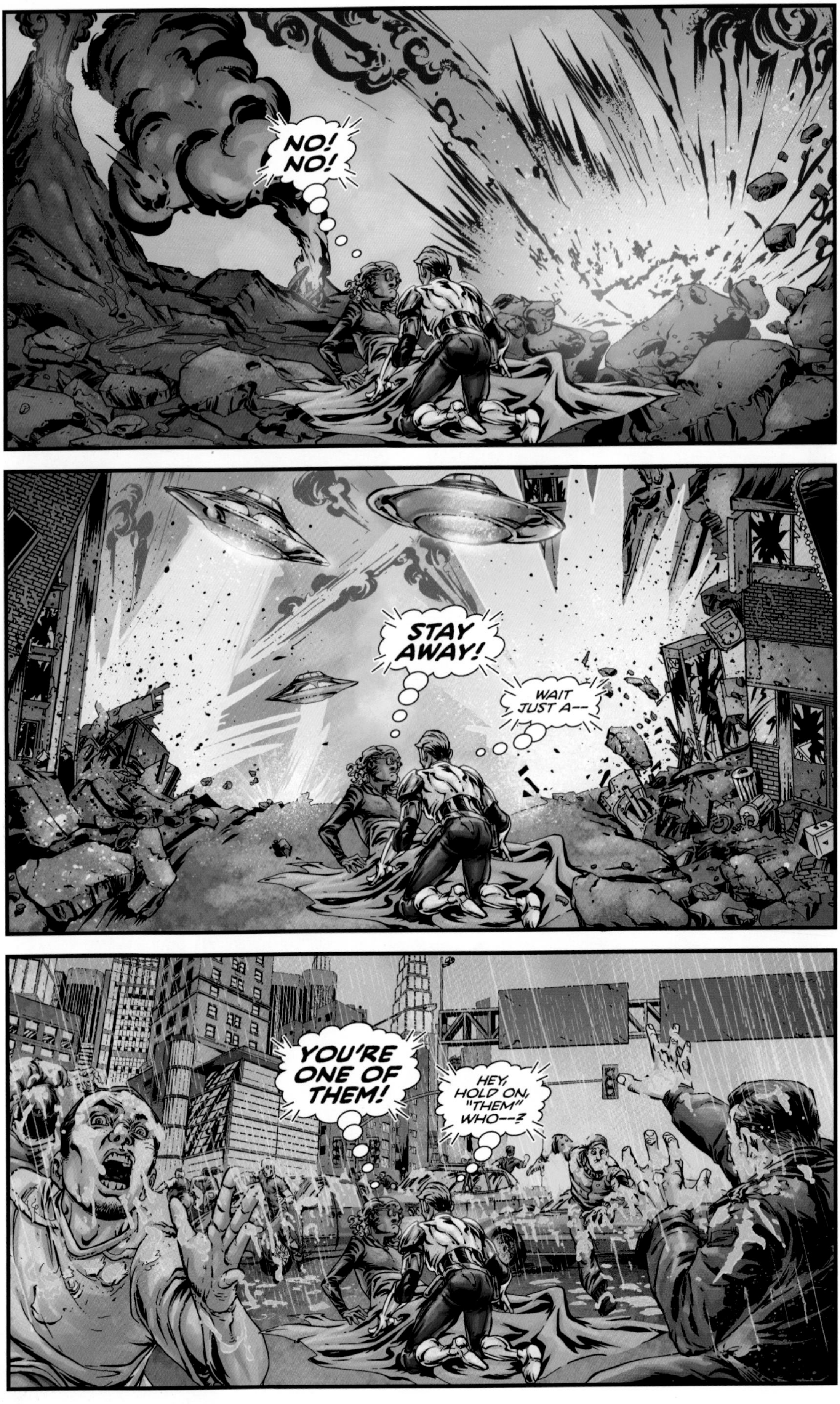
NO! NO!
STAY AWAY!
WAIT JUST A--
YOU'RE ONE OF THEM!
HEY, HOLD ON, "THEM" WHO--?

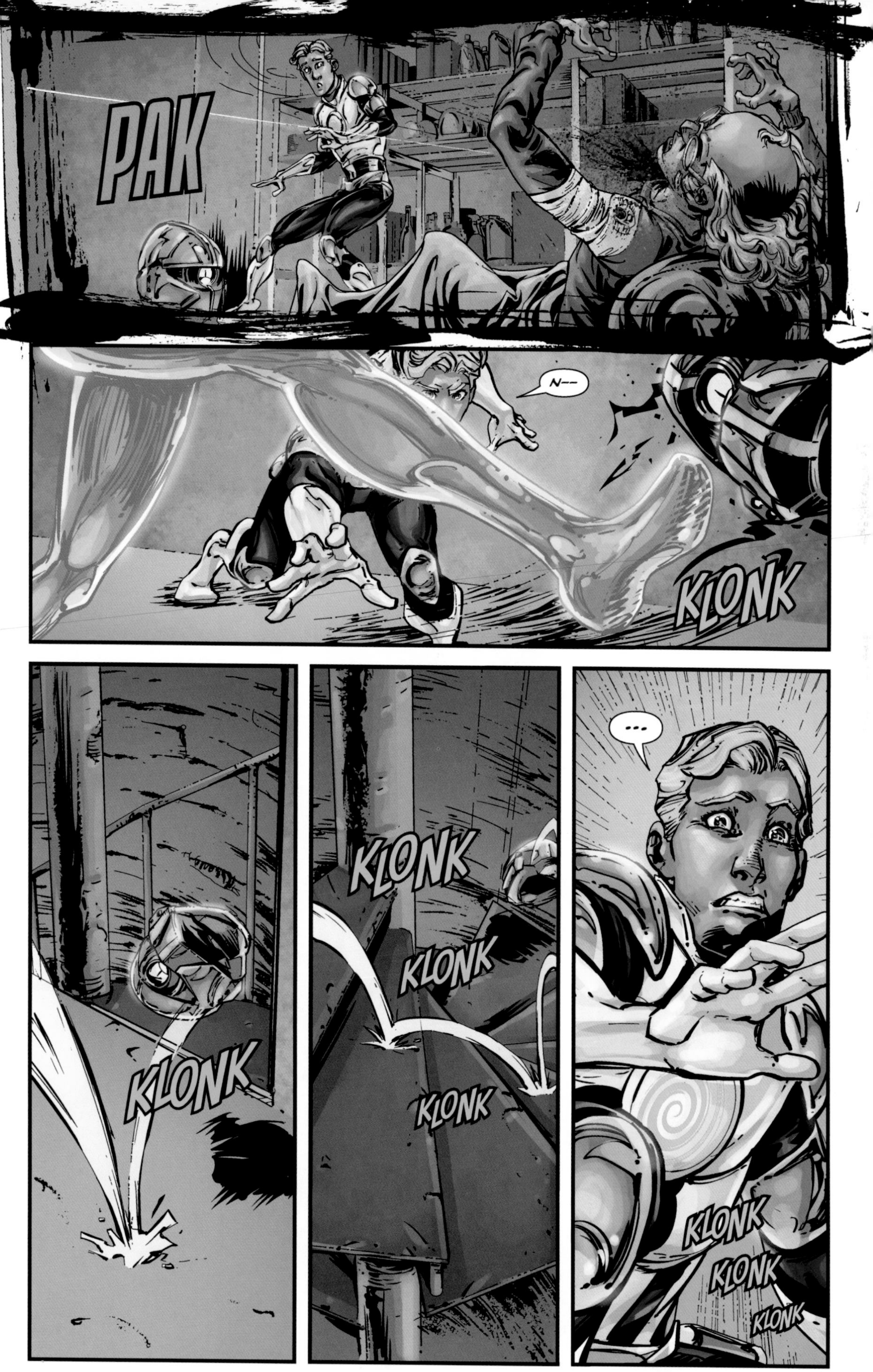
PAK
N--
KLONK
KLONK
KLONK
KLONK
KLONK
...
KLONK
KLONK
KLONK

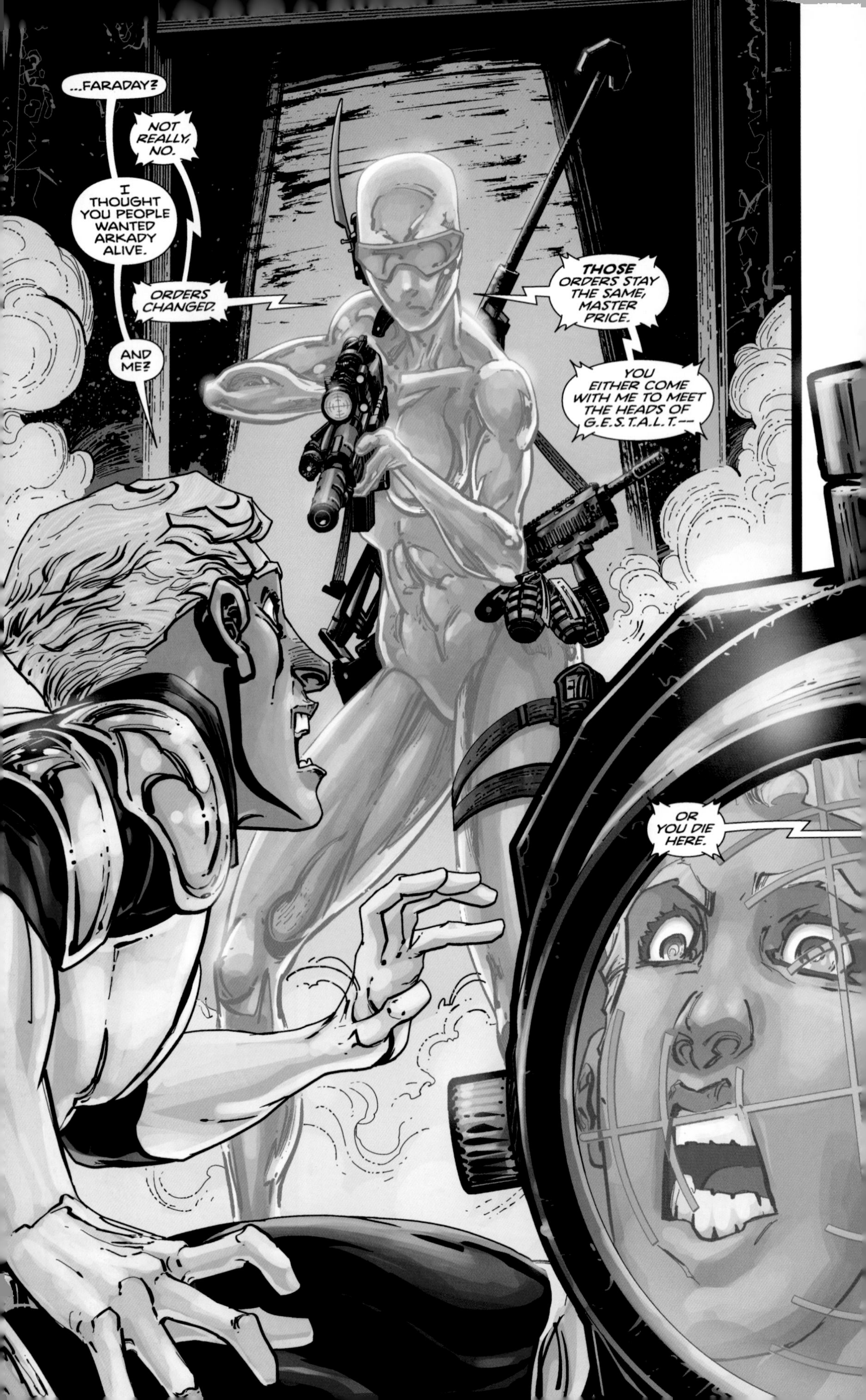
...FARADAY?
NOT REALLY, NO.
I THOUGHT YOU PEOPLE WANTED ARKADY ALIVE.
ORDERS CHANGED.
AND ME?
THOSE ORDERS STAY THE SAME, MASTER PRICE.
YOU EITHER COME WITH ME TO MEET THE HEADS OF G.E.S.T.A.L.T.--
OR YOU DIE HERE.

CHAPTER 4

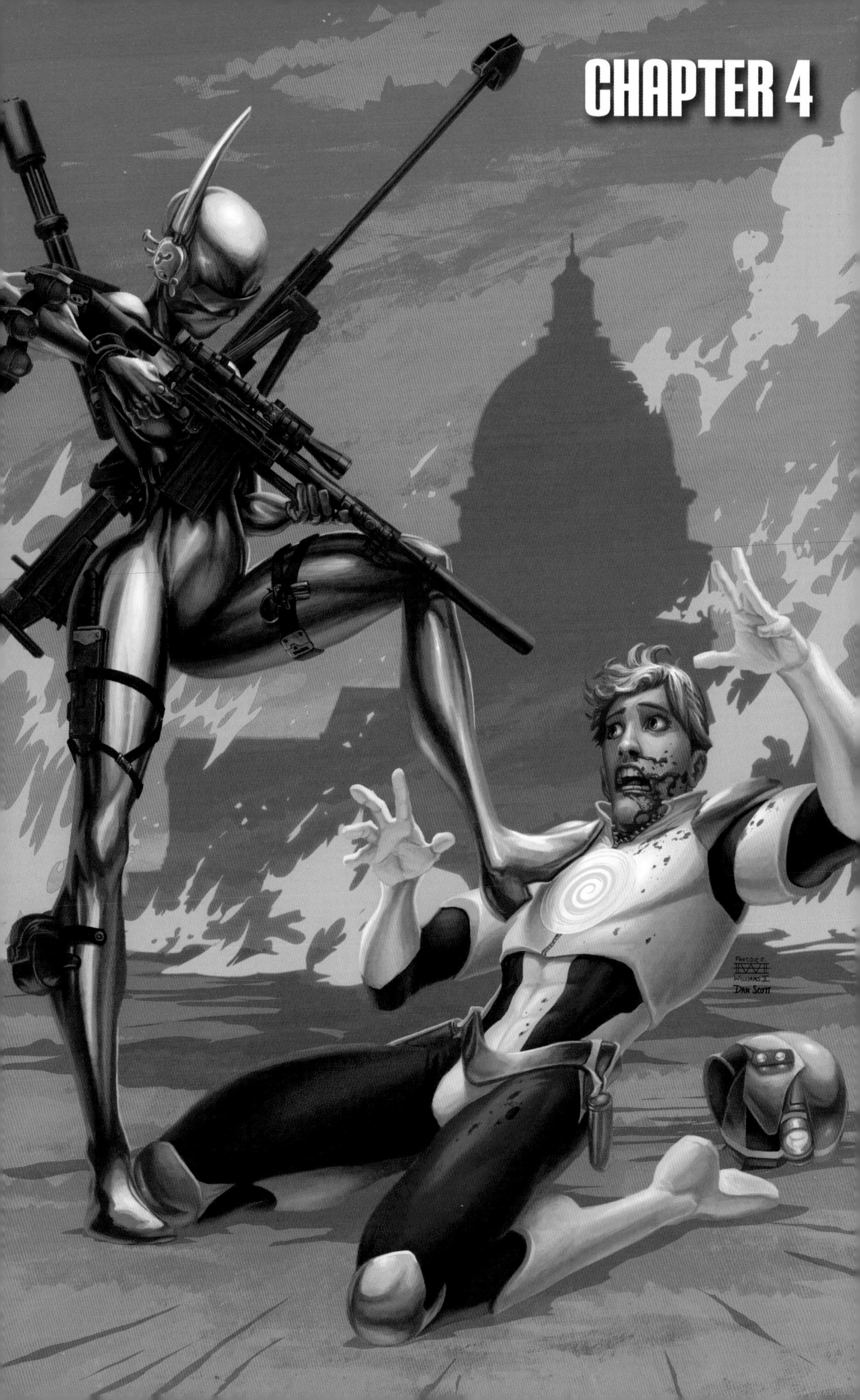
FREDDIE E. WILLIAMS II
DAN SCOTT

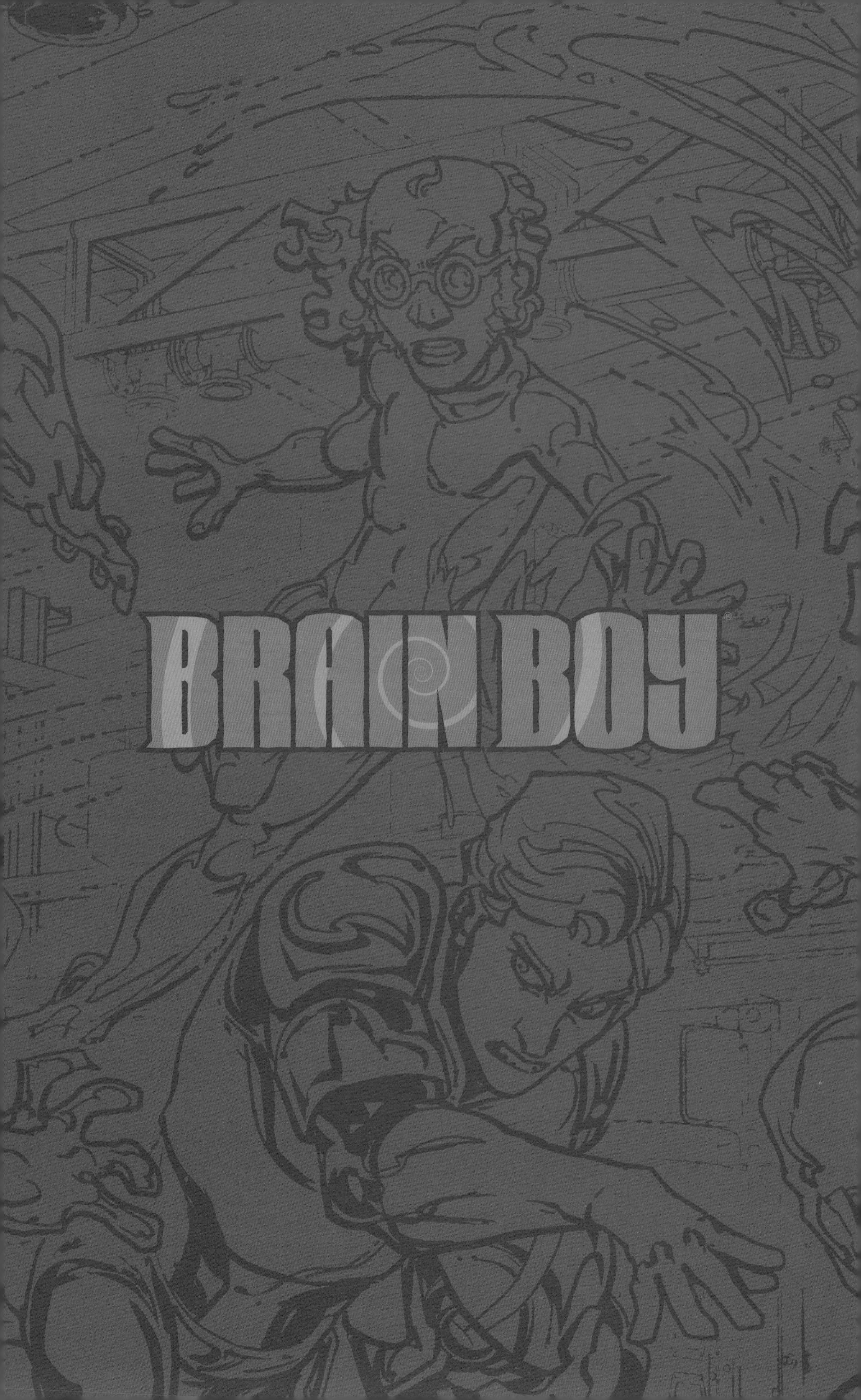
BRAIN BOY

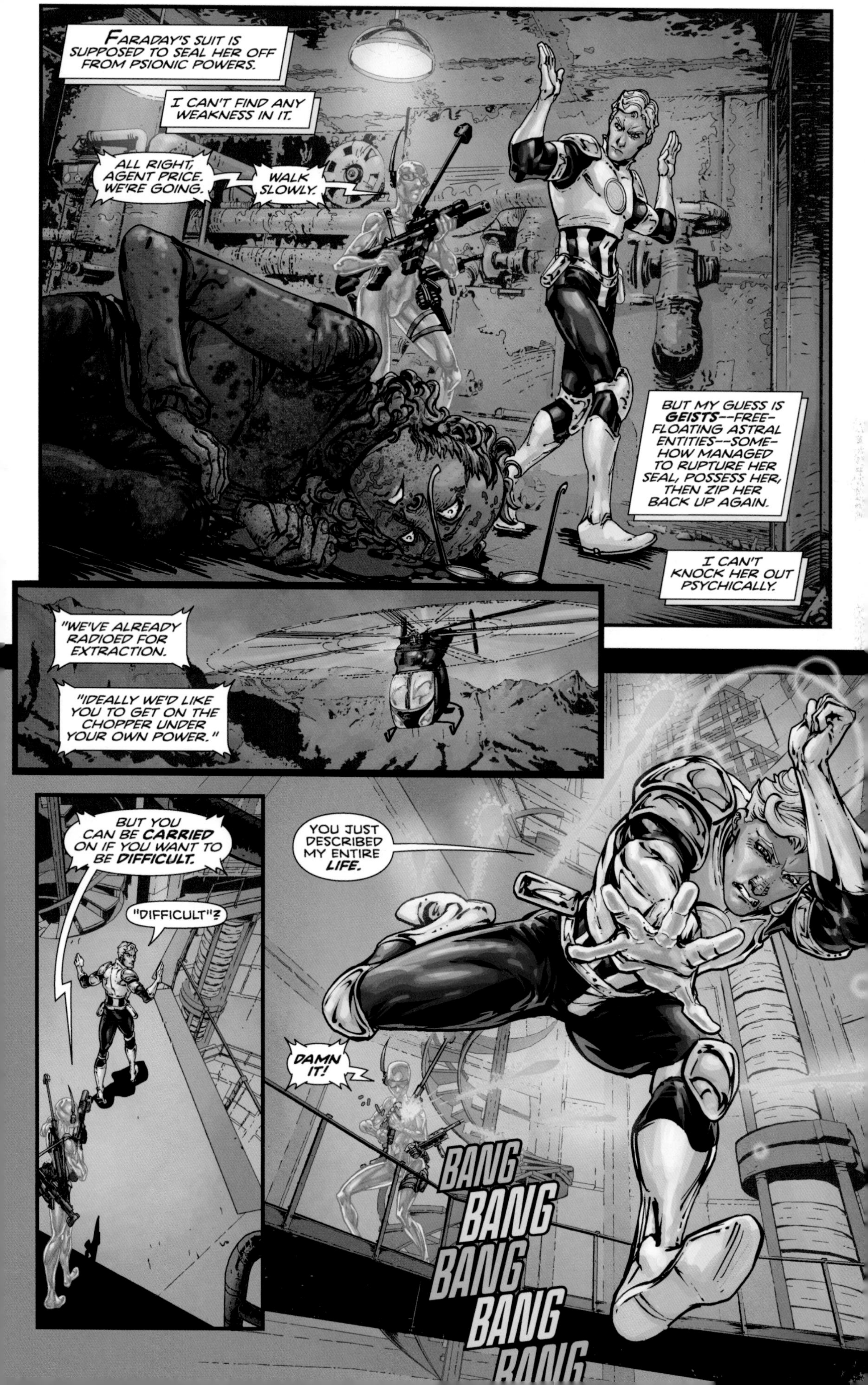
FARADAY'S SUIT IS SUPPOSED TO SEAL HER OFF FROM PSIONIC POWERS.
I CAN'T FIND ANY WEAKNESS IN IT.
ALL RIGHT, AGENT PRICE. WE'RE GOING.
WALK SLOWLY.
BUT MY GUESS IS GEISTS--FREE-FLOATING ASTRAL ENTITIES--SOMEHOW MANAGED TO RUPTURE HER SEAL, POSSESS HER, THEN ZIP HER BACK UP AGAIN.
I CAN'T KNOCK HER OUT PSYCHICALLY.
"WE'VE ALREADY RADIOED FOR EXTRACTION.
"IDEALLY WE'D LIKE YOU TO GET ON THE CHOPPER UNDER YOUR OWN POWER."
BUT YOU CAN BE CARRIED ON IF YOU WANT TO BE DIFFICULT.
"DIFFICULT"?
YOU JUST DESCRIBED MY ENTIRE LIFE.
DAMN IT!
BANG
BANG
BANG
BANG

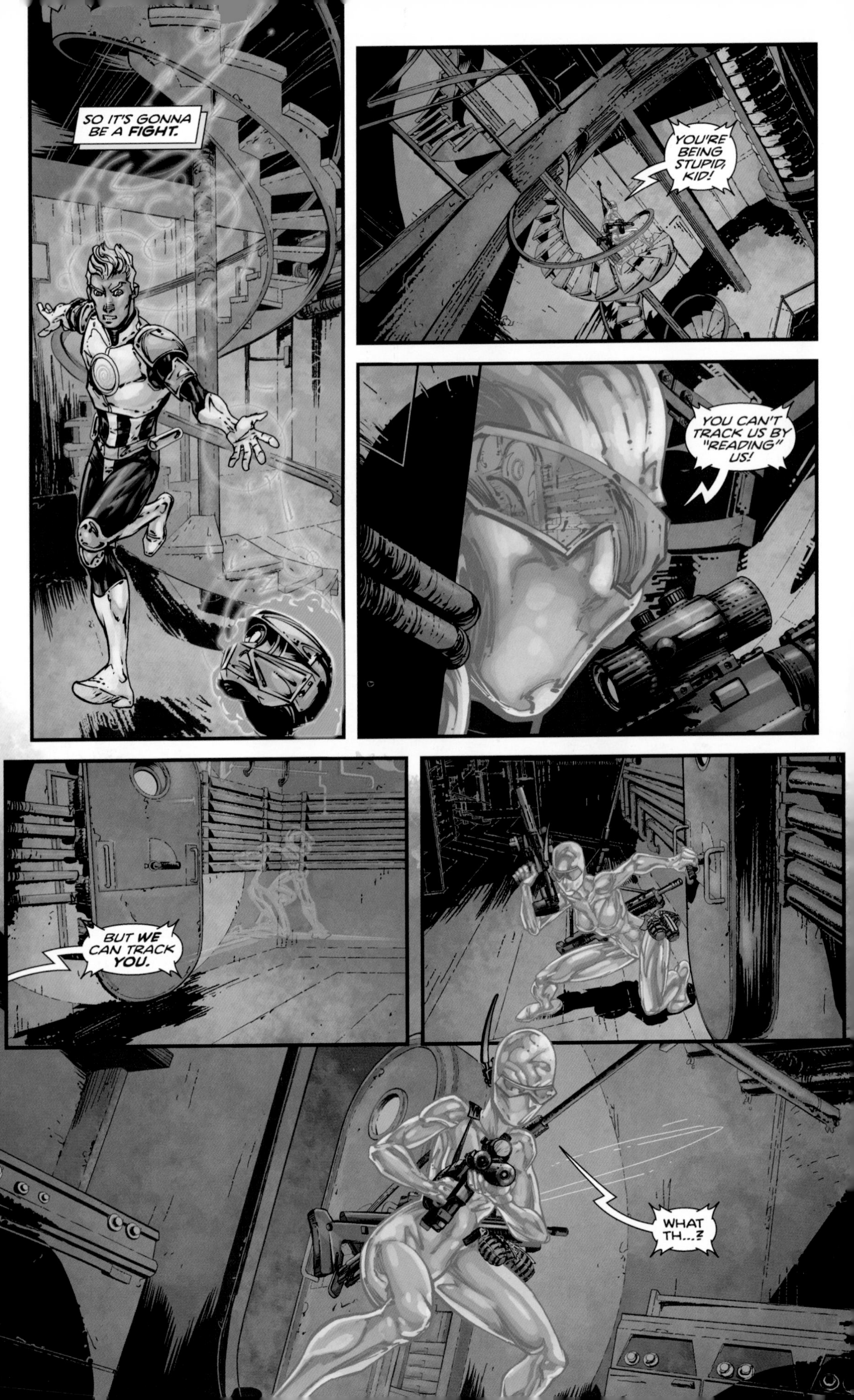
SO IT'S GONNA BE A FIGHT.
YOU'RE BEING STUPID, KID!
YOU CAN'T TRACK US BY "READING" US!
BUT WE CAN TRACK YOU.
WHAT TH...?

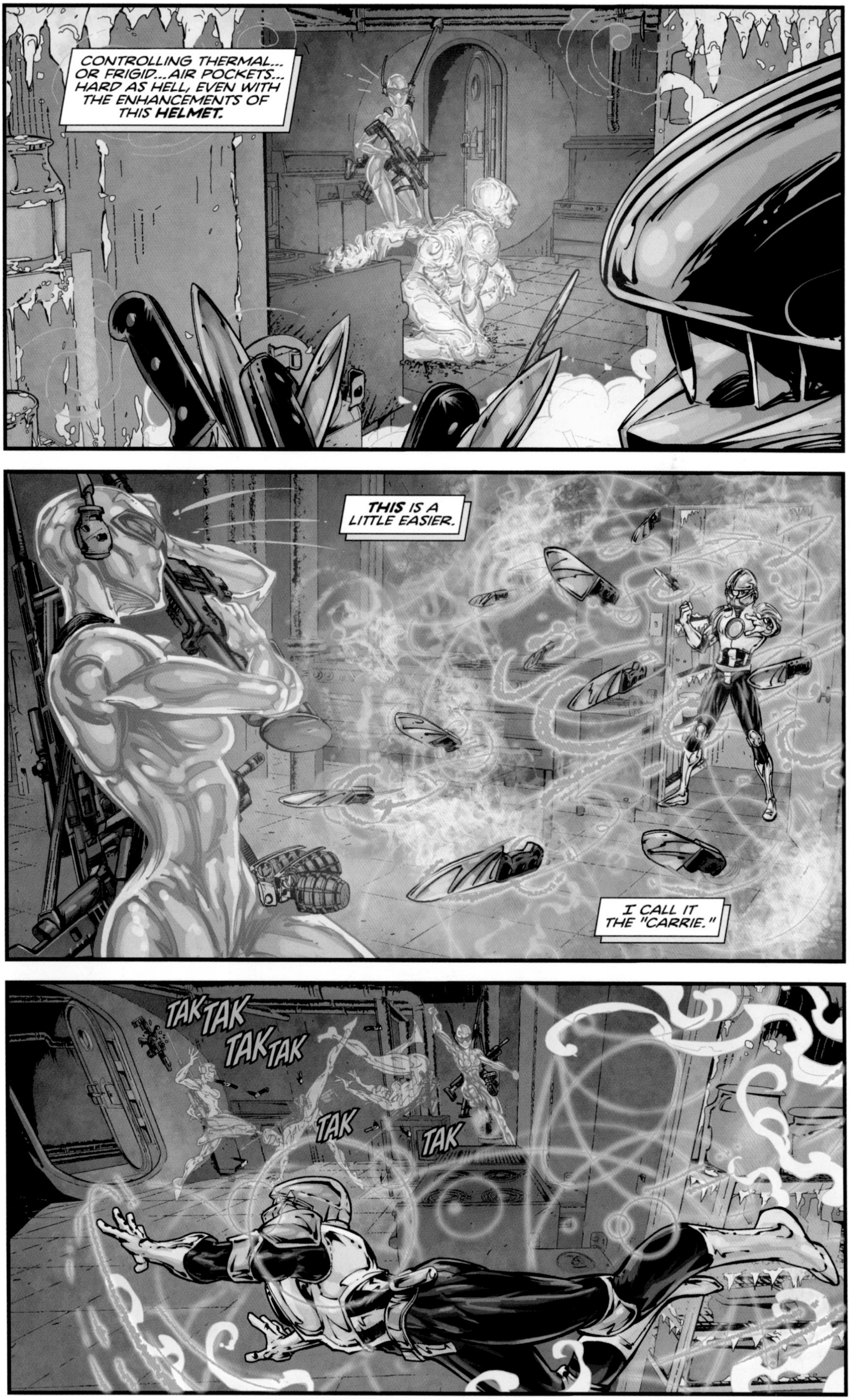
CONTROLLING THERMAL... OR FRIGID... AIR POCKETS... HARD AS HELL, EVEN WITH THE ENHANCEMENTS OF THIS **HELMET.**
THIS IS A LITTLE EASIER.
I CALL IT THE "CARRIE."
TAK TAK
TAK TAK
TAK
TAK

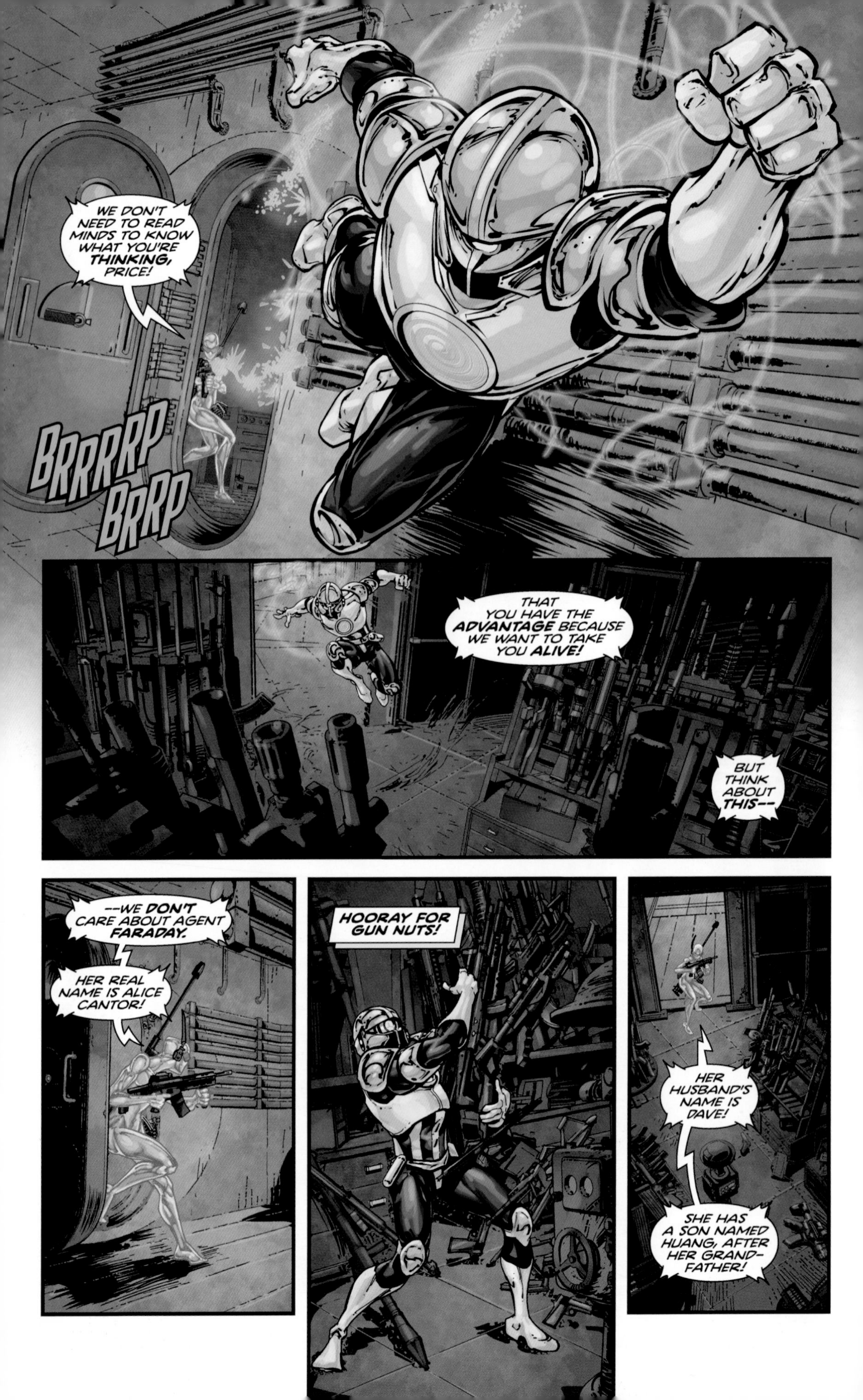
WE DON'T NEED TO READ MINDS TO KNOW WHAT YOU'RE THINKING, PRICE!
BRRRRP BRRP
THAT YOU HAVE THE ADVANTAGE BECAUSE WE WANT TO TAKE YOU ALIVE!
BUT THINK ABOUT THIS--
--WE DON'T CARE ABOUT AGENT FARADAY.
HER REAL NAME IS ALICE CANTOR!
HOORAY FOR GUN NUTS!
HER HUSBAND'S NAME IS DAVE!
SHE HAS A SON NAMED HUANG, AFTER HER GRAND-FATHER!

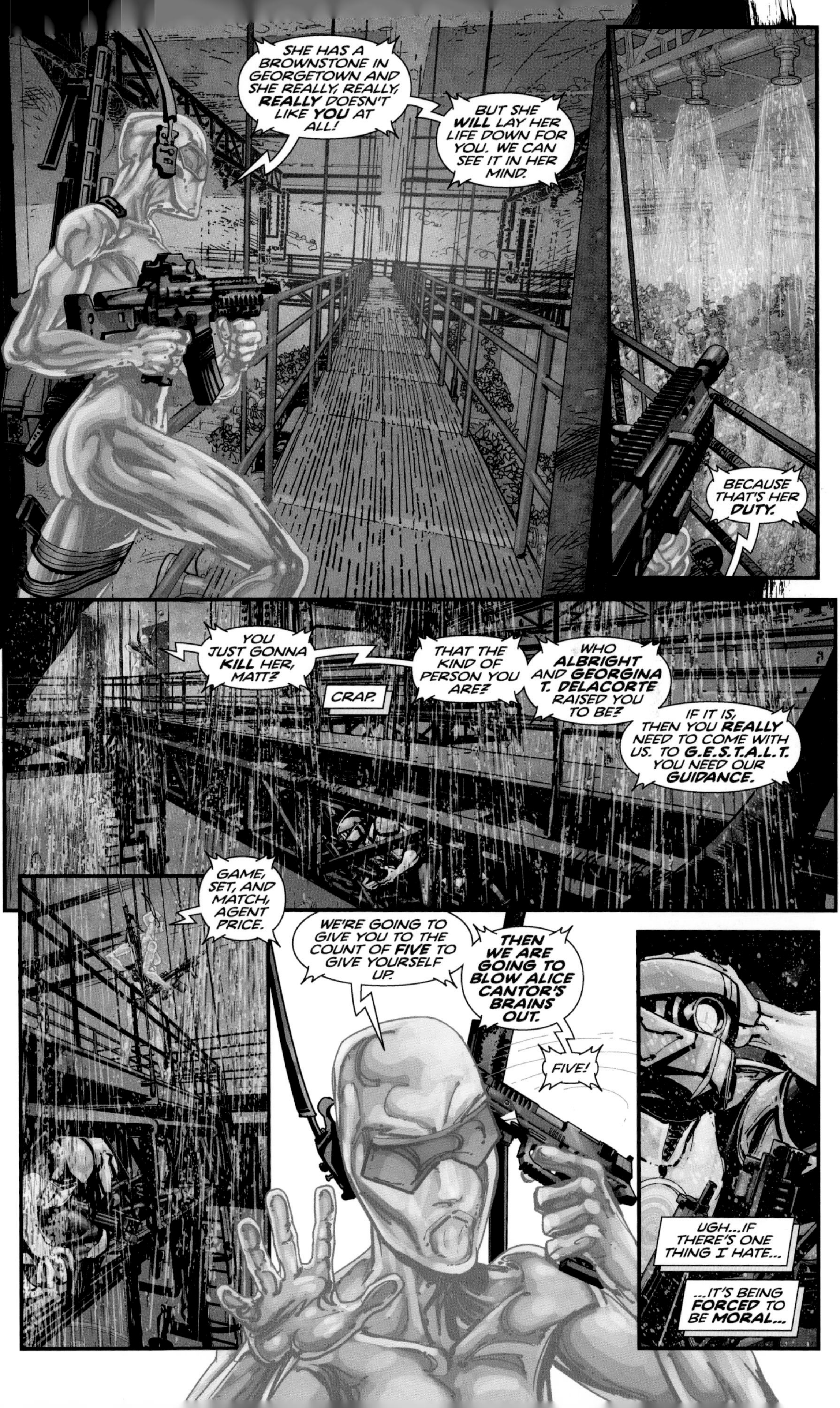
SHE HAS A BROWNSTONE IN GEORGETOWN AND SHE REALLY, REALLY, **REALLY** DOESN'T LIKE **YOU** AT ALL!
BUT SHE **WILL** LAY HER LIFE DOWN FOR YOU. WE CAN SEE IT IN HER MIND.
BECAUSE THAT'S HER **DUTY.**
YOU JUST GONNA **KILL** HER, MATT?
CRAP.
THAT THE KIND OF PERSON YOU ARE?
WHO **ALBRIGHT** AND **GEORGINA T. DELACORTE** RAISED YOU TO BE?
IF IT IS, THEN YOU **REALLY** NEED TO COME WITH US. TO **G.E.S.T.A.L.T.** YOU NEED OUR **GUIDANCE.**
GAME, SET, AND MATCH, AGENT PRICE.
WE'RE GOING TO GIVE YOU TO THE COUNT OF **FIVE** TO GIVE YOURSELF UP.
THEN WE ARE GOING TO BLOW ALICE CANTOR'S BRAINS OUT.
FIVE!
UGH... IF THERE'S ONE THING I HATE...
...IT'S BEING **FORCED** TO BE **MORAL...**

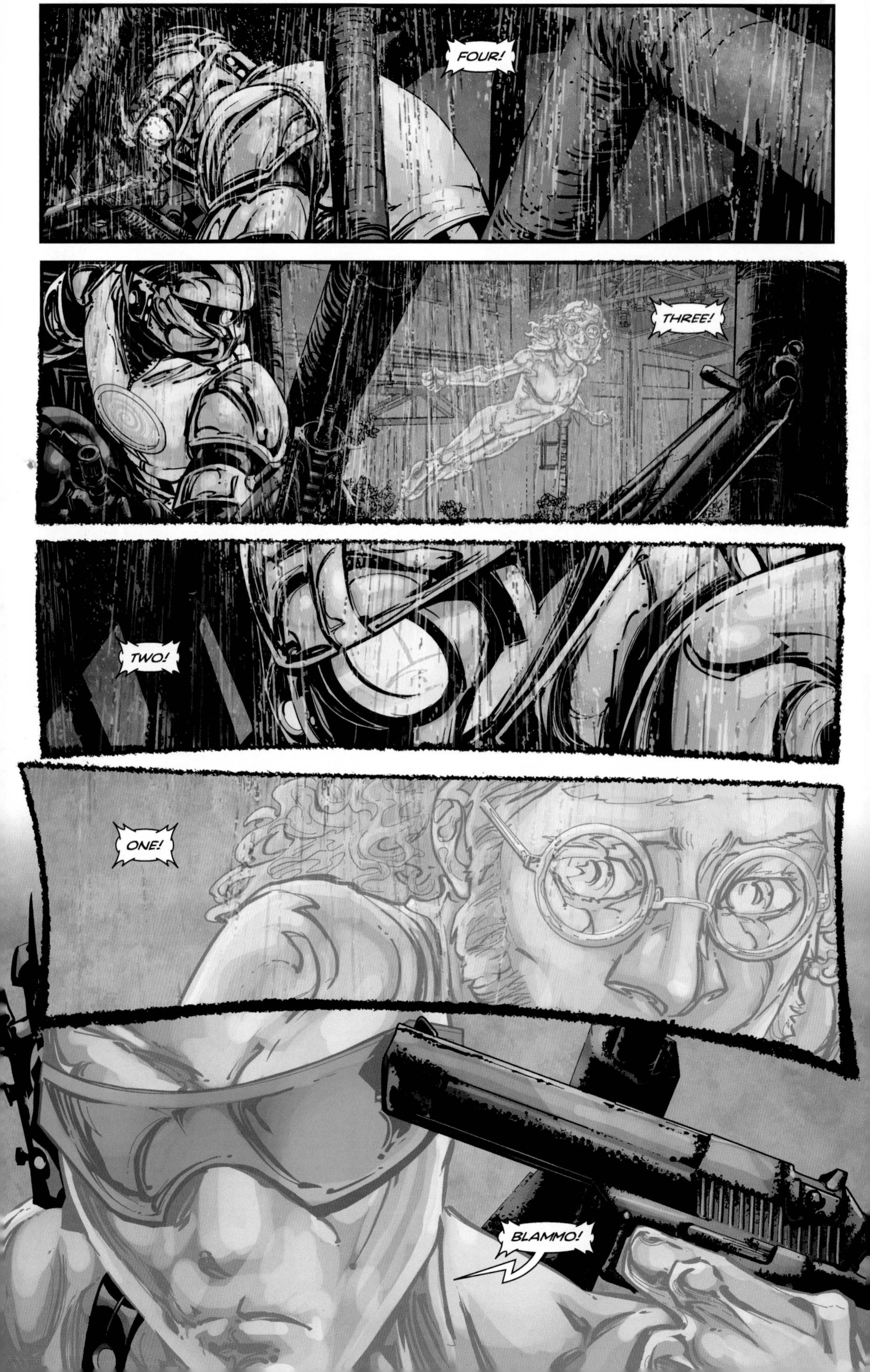
FOUR!
THREE!
TWO!
ONE!
BLAMMO!

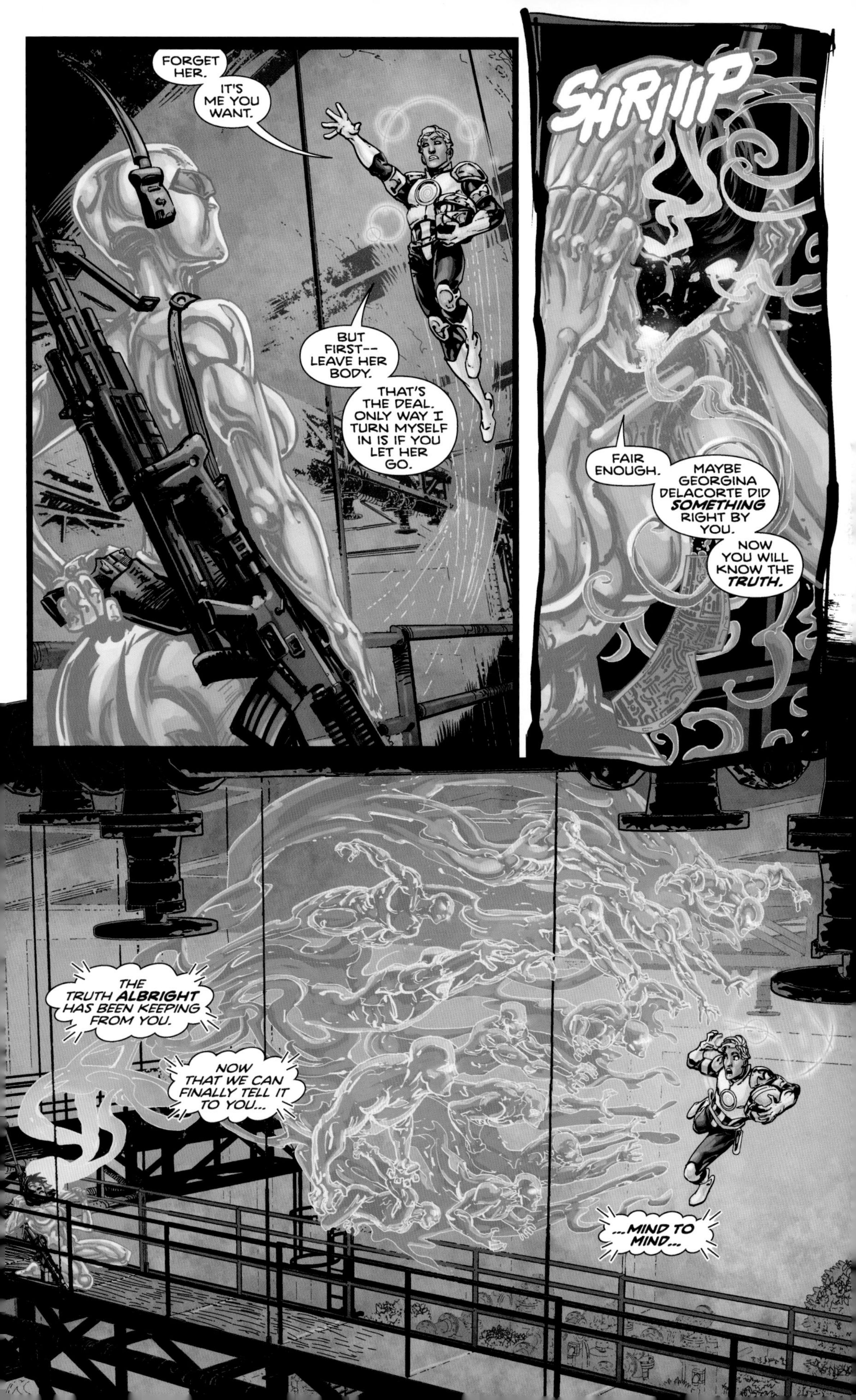
FORGET HER.
IT'S ME YOU WANT.
BUT FIRST-- LEAVE HER BODY.
THAT'S THE DEAL. ONLY WAY I TURN MYSELF IN IS IF YOU LET HER GO.
SHRIIIP
FAIR ENOUGH.
MAYBE GEORGINA DELACORTE DID SOMETHING RIGHT BY YOU.
NOW YOU WILL KNOW THE TRUTH.
THE TRUTH ALBRIGHT HAS BEEN KEEPING FROM YOU.
NOW THAT WE CAN FINALLY TELL IT TO YOU...
...MIND TO MIND...

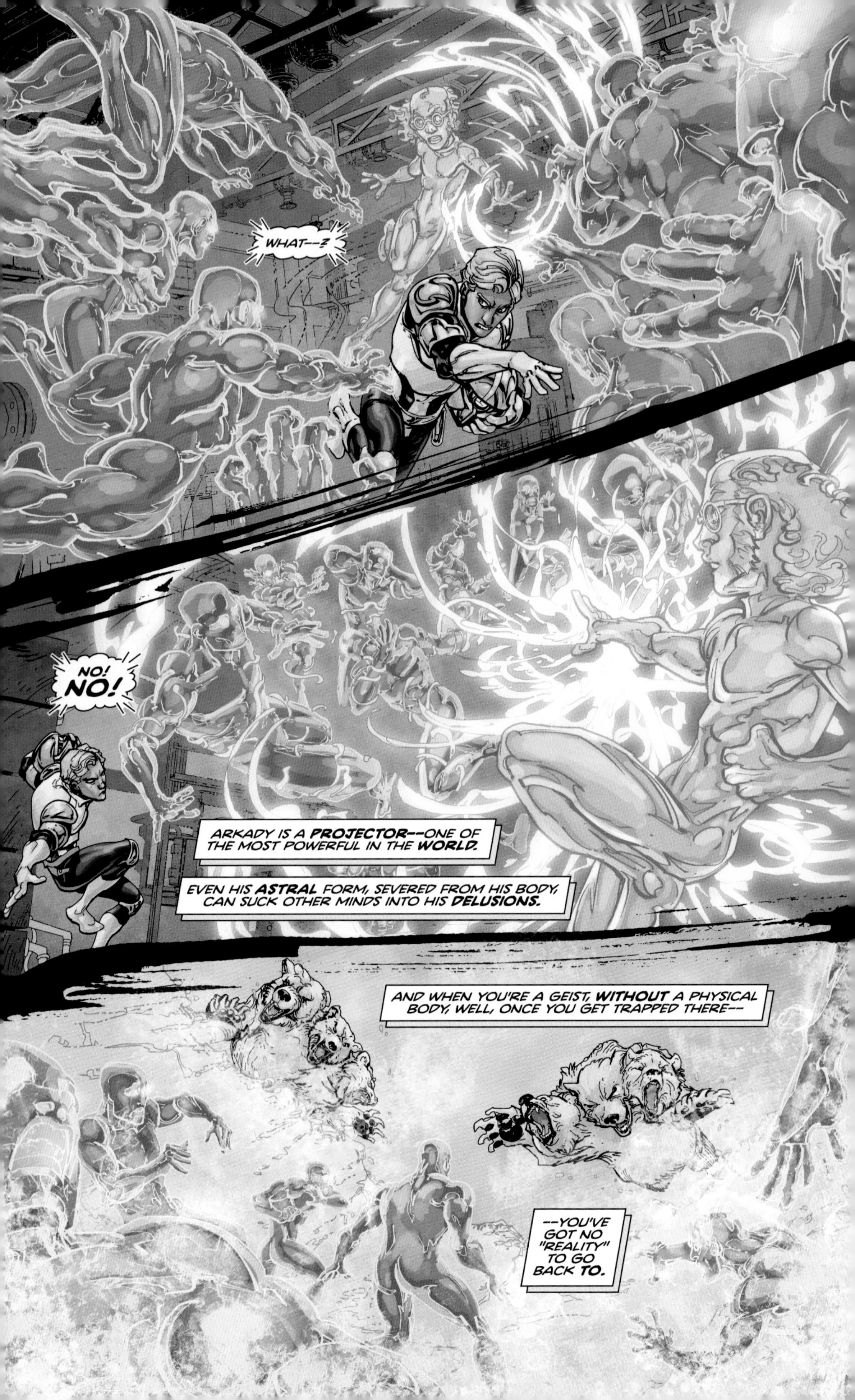
WHAT--?
NO! NO!
ARKADY IS A PROJECTOR--ONE OF THE MOST POWERFUL IN THE WORLD.
EVEN HIS ASTRAL FORM, SEVERED FROM HIS BODY, CAN SUCK OTHER MINDS INTO HIS DELUSIONS.
AND WHEN YOU'RE A GEIST, WITHOUT A PHYSICAL BODY, WELL, ONCE YOU GET TRAPPED THERE--
--YOU'VE GOT NO "REALITY" TO GO BACK TO.

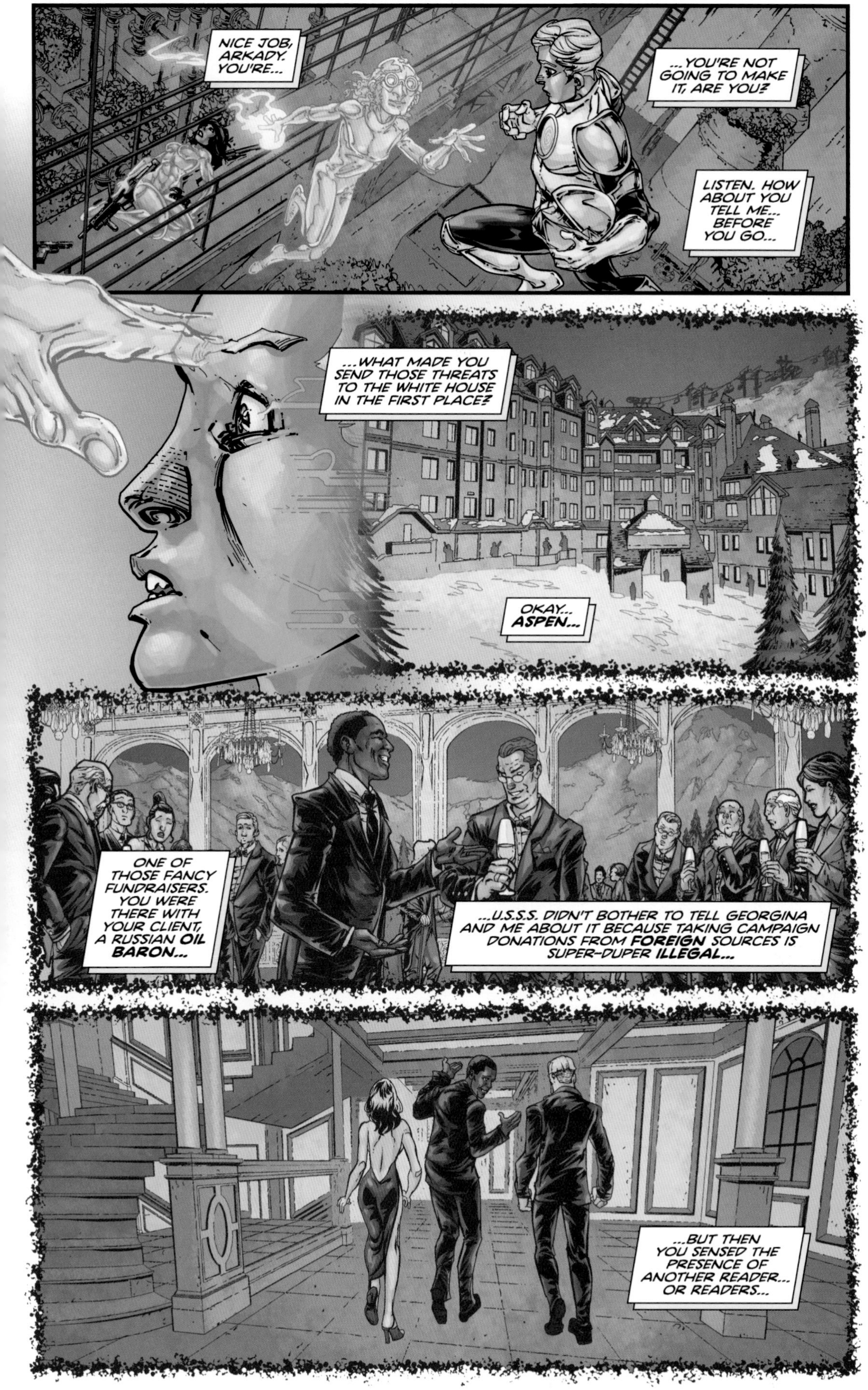
NICE JOB, ARKADY. YOU'RE...
...YOU'RE NOT GOING TO MAKE IT, ARE YOU?
LISTEN. HOW ABOUT YOU TELL ME... BEFORE YOU GO...
...WHAT MADE YOU SEND THOSE THREATS TO THE WHITE HOUSE IN THE FIRST PLACE?
OKAY... ASPEN...
ONE OF THOSE FANCY FUNDRAISERS. YOU WERE THERE WITH YOUR CLIENT, A RUSSIAN OIL BARON...
...U.S.S.S. DIDN'T BOTHER TO TELL GEORGINA AND ME ABOUT IT BECAUSE TAKING CAMPAIGN DONATIONS FROM FOREIGN SOURCES IS SUPER-DUPER ILLEGAL...
...BUT THEN YOU SENSED THE PRESENCE OF ANOTHER READER... OR READERS...

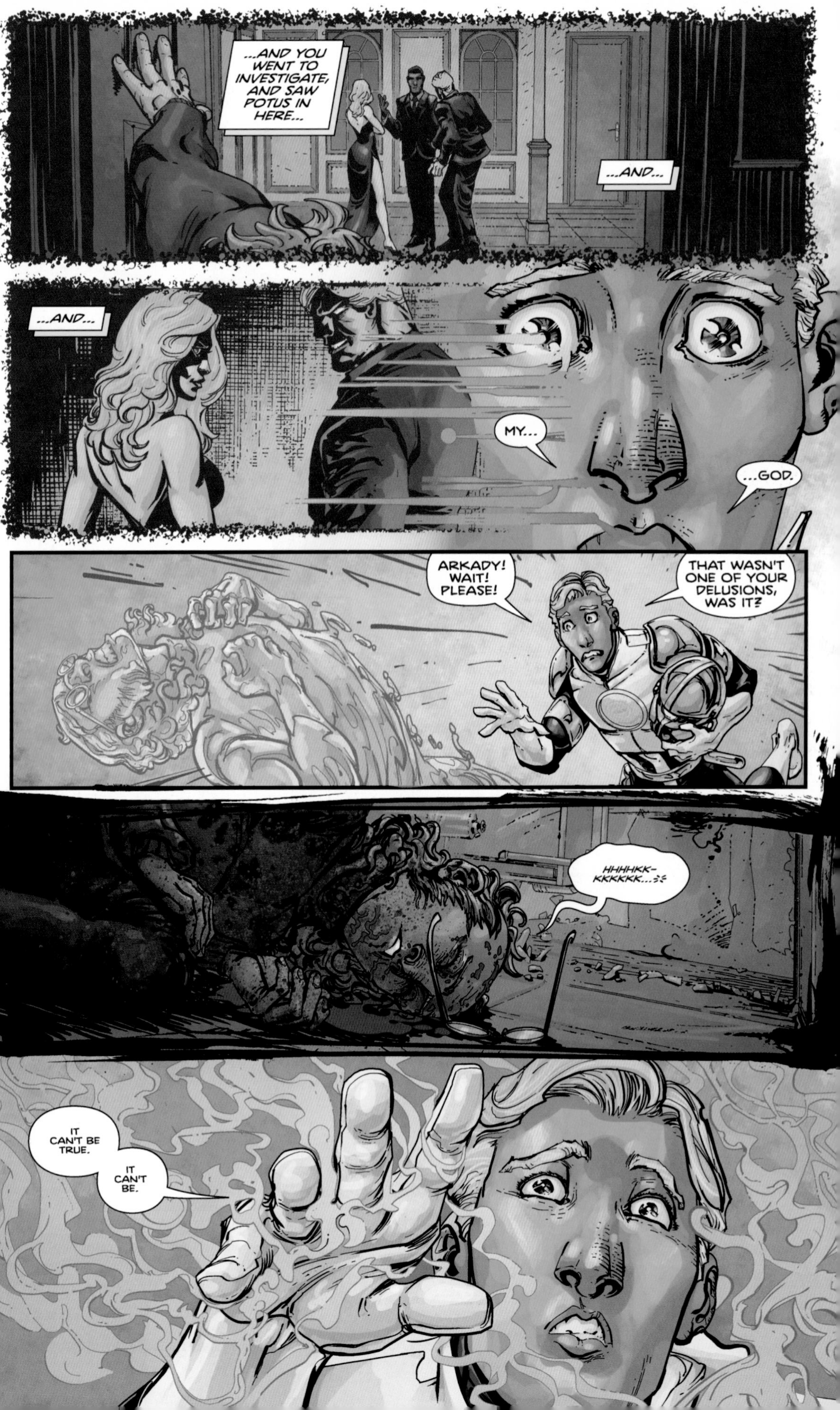
...AND YOU WENT TO INVESTIGATE, AND SAW POTUS IN HERE...
...AND...
...AND...
MY...
...GOD.
ARKADY! WAIT! PLEASE!
THAT WASN'T ONE OF YOUR DELUSIONS, WAS IT?
HHHHKK-KKKKKK...
IT CAN'T BE TRUE.
IT CAN'T BE.

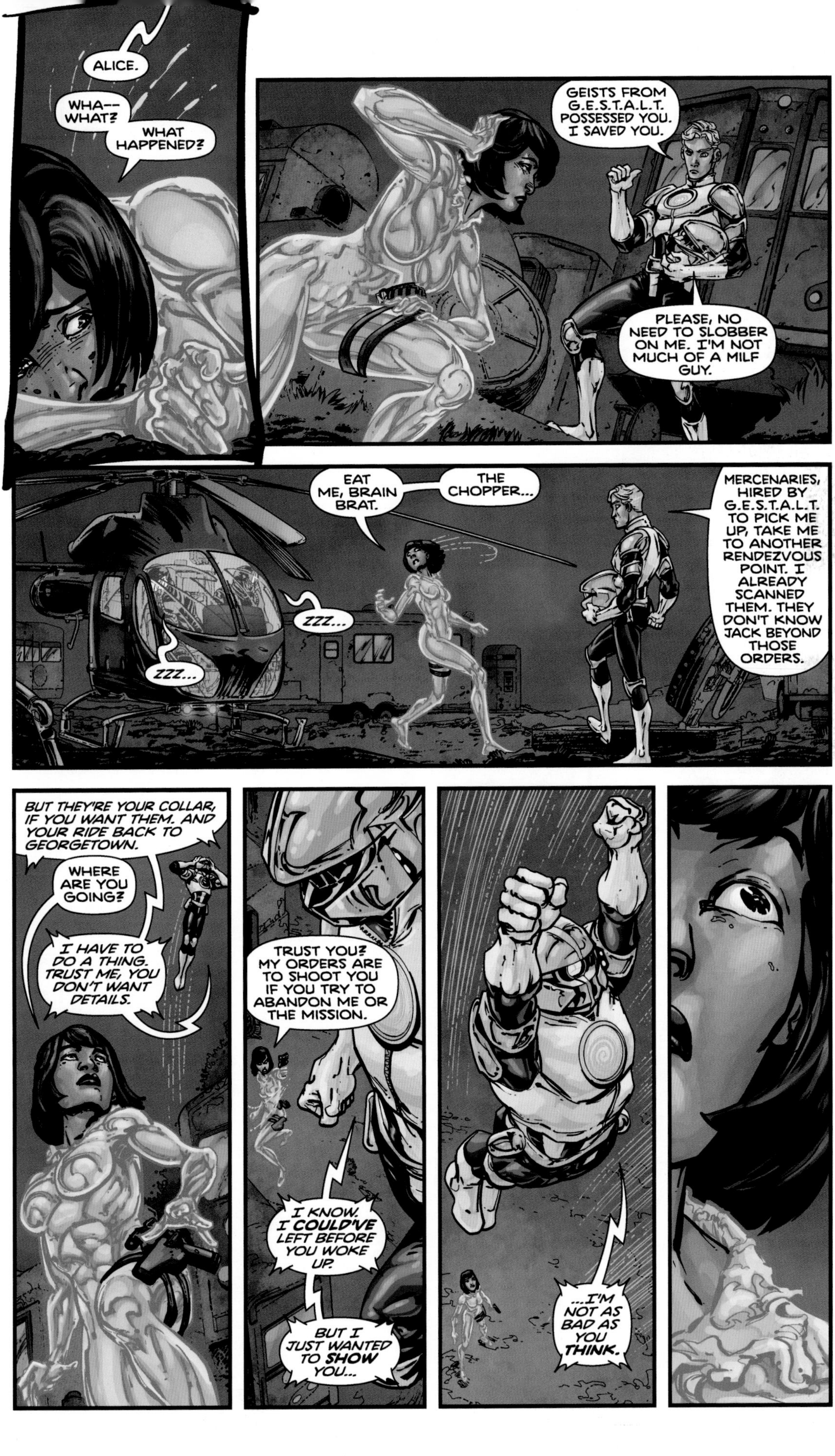
ALICE.
WHA-- WHAT?
WHAT HAPPENED?
GEISTS FROM G.E.S.T.A.L.T. POSSESSED YOU. I SAVED YOU.
PLEASE, NO NEED TO SLOBBER ON ME. I'M NOT MUCH OF A MILF GUY.
EAT ME, BRAIN BRAT.
THE CHOPPER...
MERCENARIES, HIRED BY G.E.S.T.A.L.T. TO PICK ME UP, TAKE ME TO ANOTHER RENDEZVOUS POINT. I ALREADY SCANNED THEM. THEY DON'T KNOW JACK BEYOND THOSE ORDERS.
ZZZ...
ZZZ...
BUT THEY'RE YOUR COLLAR, IF YOU WANT THEM. AND YOUR RIDE BACK TO GEORGETOWN.
WHERE ARE YOU GOING?
I HAVE TO DO A THING. TRUST ME, YOU DON'T WANT DETAILS.
TRUST YOU? MY ORDERS ARE TO SHOOT YOU IF YOU TRY TO ABANDON ME OR THE MISSION.
I KNOW. I COULD'VE LEFT BEFORE YOU WOKE UP.
BUT I JUST WANTED TO SHOW YOU...
...I'M NOT AS BAD AS YOU THINK.

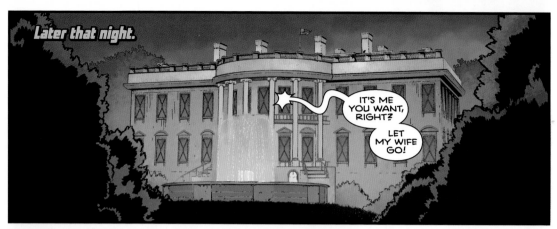

Later that night.

IT'S ME YOU WANT, RIGHT?

LET MY WIFE GO!

LET HER BE, AND I'LL GO *WITH* YOU, WITHOUT A STRUGGLE--

MR. PRESIDENT. PLEASE. WE BOTH KNOW...

...THIS ISN'T ABOUT YOUR *WIFE*.

MATT! MATT, COME IN! THIS ISN'T LIKE YOU! WHAT HAPPENED OUT THERE IN NEW MEXICO?

THE TRUTH IS WHAT HAPPENED, GEORGINA.

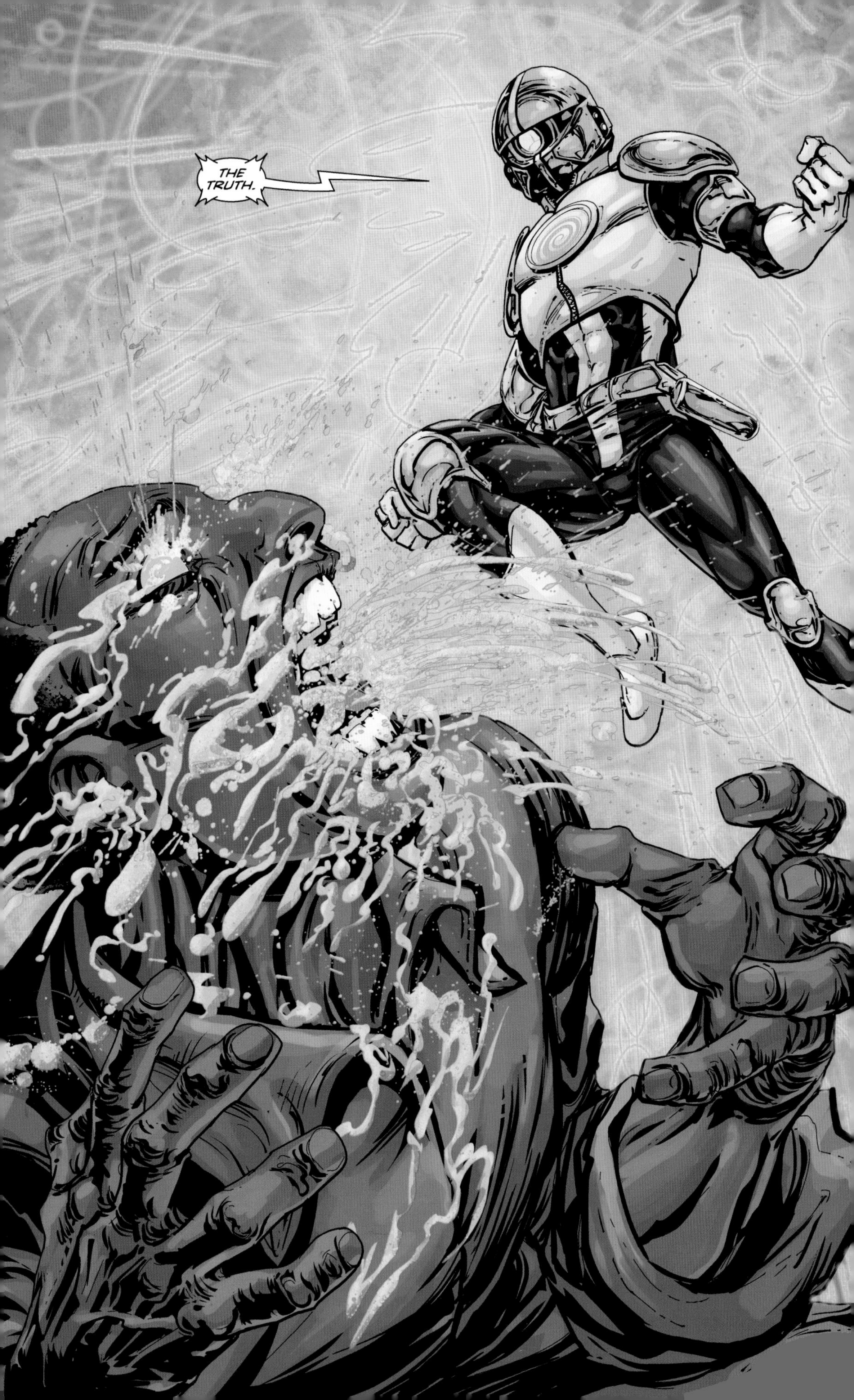
THE TRUTH.

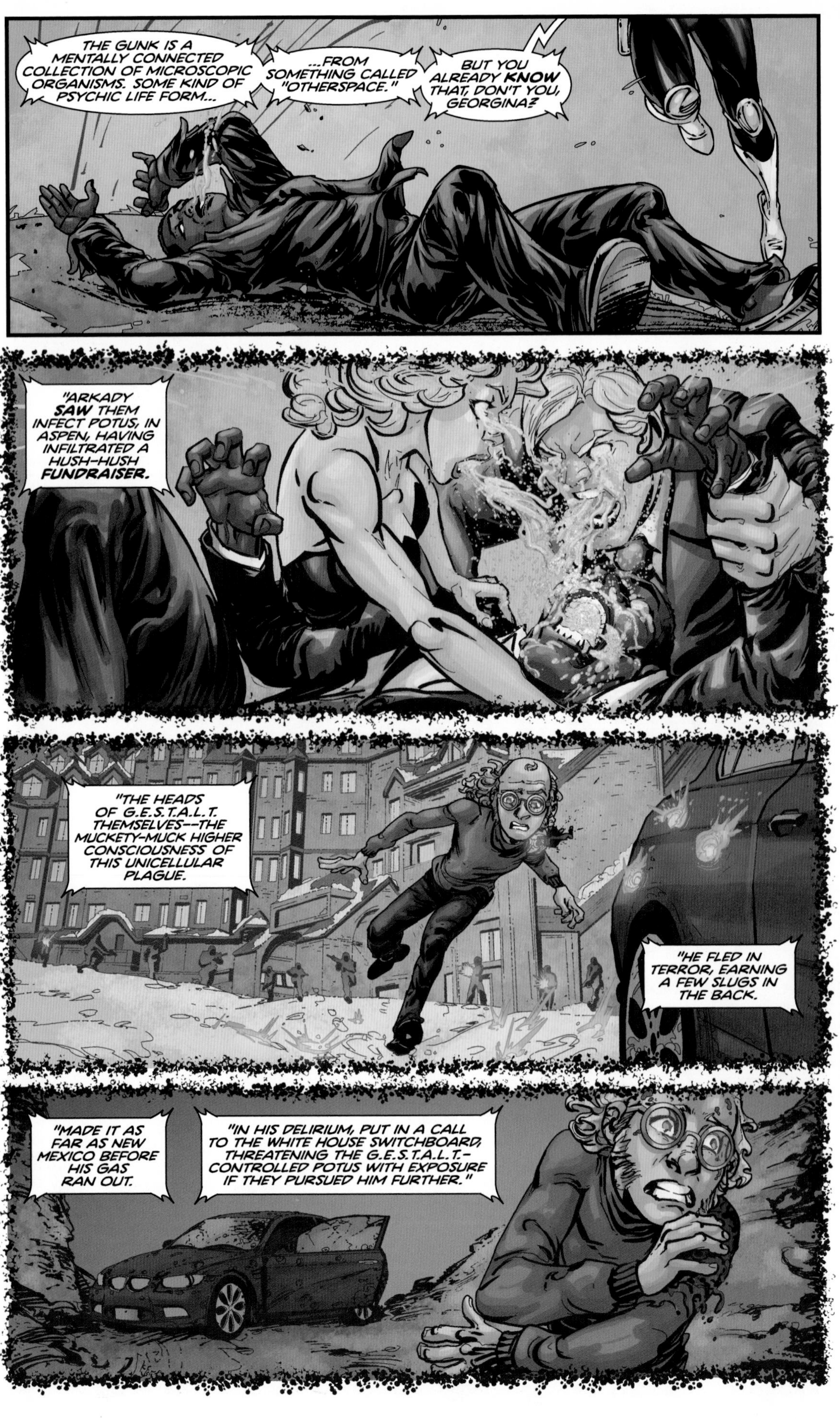
THE GUNK IS A MENTALLY CONNECTED COLLECTION OF MICROSCOPIC ORGANISMS. SOME KIND OF PSYCHIC LIFE FORM...
...FROM SOMETHING CALLED "OTHERSPACE."
BUT YOU ALREADY **KNOW** THAT, DON'T YOU, GEORGINA?
"ARKADY **SAW** THEM INFECT POTUS, IN ASPEN, HAVING INFILTRATED A HUSH-HUSH **FUNDRAISER.**
"THE HEADS OF G.E.S.T.A.L.T. THEMSELVES--THE MUCKETY-MUCK HIGHER CONSCIOUSNESS OF THIS UNICELLULAR PLAGUE.
"HE FLED IN TERROR, EARNING A FEW SLUGS IN THE BACK.
"MADE IT AS FAR AS NEW MEXICO BEFORE HIS GAS RAN OUT.
"IN HIS DELIRIUM, PUT IN A CALL TO THE WHITE HOUSE SWITCHBOARD, THREATENING THE G.E.S.T.A.L.T.-CONTROLLED POTUS WITH EXPOSURE IF THEY PURSUED HIM FURTHER."

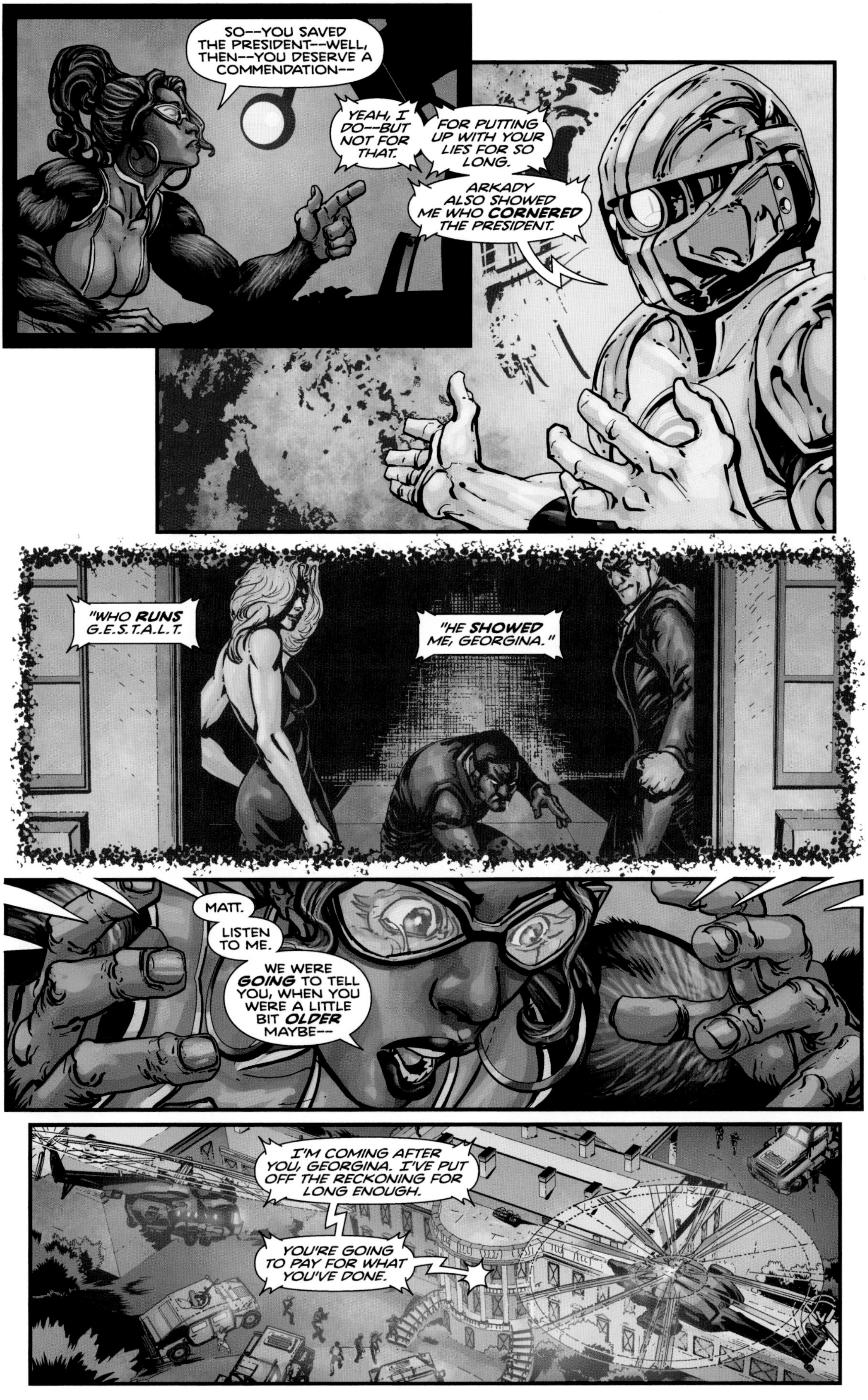
SO--YOU SAVED THE PRESIDENT--WELL, THEN--YOU DESERVE A COMMENDATION--
YEAH, I DO--BUT NOT FOR THAT.
FOR PUTTING UP WITH YOUR LIES FOR SO LONG.
ARKADY ALSO SHOWED ME WHO **CORNERED** THE PRESIDENT.
"WHO **RUNS** G.E.S.T.A.L.T.
"HE **SHOWED** ME, GEORGINA."
MATT.
LISTEN TO ME.
WE WERE **GOING** TO TELL YOU, WHEN YOU WERE A LITTLE BIT **OLDER** MAYBE--
I'M COMING AFTER YOU, GEORGINA. I'VE PUT OFF THE RECKONING FOR LONG ENOUGH.
YOU'RE GOING TO PAY FOR WHAT YOU'VE DONE.

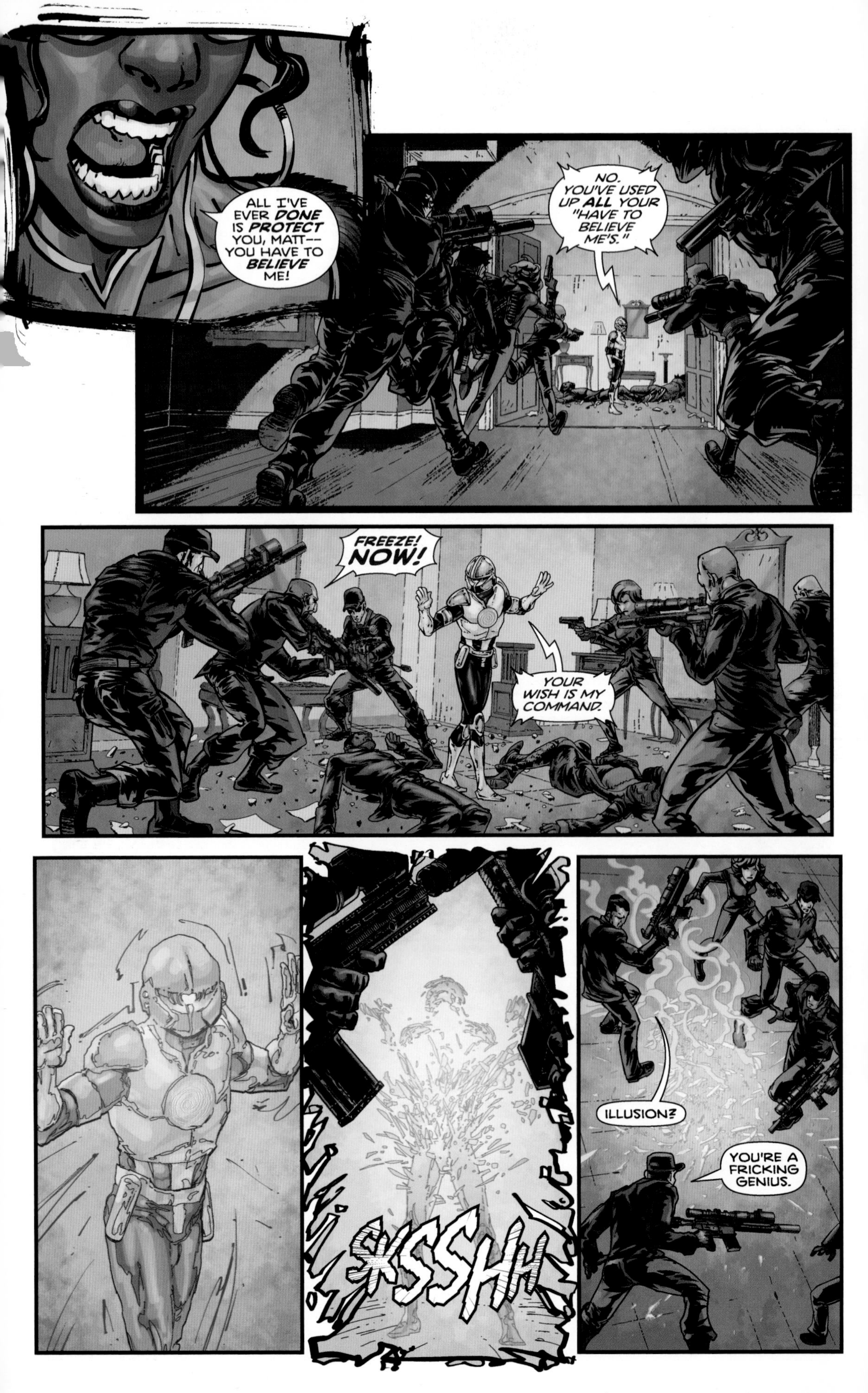
ALL I'VE EVER DONE IS PROTECT YOU, MATT-- YOU HAVE TO BELIEVE ME!
NO. YOU'VE USED UP ALL YOUR "HAVE TO BELIEVE ME'S."
FREEZE! NOW!
YOUR WISH IS MY COMMAND.
SKSSHH
ILLUSION?
YOU'RE A FRICKING GENIUS.

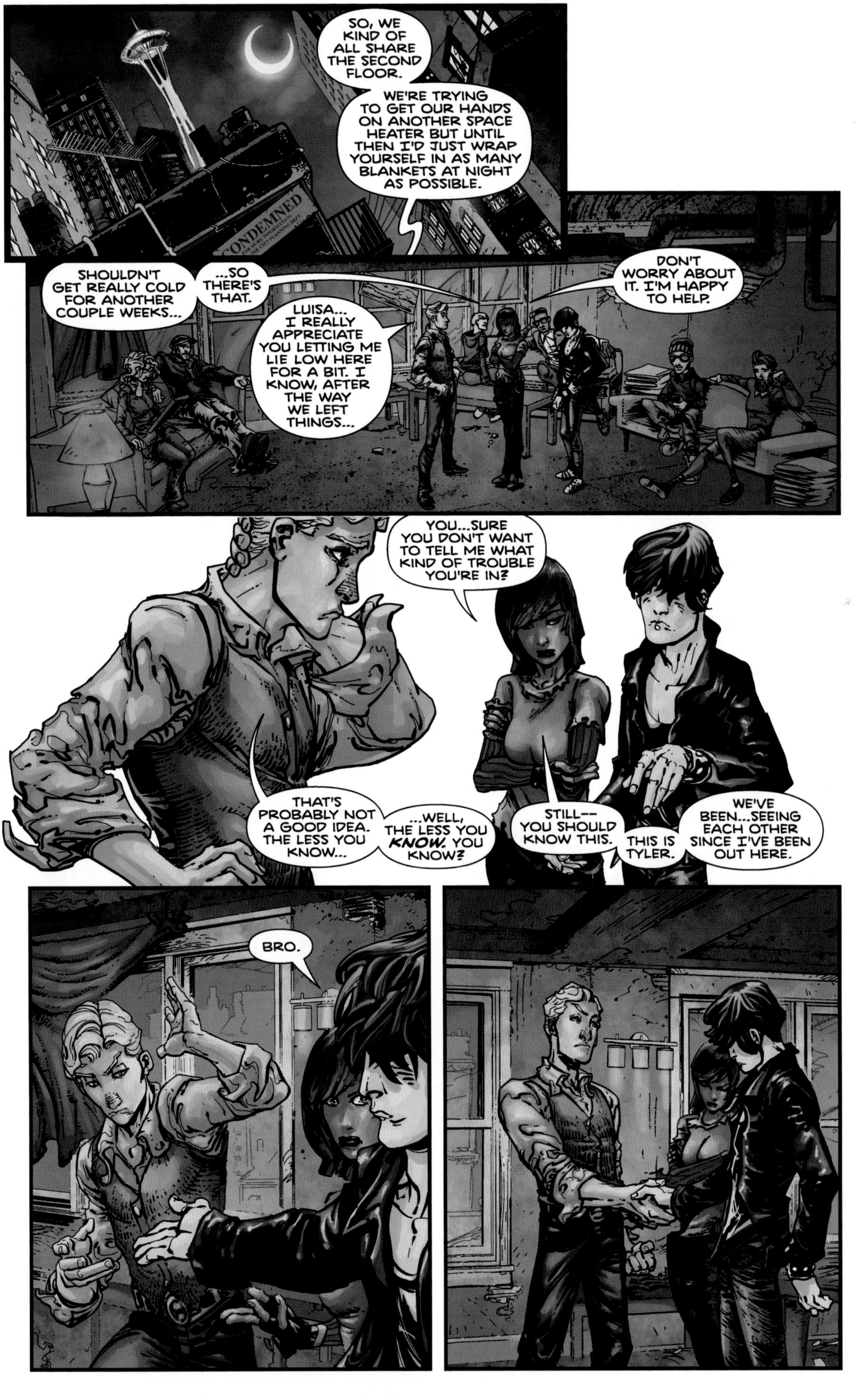
SO, WE KIND OF ALL SHARE THE SECOND FLOOR.
WE'RE TRYING TO GET OUR HANDS ON ANOTHER SPACE HEATER BUT UNTIL THEN I'D JUST WRAP YOURSELF IN AS MANY BLANKETS AT NIGHT AS POSSIBLE.
CONDEMNED
SHOULDN'T GET REALLY COLD FOR ANOTHER COUPLE WEEKS...
...SO THERE'S THAT.
LUISA... I REALLY APPRECIATE YOU LETTING ME LIE LOW HERE FOR A BIT. I KNOW, AFTER THE WAY WE LEFT THINGS...
DON'T WORRY ABOUT IT. I'M HAPPY TO HELP.
YOU...SURE YOU DON'T WANT TO TELL ME WHAT KIND OF TROUBLE YOU'RE IN?
THAT'S PROBABLY NOT A GOOD IDEA. THE LESS YOU KNOW...
...WELL, THE LESS YOU *KNOW.* YOU KNOW?
STILL-- YOU SHOULD KNOW THIS.
THIS IS TYLER.
WE'VE BEEN...SEEING EACH OTHER SINCE I'VE BEEN OUT HERE.
BRO.

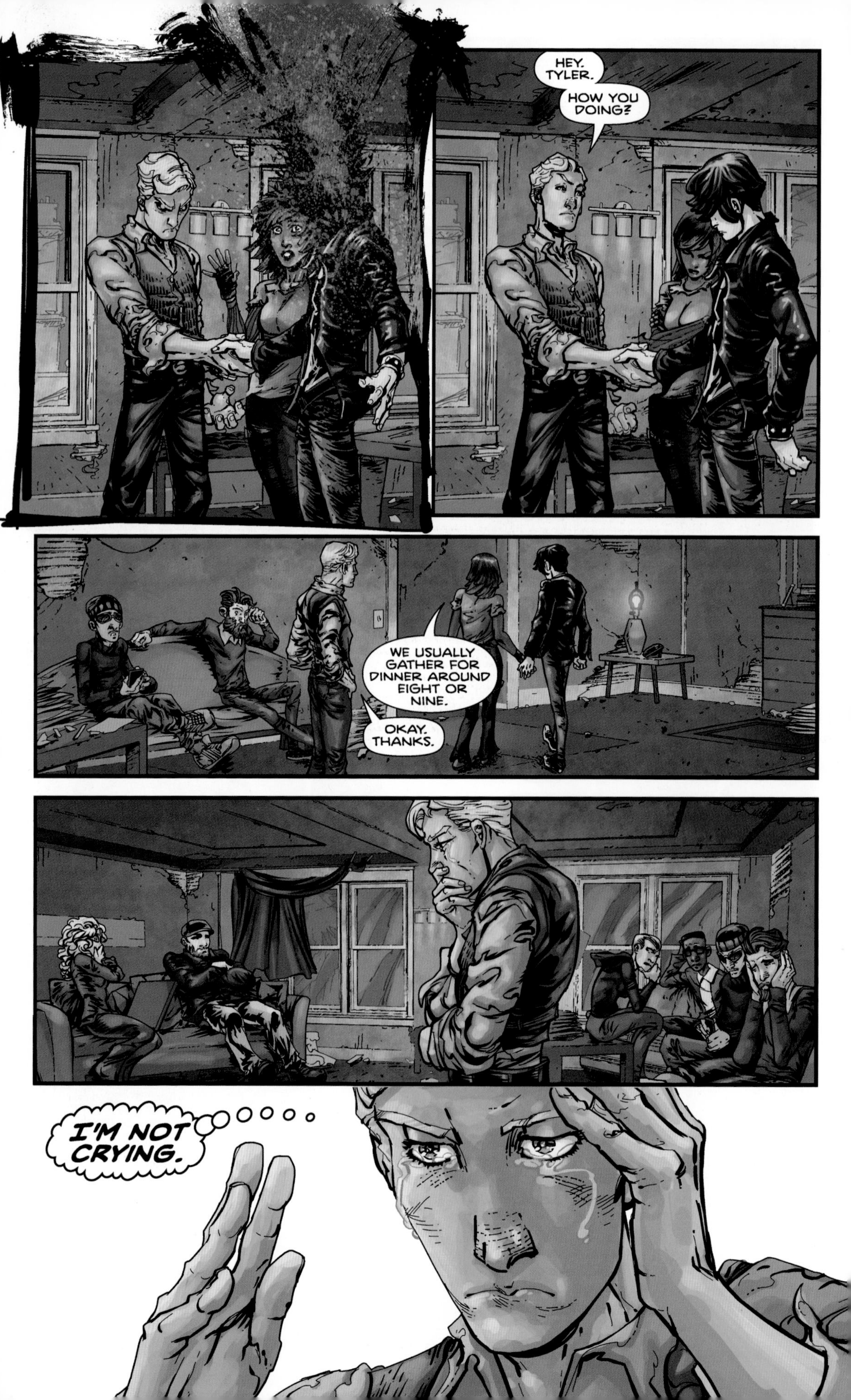
HEY. TYLER.
HOW YOU DOING?
WE USUALLY GATHER FOR DINNER AROUND EIGHT OR NINE.
OKAY. THANKS.
I'M NOT CRYING.

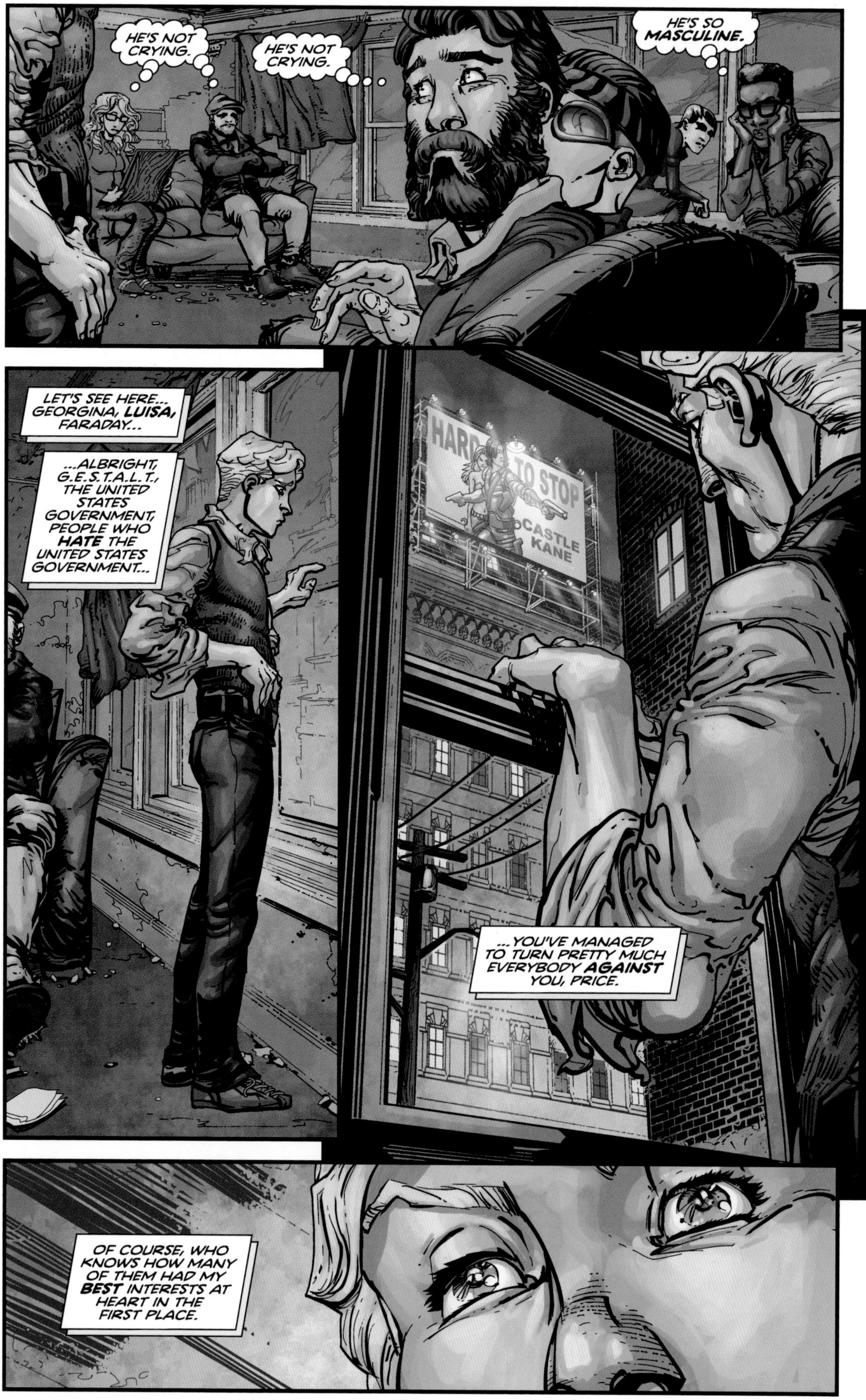
HE'S NOT CRYING.
HE'S NOT CRYING.
HE'S SO MASCULINE.
LET'S SEE HERE... GEORGINA, LUISA, FARADAY...
...ALBRIGHT, G.E.S.T.A.L.T., THE UNITED STATES GOVERNMENT, PEOPLE WHO HATE THE UNITED STATES GOVERNMENT...
HARD TO STOP
CASTLE KANE
...YOU'VE MANAGED TO TURN PRETTY MUCH EVERYBODY AGAINST YOU, PRICE.
OF COURSE, WHO KNOWS HOW MANY OF THEM HAD MY BEST INTERESTS AT HEART IN THE FIRST PLACE.

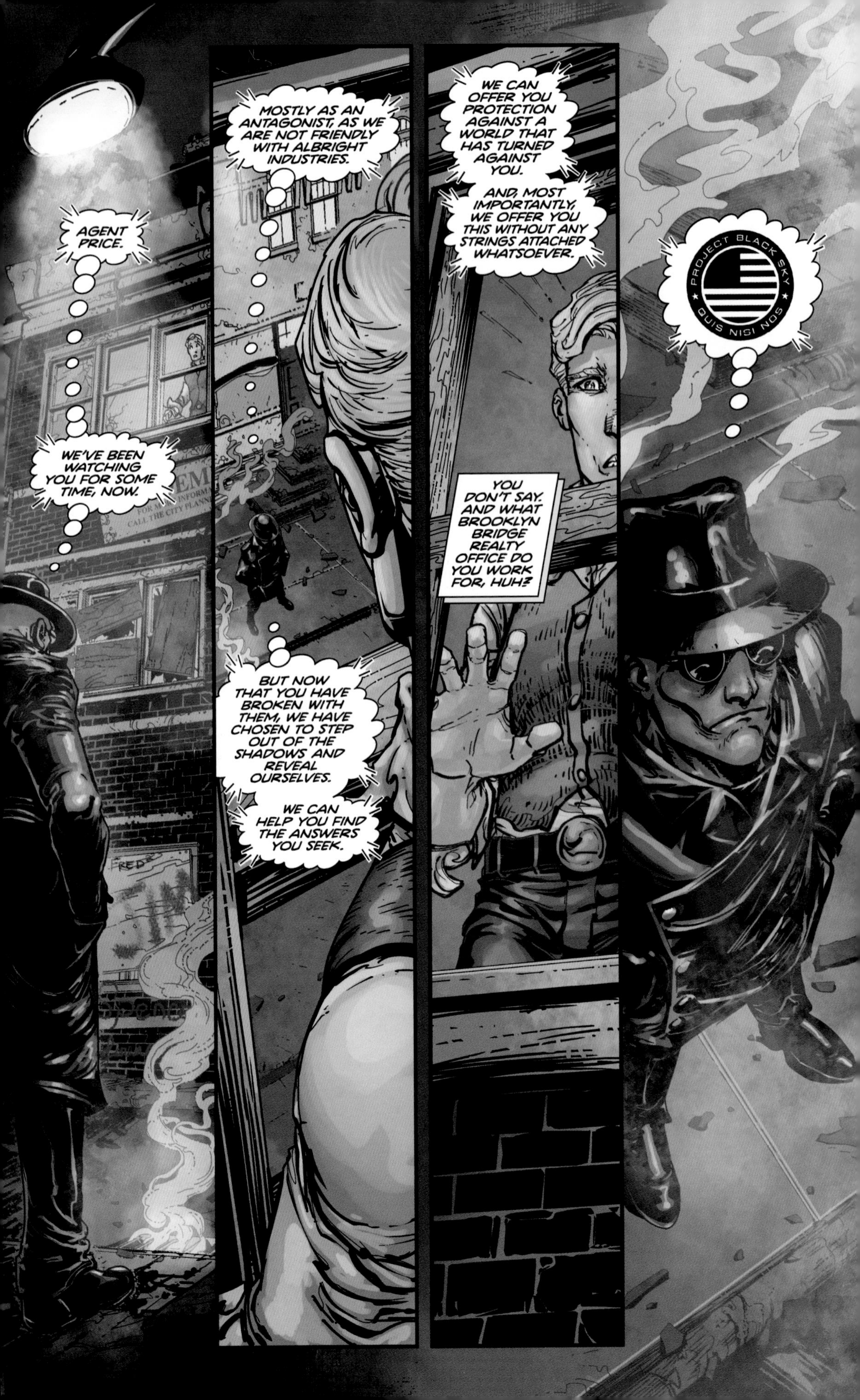
AGENT PRICE.
WE'VE BEEN WATCHING YOU FOR SOME TIME, NOW.
MOSTLY AS AN ANTAGONIST, AS WE ARE NOT FRIENDLY WITH ALBRIGHT INDUSTRIES.
BUT NOW THAT YOU HAVE BROKEN WITH THEM, WE HAVE CHOSEN TO STEP OUT OF THE SHADOWS AND REVEAL OURSELVES.
WE CAN HELP YOU FIND THE ANSWERS YOU SEEK.
WE CAN OFFER YOU PROTECTION AGAINST A WORLD THAT HAS TURNED AGAINST YOU.
AND, MOST IMPORTANTLY, WE OFFER YOU THIS WITHOUT ANY STRINGS ATTACHED WHATSOEVER.
YOU DON'T SAY. AND WHAT BROOKLYN BRIDGE REALTY OFFICE DO YOU WORK FOR, HUH?
PROJECT BLACK SKY
QUIS NISI NOS

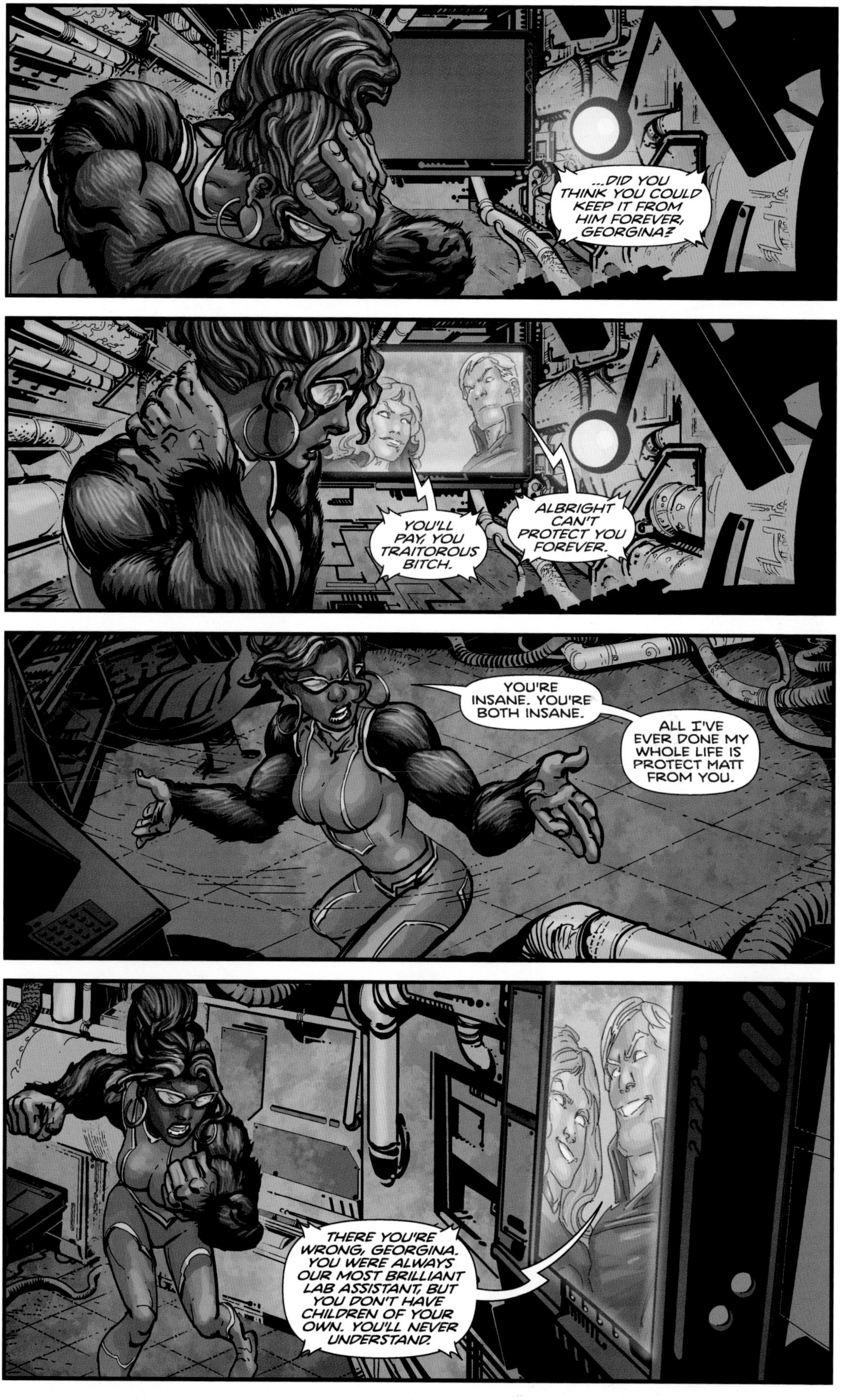
...DID YOU THINK YOU COULD KEEP IT FROM HIM FOREVER, GEORGINA?
YOU'LL PAY, YOU TRAITOROUS BITCH.
ALBRIGHT CAN'T PROTECT YOU FOREVER.
YOU'RE INSANE. YOU'RE BOTH INSANE.
ALL I'VE EVER DONE MY WHOLE LIFE IS PROTECT MATT FROM YOU.
THERE YOU'RE WRONG, GEORGINA. YOU WERE ALWAYS OUR MOST BRILLIANT LAB ASSISTANT, BUT YOU DON'T HAVE CHILDREN OF YOUR OWN. YOU'LL NEVER UNDERSTAND.

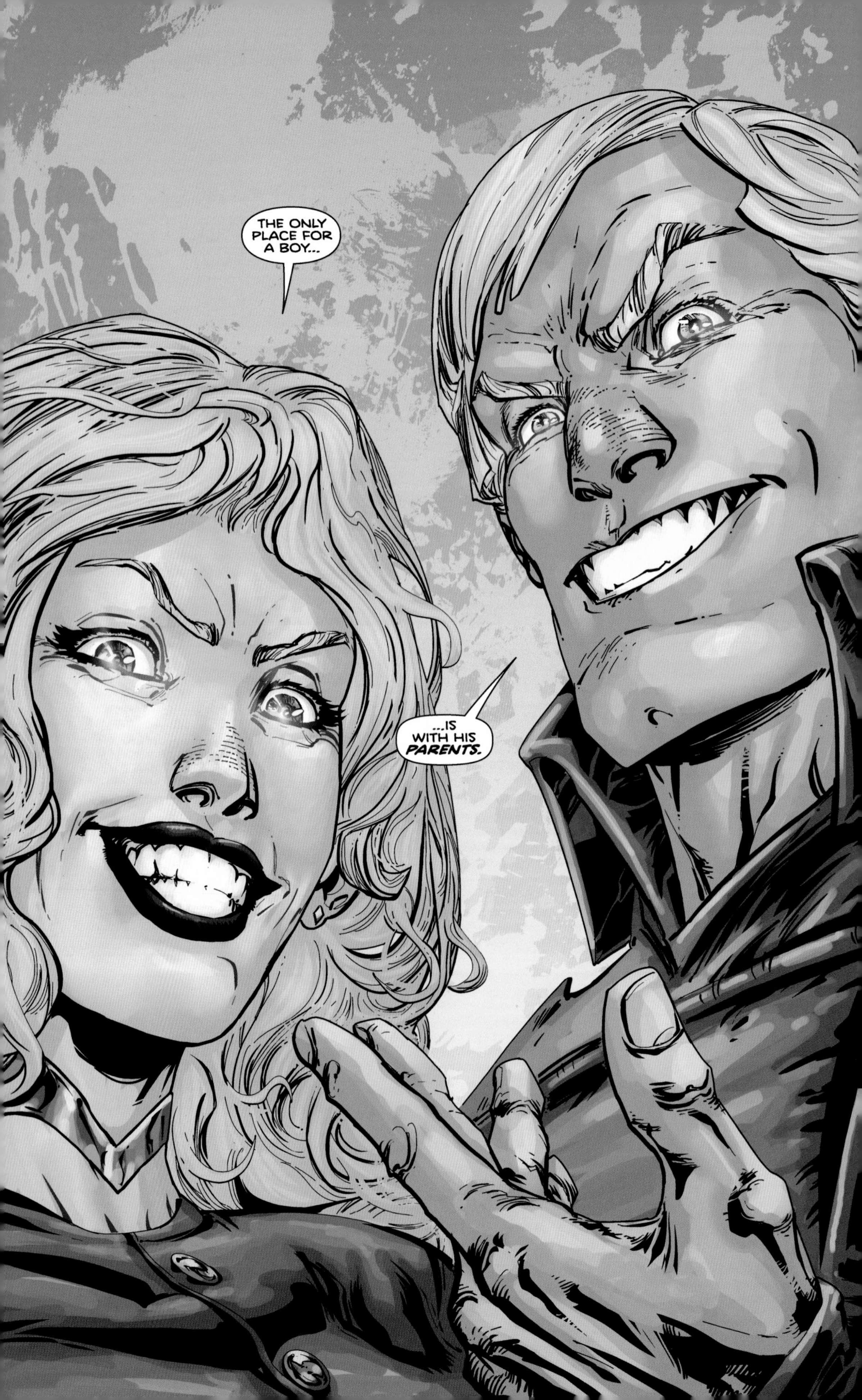
THE ONLY PLACE FOR A BOY...
...IS WITH HIS *PARENTS.*

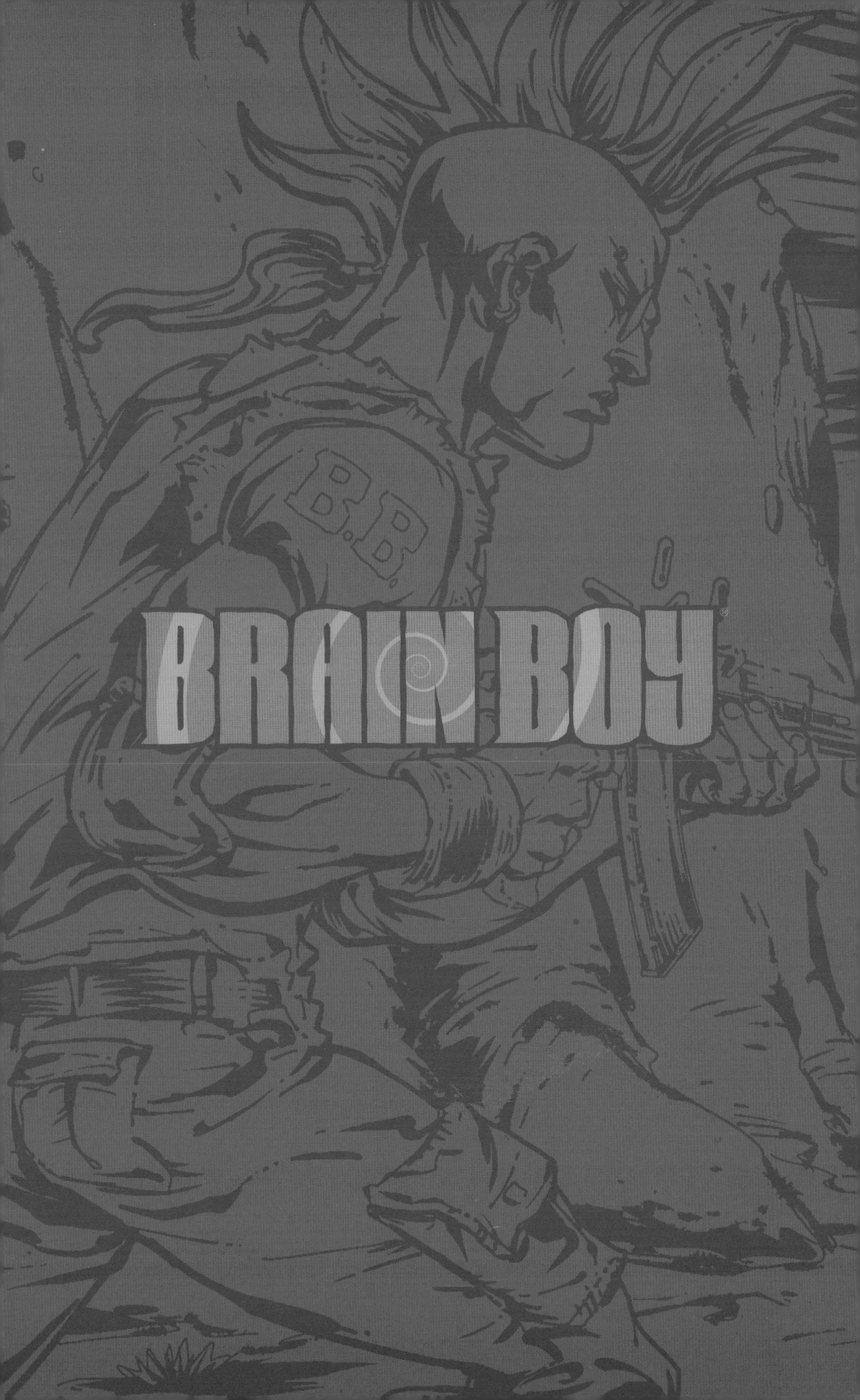
BRAIN BOY®
B.B.

BRAIN BOY®

SKETCHES AND EXTRAS

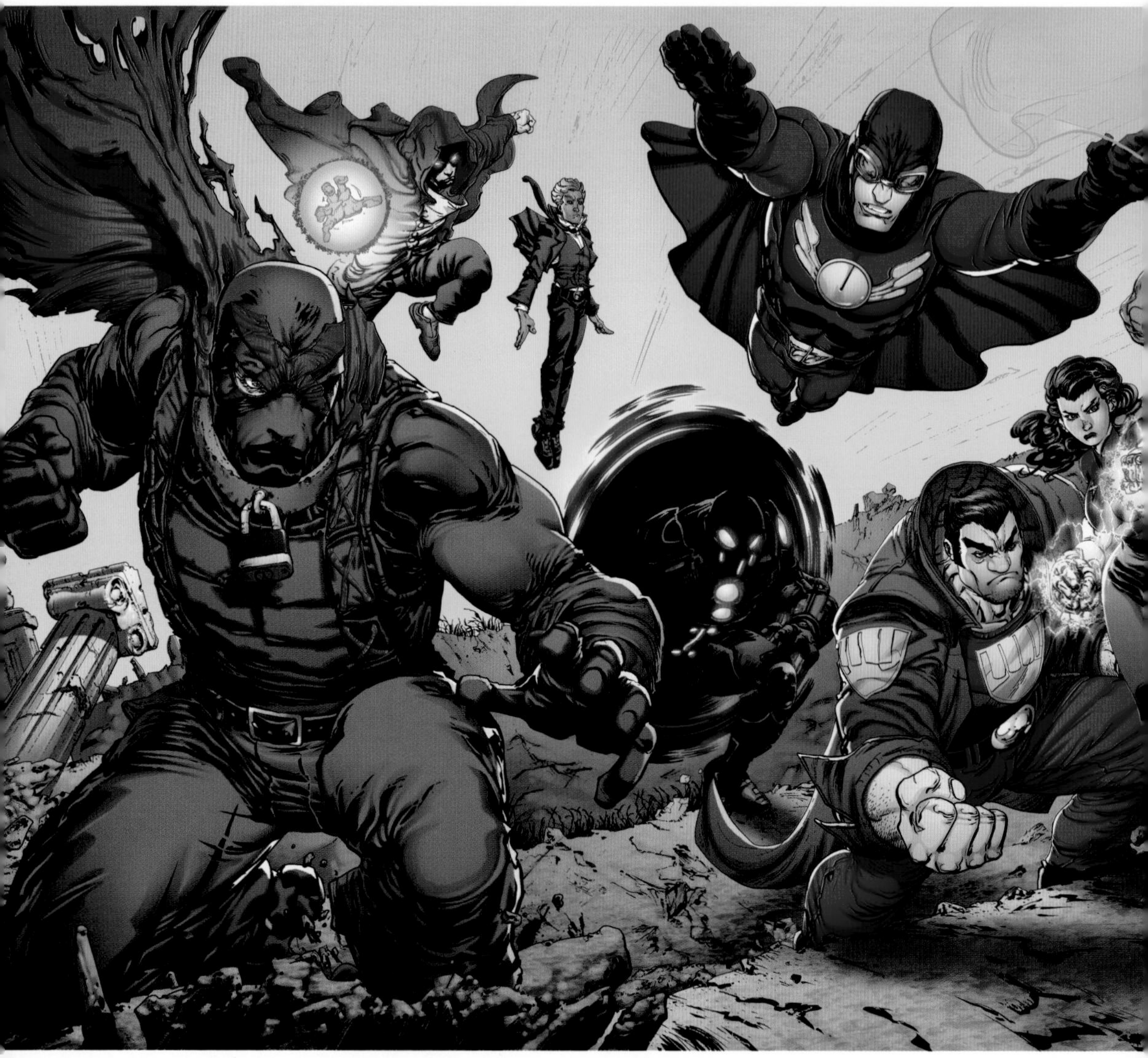

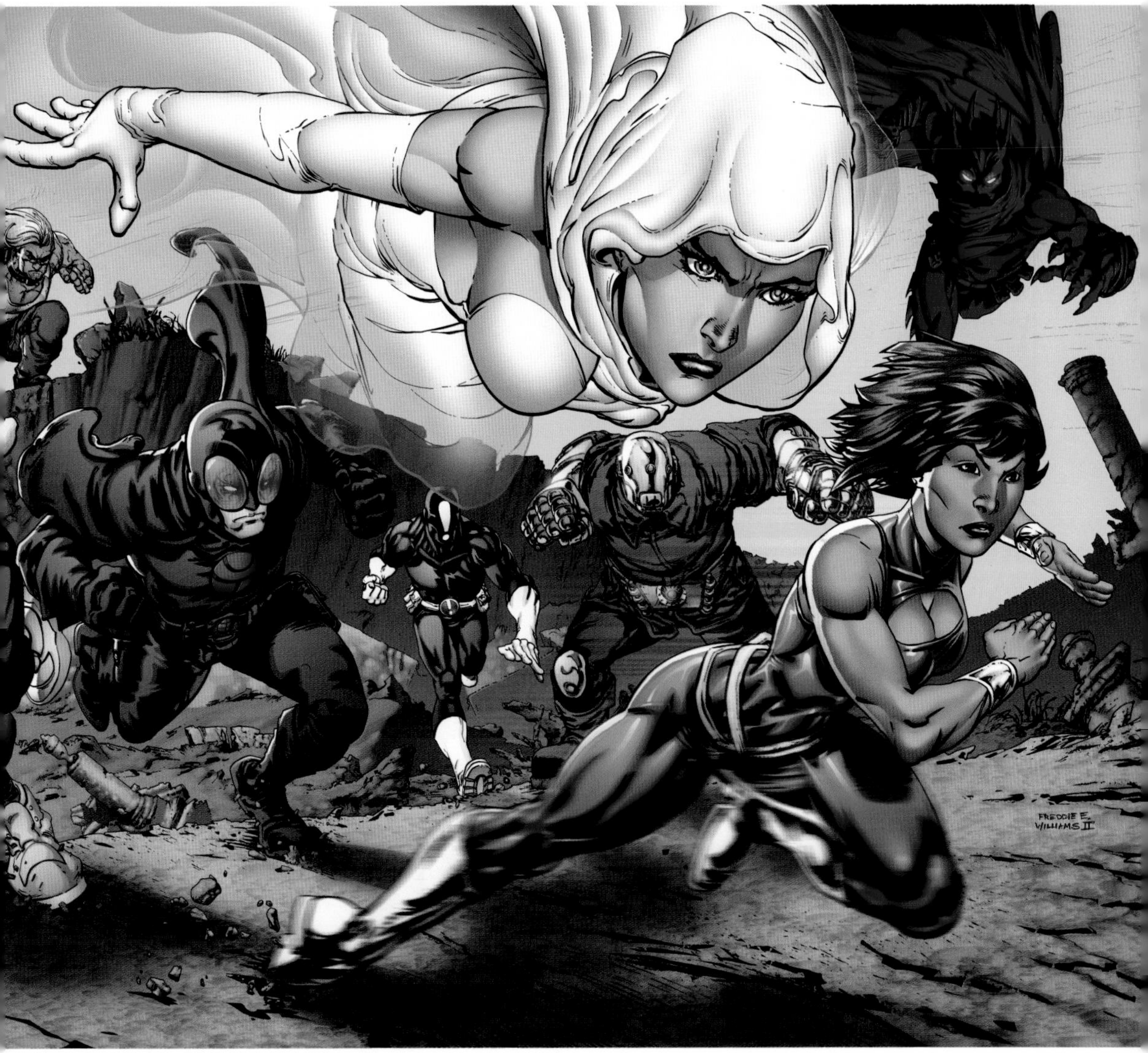
FREDDIE E. WILLIAMS II

Created for use at conventions to promote Dark Horse's company-owned and creator-owned superhero comics, this amazing pinup from Freddie Williams II with colors by Thomas Mason graced the large walls of Dark Horse's convention booths in 2013 and was available as a pullout poster in a *Super Sampler* publication given to fans at those shows.

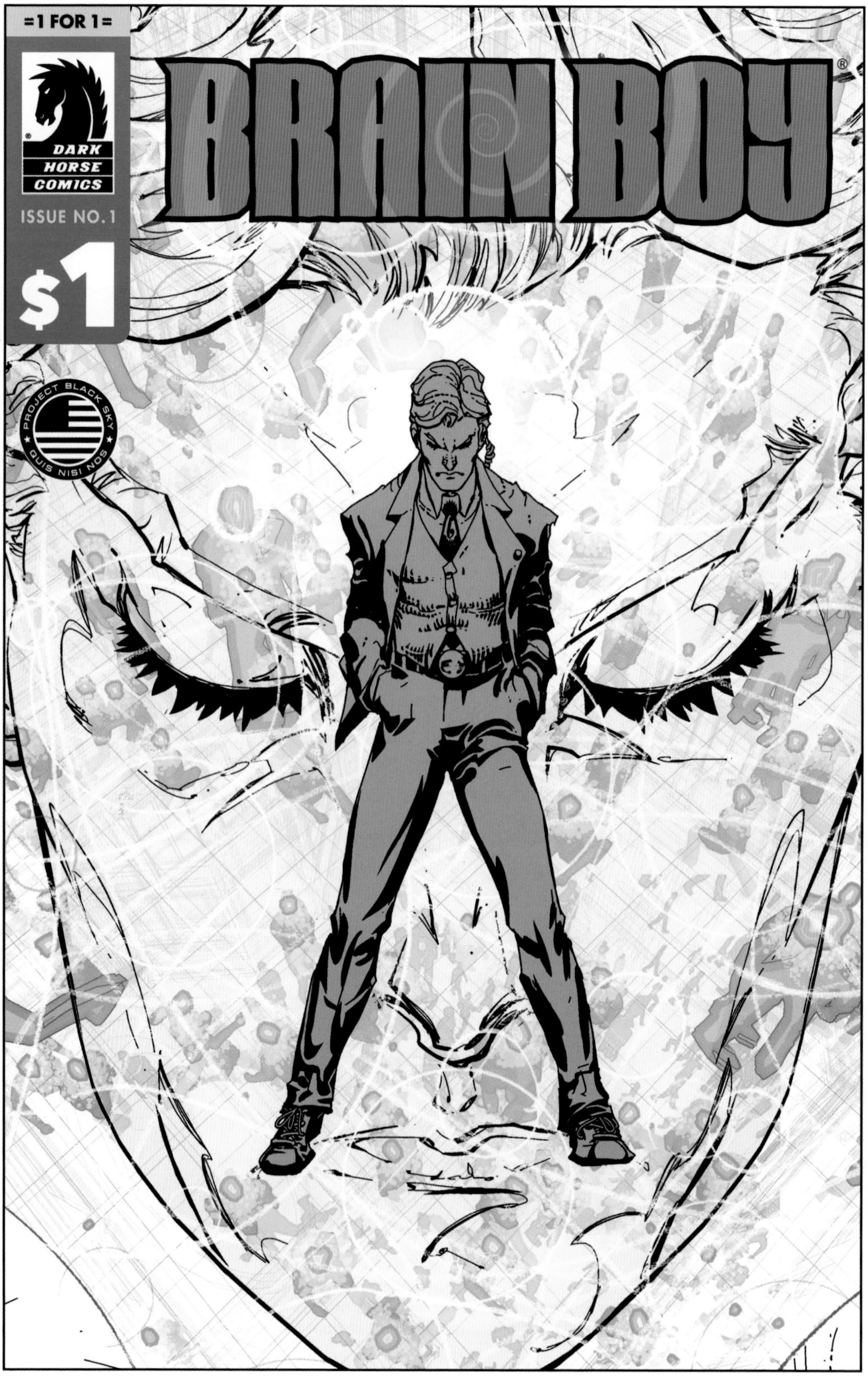
=1 FOR 1=
DARK HORSE COMICS
BRAIN BOY®
ISSUE NO. 1
$1
PROJECT BLACK SKY
QUIS NISI NOS

BRAIN BOY #1 FOR $1 COVER

When Freddie Williams II—who works digitally—sends in digital inks for complex, layered splash pages, he highlights the layers to aid the colorist. This page of inks from the first eight-page *Brain Boy* installment in *Dark Horse Presents* (eventually collected in *Brain Boy* #0) was used in mockups to showcase potential logos. The combo of the colored layers on the inks on a mock cover looked so cool that it was eventually used as the cover for a reissue of *Brain Boy* #1!

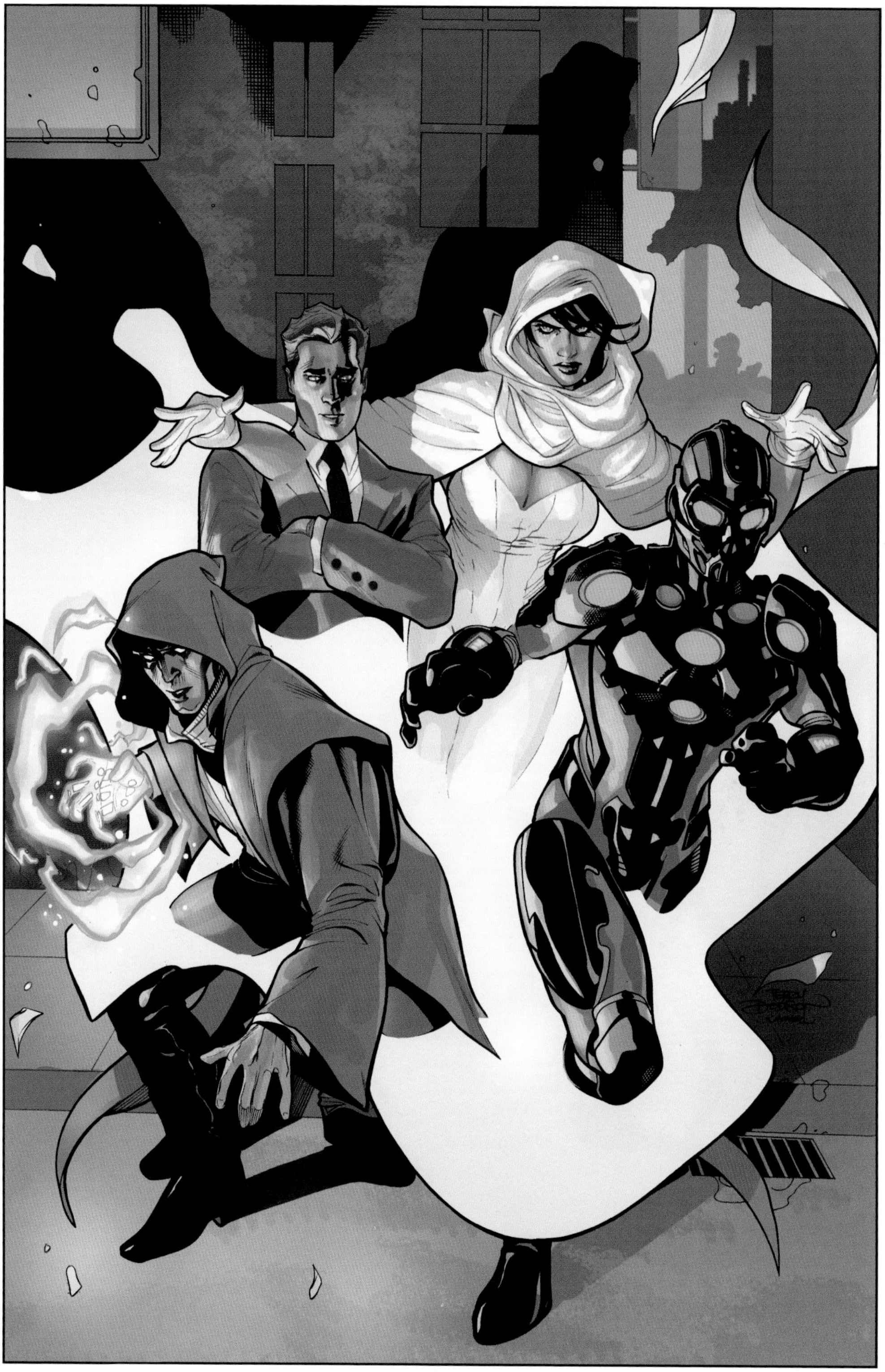

PROJECT BLACK SKY SAMPLER

Used as a cover for a collection of Project Black Sky introductory issues, including stories featuring Brain Boy, Ghost, the Occultist, and Blackout, here's Terry and Rachel Dodson's moody and cool take on these four heroes.

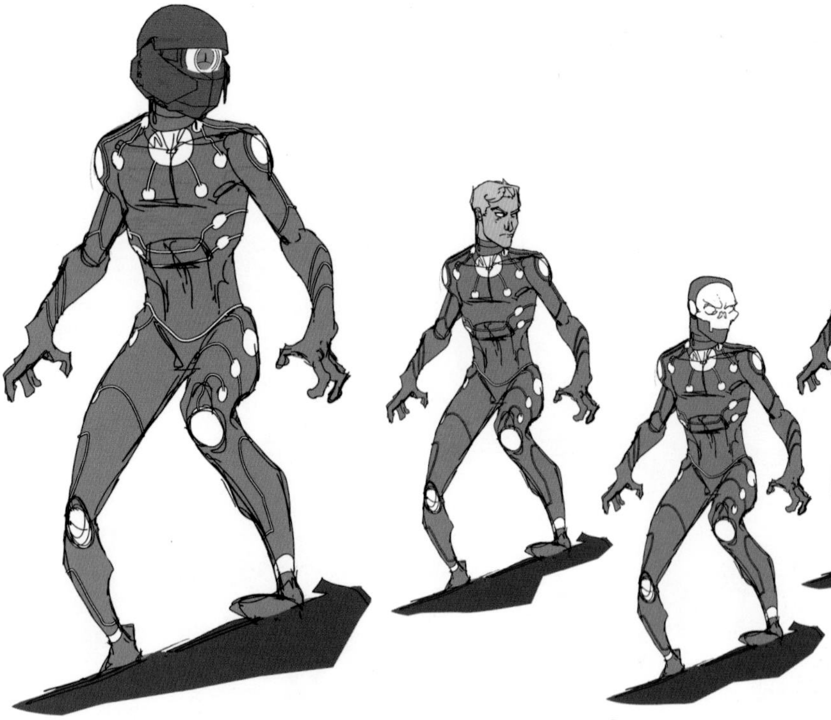

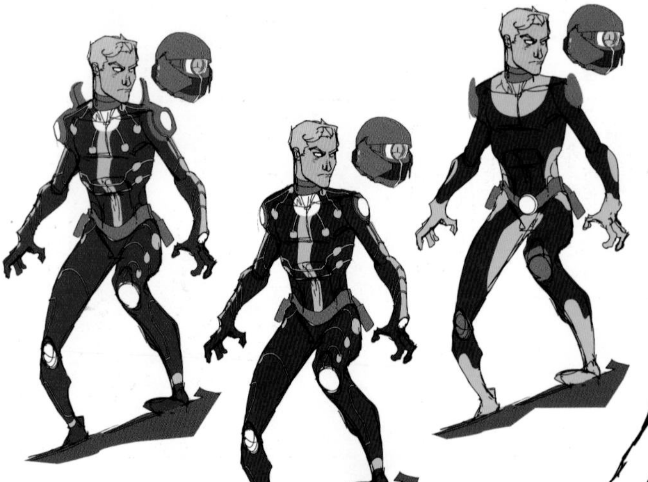

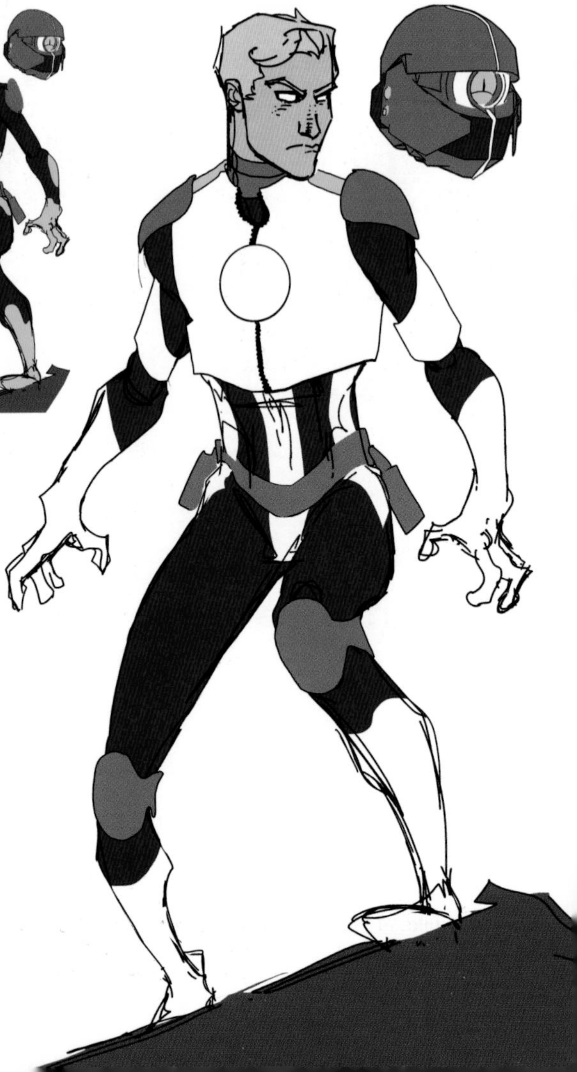

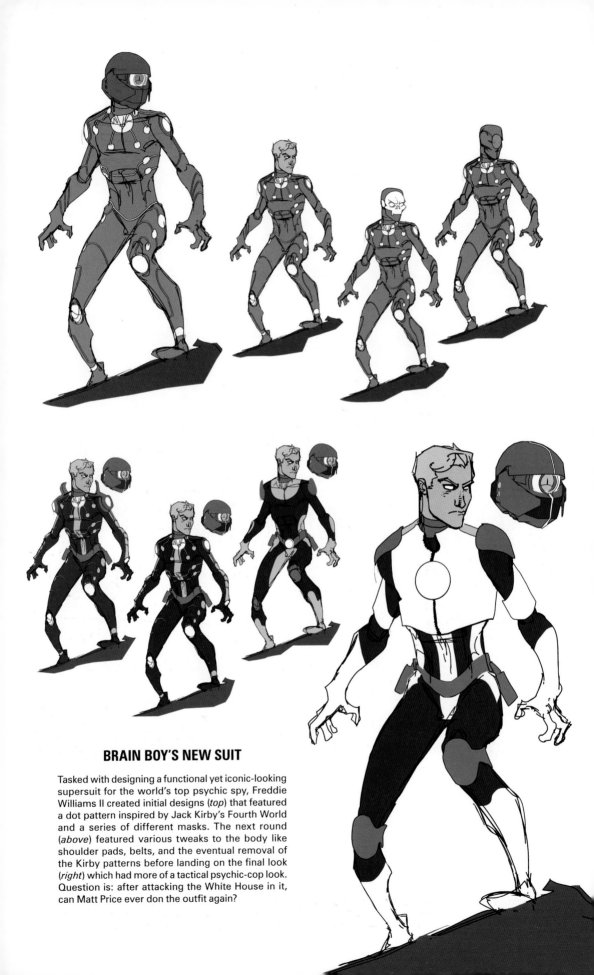

BRAIN BOY'S NEW SUIT

Tasked with designing a functional yet iconic-looking supersuit for the world's top psychic spy, Freddie Williams II created initial designs (*top*) that featured a dot pattern inspired by Jack Kirby's Fourth World and a series of different masks. The next round (*above*) featured various tweaks to the body like shoulder pads, belts, and the eventual removal of the Kirby patterns before landing on the final look (*right*) which had more of a tactical psychic-cop look. Question is: after attacking the White House in it, can Matt Price ever don the outfit again?

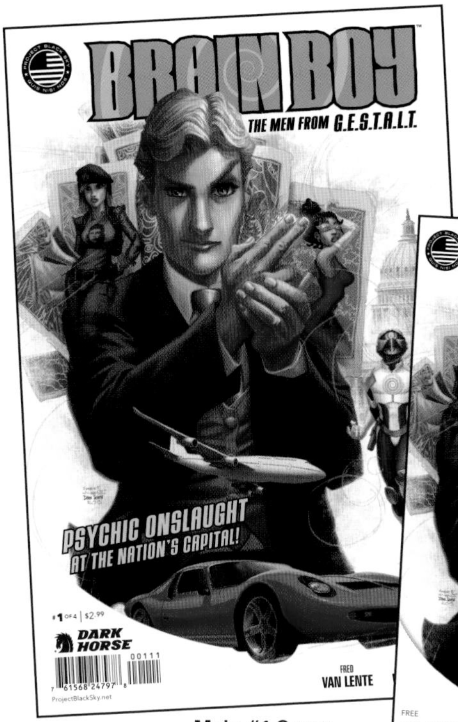
BRAIN BOY
THE MEN FROM G.E.S.T.A.L.T.
PSYCHIC ONSLAUGHT AT THE NATION'S CAPITAL!
#1 OF 4 | $2.99
DARK HORSE
FRED VAN LENTE
ProjectBlackSky.net

Main #1 Cover

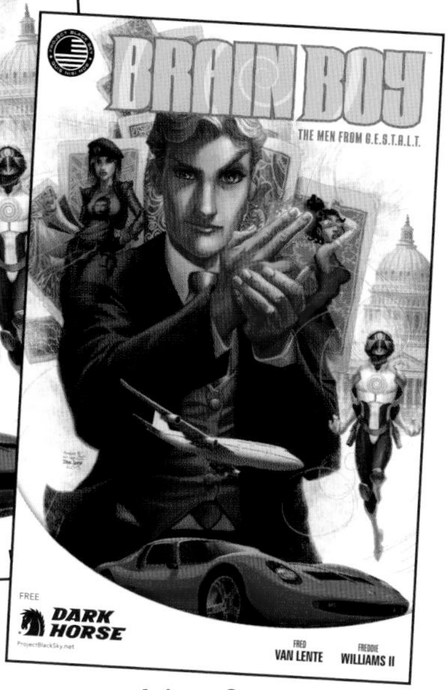
BRAIN BOY
THE MEN FROM G.E.S.T.A.L.T.
FREE
DARK HORSE
ProjectBlackSky.net
FRED VAN LENTE
FREDDIE WILLIAMS II

Ashcan Cover

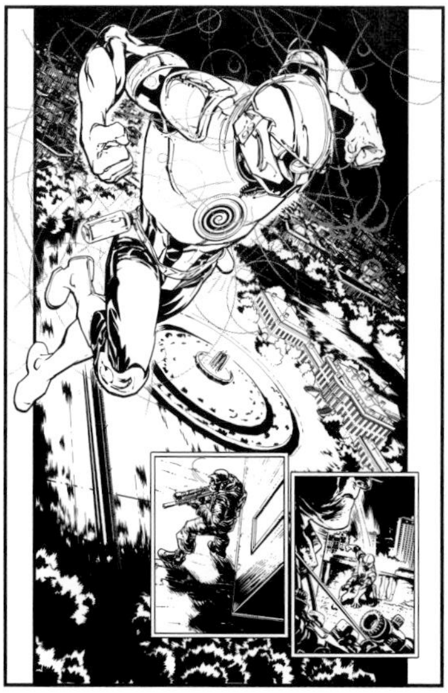

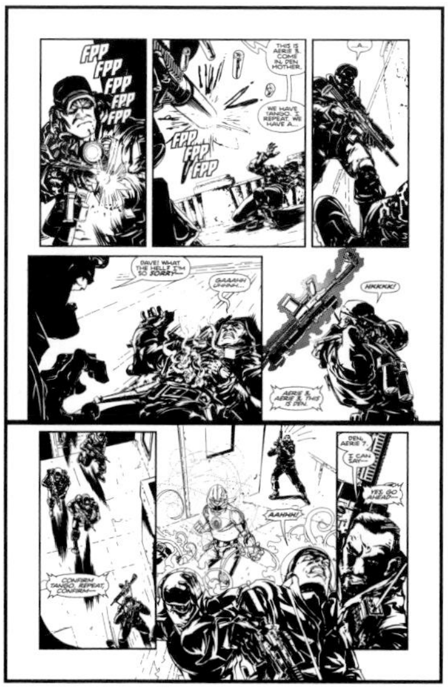

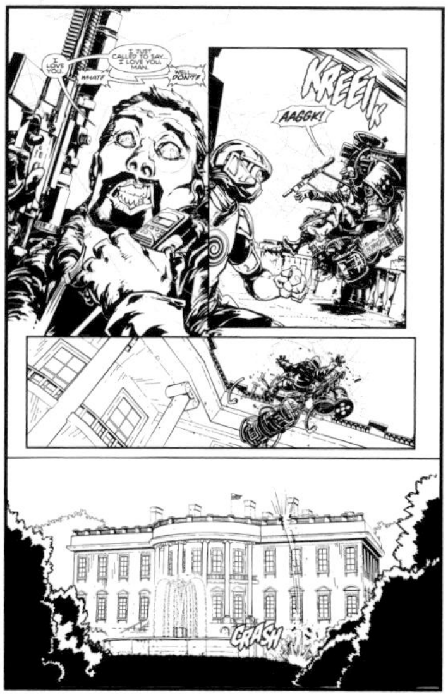

THE BRAIN BOY ASHCAN

To build support for the series, a free black-and-white ashcan of issue #1 of *Brain Boy: The Men from G.E.S.T.A.L.T.* was given to retailers at the ComicsPro summit. Featuring a slightly different cover design, this uncolored version of the issue was printed at smaller dimensions—the most rare *Brain Boy* publication to date!

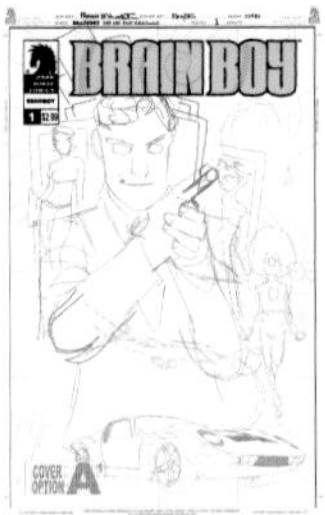
BRAINBOY
COVER OPTION A

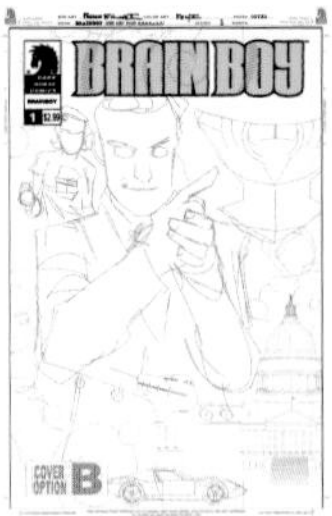
BRAINBOY
COVER OPTION B

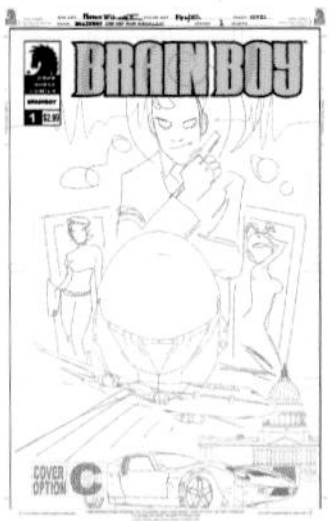
BRAINBOY
COVER OPTION C

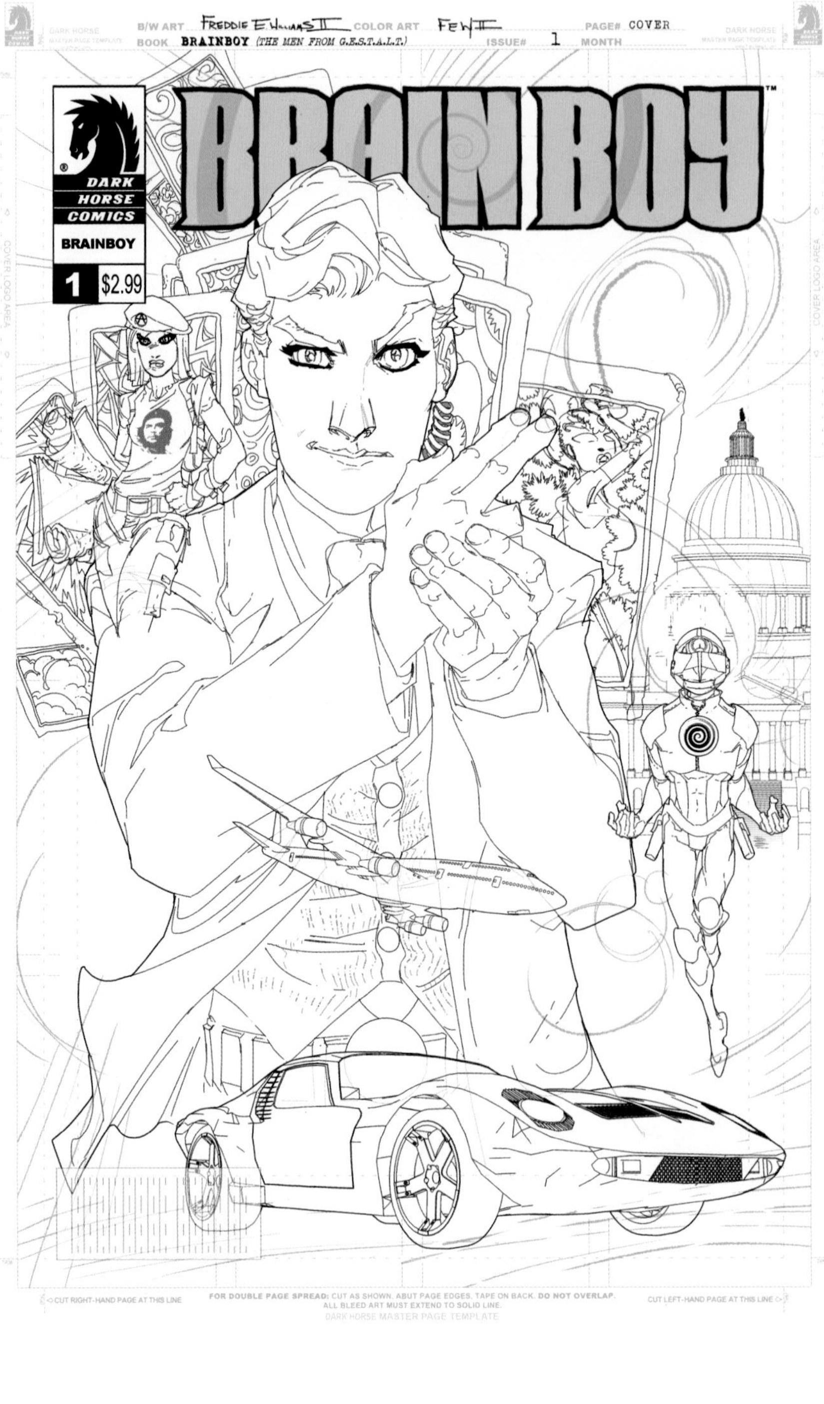
B/W ART Freddie E Williams II COLOR ART FEW II PAGE# COVER
BOOK BRAINBOY (THE MEN FROM G.E.S.T.A.L.T.) ISSUE# 1 MONTH
BRAINBOY™
DARK HORSE COMICS
BRAINBOY
1 $2.99
FOR DOUBLE PAGE SPREAD: CUT AS SHOWN. ABUT PAGE EDGES. TAPE ON BACK. DO NOT OVERLAP.
ALL BLEED ART MUST EXTEND TO SOLID LINE.

FREDDIE'S #1 COVER SKETCHES

Devised as an homage to a certain well-known British spy's movie posters and old-school pulp espionage novels, Freddie Williams II's cover showcases Agent Price wielding a finger pistol (as he can kill ya with his mind . . . HIS MIND!) and a tease of many of the intriguing elements that would show up in the series.

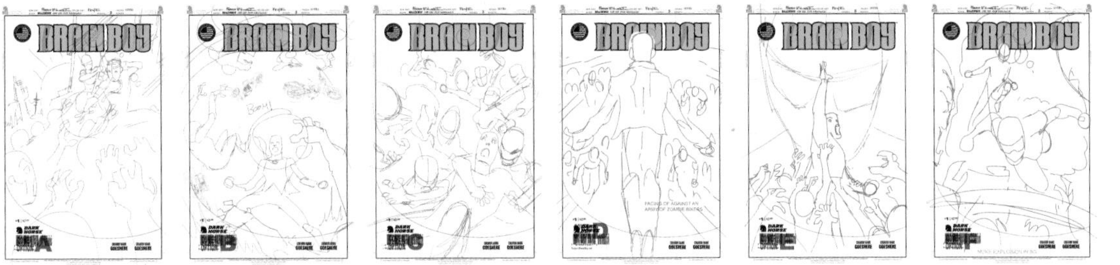

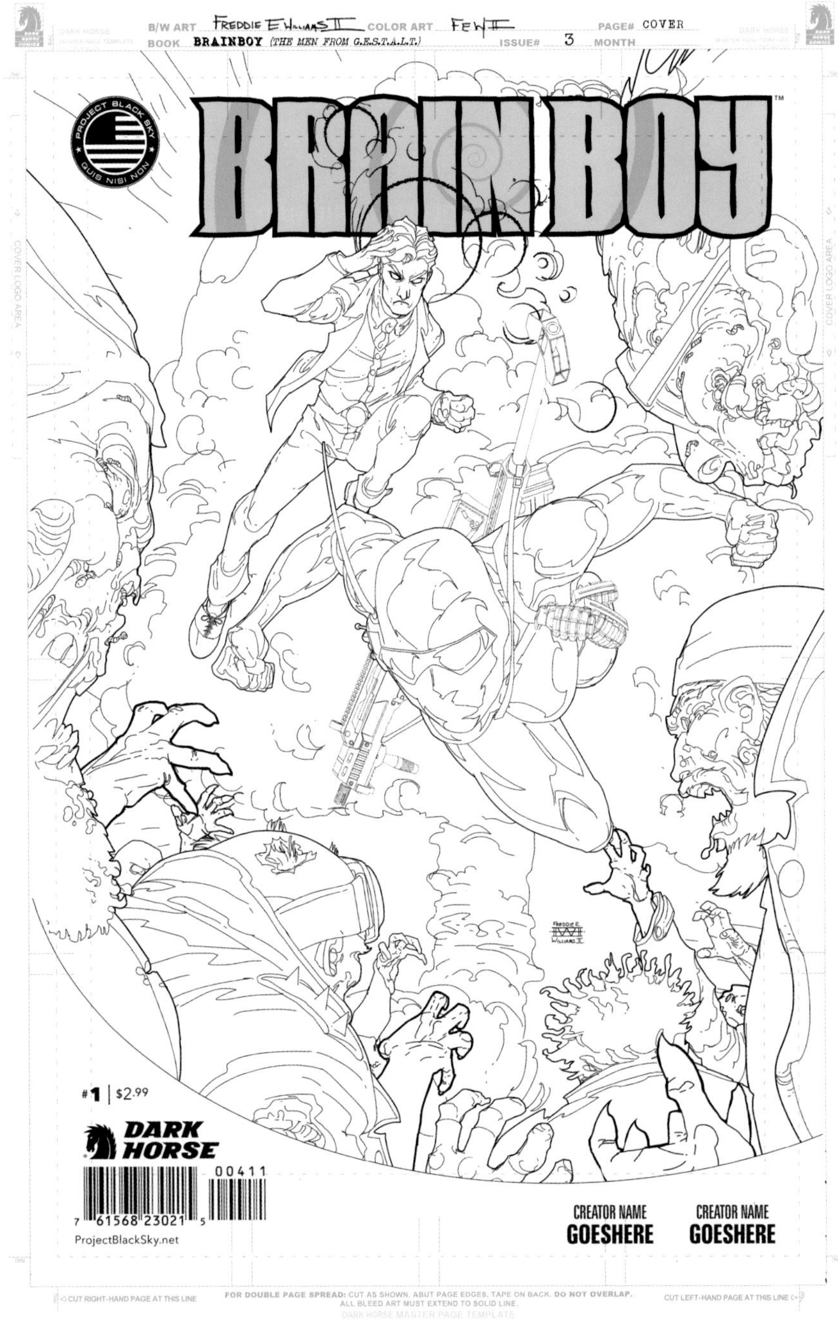
B/W ART FREDDIE E WILLIAMS II COLOR ART FEW II PAGE# COVER
BOOK BRAINBOY (THE MEN FROM G.E.S.T.A.L.T.) ISSUE# 3 MONTH
BRAIN BOY
PROJECT BLACK SKY
QUIS NISI NON
#1 $2.99
DARK HORSE
ProjectBlackSky.net
CREATOR NAME GOESHERE
CREATOR NAME GOESHERE
FOR DOUBLE PAGE SPREAD: CUT AS SHOWN. ABUT PAGE EDGES. TAPE ON BACK. DO NOT OVERLAP.
ALL BLEED ART MUST EXTEND TO SOLID LINE.
CUT RIGHT-HAND PAGE AT THIS LINE
CUT LEFT-HAND PAGE AT THIS LINE

FREDDIE'S #3 COVER SKETCHES

We had a bunch of options for this epic team-up cover featuring Brain Boy and Faraday, as the sketches above showcase, but the decision was unanimous: whatever highlighted the zombie bikers and looming mushroom cloud most prominently was best! Mission accomplished!

PROJECT BLACK SKY

X

Duane Swierczynski and Eric Nguyen
A masked vigilante dispenses justice without mercy to the criminals of the decaying city of Arcadia. Nonstop, visceral action, with Dark Horse's most brutal and exciting character—X!

VOLUME 1: BIG BAD
978-1-61655-241-1 | $14.99

VOLUME 2: THE DOGS OF WAR
978-1-61655-327-2 | $14.99

VOLUME 3: SIEGE
978-1-61655-458-3 | $14.99

GHOST

Kelly Sue DeConnick, Chris Sebela, Phil Noto, and Ryan Sook
Paranormal investigators accidentally summon a ghostly woman. The search for her identity uncovers a deadly alliance between political corruption and demonic science! In the middle stands a woman trapped between two worlds!

VOLUME 1: IN THE SMOKE AND DIN
978-1-61655-121-6 | $14.99

VOLUME 2: THE WHITE CITY BUTCHER
978-1-61655-420-0 | $14.99

THE OCCULTIST

Mike Richardson, Tim Seeley, and Victor Drujiniu
With a team of hit mages hired by a powerful sorcerer after him, it's trial by fire for the new Occultist, as he learns to handle his powerful magical tome, or suffer at the hands of deadly enemies. From the mind of Dark Horse founder Mike Richardson (*The Secret, Cut, The Mask*)!

VOLUME 1
978-1-59582-745-6 | $16.99

VOLUME 2: AT DEATH'S DOOR
978-1-61655-463-7 | $16.99

DARK HORSE BOOKS

AVAILABLE AT YOUR LOCAL COMICS SHOP OR BOOKSTORE! • To find a comics shop in your area, call 1-888-266-4226.
For more information or to order direct visit DarkHorse.com or call 1-800-862-0052 Mon.–Fri. 9 AM to 5 PM Pacific Time. Prices and availability subject to change without notice.

DarkHorse.com   Dark Horse Books® and the Dark Horse logo are registered trademarks of Dark Horse Comics, Inc. (BL 6074)

PROJECT BLACK SKY

★ PROJECT BLACK SKY ★
QUIS NISI NOS

CAPTAIN MIDNIGHT

Joshua Williamson, Fernando Dagnino, Eduardo Francisco, Victor Ibáñez, Pere Pérez, and Roger Robinson

In the forties, he was an American hero, a daredevil fighter pilot, a technological genius . . . a superhero. Since he rifled out of the Bermuda Triangle and into the present day, Captain Midnight has been labeled a threat to homeland security. Can Captain Midnight survive in the modern world, with the US government on his heels and an old enemy out for revenge?

VOLUME 1: ON THE RUN
978-1-61655-229-9 | $14.99

VOLUME 2: BRAVE OLD WORLD
978-1-61655-230-5 | $14.99

BRAIN BOY

Fred Van Lente, Freddie Williams II, and R. B. Silva

Ambushed while protecting an important statesman, Matt Price Jr., a.k.a. Brain Boy, finds himself wrapped up in political intrigue that could derail a key United Nations conference and sets the psychic spy on a collision course with a man whose mental powers rival his own!

VOLUME 1: PSY VS. PSY
978-1-61655-317-3 | $14.99

SKYMAN

Joshua Hale Fialkov and Manuel Garcia

The Skyman Program turns to US Air Force Sgt. Eric Reid: a wounded veteran on the ropes, looking for a new lease on life. *Ultimates* writer Joshua Hale Fialkov pens an all-new superhero series from the pages of *Captain Midnight*!

VOLUME 1: THE RIGHT STUFF
978-1-61655-439-2 | $14.99

BLACKOUT

Frank Barbiere, Colin Lorimer, and Micah Kaneshiro

Scott Travers possesses a special suit bearing technology that allows Travers to move in and out of our world through a shadowy parallel dimension—but he doesn't know how the device works or where it came from. With his benefactor missing, and powerful adversaries after his "Blackout" gear, Scott must master the suit's mysterious powers and find answers before the answers find him!

VOLUME 1: INTO THE DARK
978-1-61655-555-9 | $12.99

DARK HORSE BOOKS

AVAILABLE AT YOUR LOCAL COMICS SHOP OR BOOKSTORE! • To find a comics shop in your area, call 1-888-266-4226.
For more information or to order direct visit DarkHorse.com or call 1-800-862-0052 Mon.–Fri. 9 AM to 5 PM Pacific Time. Prices and availability subject to change without

SUPER:POWERED BY CREATORS!

"These superheroes ain't no boy scouts in spandex. They're a high-octane blend of the damaged, quixotic heroes of pulp and detective fiction and the do-gooders in capes from the Golden and Silver Ages." —Duane Swierczynski

SLEDGEHAMMER 44
Mike Mignola, John Arcudi, and Jason Latour
ISBN 978-1-61655-395-1 | $19.99

DREAM THIEF
Jai Nitz and Greg Smallwood
ISBN 978-1-61655-283-1 | $17.99

BUZZKILL
Mark Reznicek, Donny Cates,
and Geoff Shaw
ISBN 978-1-61655-305-0 | $14.99

THE BLACK BEETLE
Francesco Francavilla
VOLUME 1: NO WAY OUT
ISBN 978-1-61655-202-2 | $19.99

THE ANSWER!
Mike Norton and Dennis Hopeless
ISBN 978-1-61655-197-1 | $12.99

BLOODHOUND
Dan Jolley, Leonard Kirk, and Robin Riggs
VOLUME 1: BRASS KNUCKLE PSYCHOLOGY
ISBN 978-1-61655-125-4 | $19.99
VOLUME 2: CROWBAR MEDICINE
ISBN 978-1-61655-352-4 | $19.99

**MICHAEL AVON OEMING'S
THE VICTORIES**
Michael Avon Oeming
VOLUME 1: TOUCHED
ISBN 978-1-61655-100-1 | $9.99
VOLUME 2: TRANSHUMAN
ISBN 978-1-61655-214-5 | $17.99
VOLUME 3: POSTHUMAN
ISBN 978-1-61655-445-3 | $17.99

ORIGINAL VISIONS—
THRILLING TALES!

DARK HORSE

AVAILABLE AT YOUR LOCAL COMICS SHOP OR BOOKSTORE! • To find a comics shop in your area, call 1-888-266-4226.
For more information or to order direct visit DarkHorse.com or call 1-800-862-0052 Mon.–Fri. 9 a.m. to 5 p.m. Pacific Time. Prices and availability subject to change without notice.

Sledgehammer 44™ and © Mike Mignola. The Black Beetle™: No Way Out © Francesco Francavilla. Bloodhound™ © Dan Jolley. The Answer!™ © Mike Norton and Dennis Hopeless. Victories™ © Michael Avon Oeming.